12098

BAROQUE
MUSIC

BAROQUE MUSIC

A Practical Guide
for the Performer

Victor
Rangel-Ribeiro

SCHIRMER BOOKS

A Division of Macmillan Publishing Co., Inc.
New York

Collier Macmillan Publishers
London

Schirmer Books
A Division of Macmillan Publishing Co., Inc.
866 Third Avenue, New York, N. Y. 10022

Collier Macmillan Canada, Ltd.

Library of Congress Catalog Card Number: 80-5222

Printed in the United States of America

printing number
1 2 3 4 5 6 7 8 9 10

Library of Congress Cataloging in Publication Data

Rangel-Ribeiro, Victor.
      Baroque music.

        1. Music, Baroque. 2. Music—Interpretation (Phras-
ing, dynamics, etc.) I. Title.
MT75.R3   781.6′3   80-5222
ISBN 0-02-871980-8   AACR2

To my dear friend
David Simpson —
An upright man
with Baroque leanings

Victor Rangel-Ribeiro
March 23 1989

To the composers and performers
of the Baroque era,
and to the musicians and audiences of today,
this work is respectfully dedicated;
but most of all I dedicate it to Yehudi Menuhin,
for his great encouragement,
and to Lea, Eva, Eric, and Richard

Contents

Acknowledgments

My thanks are due the following music and book publishers and publishers' agents for permission to quote material copyrighted by them:

Associated Music Publishers, Inc.
Bärenreiter Verlag
Belwin-Mills, Inc.
Breitkopf & Härtel
Franco Colombo, Inc.
Verlag Doblinger
Dover Publications, Inc.
Edition Moeck
Faber & Faber
The Free Press

G. Henle Verlag
The Macmillan Company
Magnamusic, Inc.
W. W. Norton & Company, Inc.
Oxford University Press
C. F. Peters Corp.
G. Ricordi & Co.
St. Martin's Press
G. Schirmer, Inc.
B. Schött's Söhne
University of California Press

Particular thanks are due the following individuals for their very special cooperation:

The eminent musicologist Emanuel Barblan for encouragement given during all-too-brief conferences in Milan in the fall of 1970; Edward Brewer, harpsichordist, for reading much of the manuscript and commenting thereon; Frances Cole, harpsichordist, at whose 1973 "Harpsichord Festival" in Princeton some of these ideas were first tested, particularly some in Chapters 9 and 10; Adolf Dingfelder for his unfailing encouragement; Ingrid Dingfelder, flutist, for reading the manuscript and testing its ideas with enthusiasm; Ginette Fowler, violinist, who played through some of the elaborations and made very practical, constructive suggestions; Sam Goody, of the record stores that bear his name; soprano Hedi Klebe, for singing "Bist du bei mir" in its ornamented version on a very special occasion; Doris Ornstein, Music Director of the Cleveland Baroque Soloists, for reading much of the manuscript and being greatly supportive; the late Morris Rubinstein, of Broude Bros., New York, for making several of his company's splendid facsimile editions available for study; and most particularly Oscar Schonfeld, for having started me on this project, for his constructive criticism, and above all for having persuaded me to compress the work into its present readable size. To all of these, and to others that I inadvertently might have overlooked, my heartfelt thanks; the book is better for their helpfulness. Such flaws as may be found in my text, however, are my sole responsibility and should in no way be laid at their door.

Introduction

This book is meant to help any practicing musician, professional or amateur, who has ever picked up a piece of Baroque music and asked himself: "What am I supposed to do with this?" Even more is it aimed at the practicing musician who has never asked himself that question; I hope that after reading this book, he will realize that he should have asked it. It is written for critics and conductors; for students of music—in fact, for anybody who is involved with music and has a questioning mind.

For reasons of space and clarity, this book deals mostly with music written by major composers or members of their respective schools in the last hundred years or so of the Baroque period; that is to say, roughly between 1700 and 1800, when the last waves of the Baroque movement finally expended themselves.

You can see right away that this is not a "safe" book—that the author does not hesitate to express strong and often controversial opinions. Truth is often uncovered as the result of a swirling controversy. So if this book provokes you into reexamining musical values, into disputing fixed positions, into asking questions and demanding logical answers, then it will have fulfilled its three prime purposes—to share information, to challenge, and to act as a catalyst.

The author also hopes that the book will help set certain musical events in a truer historical perspective. The first step in doing this is to establish the fact that the Baroque period survived to the end of the eighteenth and the beginning of the nineteenth centuries. As proof he wishes to point out that while four major books by the great codifiers of late Baroque practice—Johann Joachim Quantz, Carl Philipp Emanuel Bach, Francesco Geminiani and Leopold Mozart—all appeared within a few years of each other in the 1750s, the very greatest anthology of late-late-Baroque violin literature, Jean-Baptiste Cartier's *L'Art du Violon*, was published in Paris in 1798, and sold well enough to be reprinted. The value of this great anthology to us is inestimable, for not only did Cartier include complete versions of major violin works as they were first published, but he also printed in full the very elaborately ornamented versions it had become customary to play in the latter part of the century. This ornamented version appeared on a separate staff immediately below the original, making comparison easy. (See Appendix 2, page 293.)

This was in the year 1798. Wolfgang Amadeus Mozart had lived out his entire life and died seven years before this great Baroque anthology began enjoying its success in Paris; Beethoven, by then settled in Vienna, was twenty-eight years old. A new wave, which came to be known as the Classical period, was foaming and cresting in Germany and Austria even before the old wave had quite peaked out in France. We shall come across this national time-lag often in the course of our study; it was one of the characteristics of the period. Even allowing for this time-lag, however, there is an increasing awareness amongst musicians that Mozart received a quite Baroque training at the hands of his father, the justly celebrated Leopold, particularly in the arts of ornamentation and improvisation; and Beethoven's own training during his earliest years was also Baroque-oriented. Strong traces of this training may be found in Beethoven's keyboard and chamber music until about 1803, and vestiges of it may be found in his later work.

Having thus briefly conjured up the ghosts of Mozart and Beethoven, let us dismiss them for now, so we can call on them again later. At this moment, we should turn our attention to ways in which we can best use this book. Readers who are just beginning their study of Baroque music should begin with chapter 1. Others can begin anywhere and read in any order they please. Chapters 2, 3, and 7 provide us with guidelines that will help us to cope with music written in the first half of the eighteenth century. Chapter 13 has contributions by Leopold Mozart and Tartini that introduce us to the increasingly elaborate ornaments that were used in the second half of the century.

From chapter 4 on we work mainly with music. We begin with Handel because his style is familiar, approachable, and easy to work with. At the same time it is not regarded as sacrosanct, the way Johann Sebastian Bach's is. We can therefore elaborate it, ornament it, even change it, without feeling too guilty or running into too much opposition. Even here our approach will be careful and experimental. We must get used to the idea of ornamenting before we plunge fully into ornamentation.

After dealing with Handel and before dealing with Bach, I have found it practical to examine the music of Antonio Vivaldi. Not only can Vivaldi's music be treated with the same freedom we use with Handel's, and for the same reasons, but it also strongly influenced Bach's style and development and should therefore be studied first. In fact Vivaldi helped shape the course of music for the greater part of the eighteenth century. Consider this line of succession: through J. S. Bach he influenced Bach's son Carl Philipp Emanuel; through his own pupil, the violin-virtuoso and composer Pisendel, he influenced the flute-virtuoso and composer J. J. Quantz. By a quirk of fate both C. P. E. Bach and Quantz became important musicians at the court of Frederick the Great of Prussia, and each man published a book within a year of the other—Quantz in 1752, C. P. E. in 1753—codifying the laws and practices of the late Baroque for their own age and for all time.

C. P. E. Bach and Quantz have provided much of the background for this volume. Their knowledge was not confined to any one instrument; in fact, it was spectacularly broad. Both had an excellent grounding in composition and musicianship—C. P. E. from his great father, Quantz from Zelenka, who was a pupil of Fux. C. P. E. was proficient on the harpsichord, clavichord, and organ; he functioned as soloist, continuo player, accompanist, and composer. Quantz functioned as a composer and flute virtuoso; but he had also studied the violin, oboe, trumpet, cornetto, trombone, horn, recorder, bassoon, cello, viola da gamba, and contrabass. Their pages therefore are filled with practical advice born of long experience.

Whenever possible we have gone to the best of all sources—the variants that composers wrote or that were published during or soon after their lifetime. Material of this type forms the basis of the chapters on Vivaldi, Bach, Telemann, Corelli, Geminiani, and Tartini. Enough exists to give us a starting point; more will undoubtedly be uncovered as scholars continue their researches.

But the growth of Baroque scholarship in itself is not enough. The danger is that too few active musicians are making use of what has been learned regarding the Baroque period and its practices. To be sure, large numbers of scholars have read David D. Boyden's magnificent *The History of Violin Playing from Its Origins to 1761* (New York: Oxford, 1965). But we ask, how many violinists have read it? Of those that have, how many have absorbed and are applying its ideas? A good many, certainly, but not nearly enough!

The musical public is fickle, and its taste runs in cycles. There is therefore a real danger that the Baroque revival may run its course and pass into history before the vast body of our musicians ever learns what Baroque music is all about; then several generations will be deprived of the knowledge of one of the great treasures of mankind.

The prime purpose of this book is to involve the amateur as well as the professional musician directly in the delights and excitement of Baroque music-making, as Baroque music should properly be played. The player is invariably encouraged to perform more perceptively at his own level, even as he begins to perfect himself. As his skill and knowledge increase, he will be able to use more and more complex ideas in his interpretations. As musical performance of Baroque music improves, audiences will become more discerning and more demanding; it is hoped that this will encourage musicologists to intensify their own efforts. The ultimate reward will come if performing musicians in increasing numbers take the time to do some musicological digging of their own. If just one violinist with the stature of a Menuhin, for example, would bend his talents and his technique to restudying the violin music of Corelli, Legrenzi, Leclair, Geminiani, Vivaldi, Viotti, and Tartini in a Baroque context and then play this music in the manner the public has a right to expect, 'twere a consummation devoutly to be wished.

1

Problems of Baroque Performance Today

In a recording studio in Europe not too long ago, the big-maned, big-named conductor sat in his high rehearsal chair, clothed in authority. The virtuoso recorder soloist, renowned in his own field, sat alert and waiting. The musicians leaned forward in their chairs, instruments at the ready, eyes on the conductor. The music began to flow, smooth and professional; the solo line soared—and within seconds the conductor stopped the orchestra, incredulous.

"Just what do you think you're doing?" he demanded.

"Why, I'm ornamenting the melodic line," said the soloist, rather taken aback.

"And you'd better stop!" shouted the conductor, suddenly enraged. "If Handel had wanted the solo line ornamented, he would have written in the ornaments himself! We'll play the music as written!"

"I'm sorry," said the soloist, bristling, "but to play this music as written would be barbaric. I must play it with the ornaments that the style calls for."

"I'll be damned if you do!" cried the conductor.

"God rest your soul!" retorted the soloist.

And the conductor stomped off in a rage, expecting that the recording company would have the soloist replaced. Instead, a new conductor took the chair half an hour later, and the recording proceeded without further incident.

Fiction? The dialogue has been fictionalized, but the incident did occur.

How is it, you ask, that a prominent conductor could be so ignorant of the laws that govern the performance of Baroque music? Doesn't everybody know the rules? "What everybody knows" can probably be summarized as follows: The Baroque period ran approximately from 1600 to 1750. Music written during this period shared certain characteristics: It was largely contrapuntal and became increasingly harmonic; it relied heavily on ornamentation; one of its most characteristic marks was the use of the basso continuo, where a harpsichordist played from a score or a single bass line with small numerals written under it; these figures told him what harmonies to use as the music unfolded. A gamba player played the same bass line as the harpsichordist, but without the chords, of course.

"What everybody knows" does not include the fact that strong Baroque influences began around 1575 and persisted to around 1800. Nor does it include the

1

fact that ornamentation could either be written out in full, as in many of the keyboard works of Bach; or jotted down in a sort of musical shorthand, as in the works of Couperin le Grand; or left out entirely with the understanding that the performer would put in his own. Here it not only called for a solid knowledge of the rules but also made great demands on an artist's powers of improvisation. Let me illustrate this point: Today one can go hear Maestro X conduct a Beethoven concerto with a Russian pianist and a Soviet orchestra in Moscow, and hear him lead the same music performed by American musicians in New York a month later, or by German musicians in Stuttgart the week after that, and the music will sound unmistakably the same, allowing for regional differences in orchestral discipline and tone color and the inspiration born of the moment. But in the eighteenth century one could go to hear a group of Baroque performers play a trio sonata by Handel one day and go hear the same group play the same work again the next day, and it would not come out the same at all—not if they knew what they were doing.

Research into Baroque performance practice is a relatively new phenomenon. In the early decades of the twentieth century, very few traditionally trained musicians concerned themselves with the Baroque period, and of those who did, only a very small percentage specialized to the point where they could perform early works with knowledge, sensitivity, and authority. Because knowledge by itself is not enough: in large doses it can degenerate into pedantry. And the air of authority by itself is not enough, as the anecdote at the beginning of this chapter illustrates. Sensitivity is the important ingredient that brings a performance to life, because it involves sympathy for the music, for the composer, and for the period in which he lived; sensitivity involves perceptiveness in choosing an appropriate style of Baroque ornamentation for a particular piece; and above all it combines with inspiration to allow the artist to adapt Baroque style with subtlety to the conditions of our own environment.

To understand this better, let us consider the kindred art of painting. A Baroque master sets down a portrait in oils; the subject, whether doge, prince, or noblewoman, is immortalized. Generations pass; art teachers dutifully tell their students about the famous portrait; it is studied and copied a thousand times a year. Comes the twentieth century, and the teachers and art critics are still at it. Behold, they say, those somber hues, how somber! That shaft of light, how exquisitely placed! That death's head in the corner—magnificent! And while the pedants are talking, a genuine inquisitive art historian comes along. "Ahem," he says, "this old masterpiece—what secrets does it hold? Perhaps we should clean it? X-ray it? Such ingrained layers of dust! Ah, well, here goes!" He sets to work with careful delicate hands and lo—the dust of the ages is lifted off, the somber hues turn out to be rich browns and yellows, the shaft of light is the section a long-dead custodian had begun to clean with a damp rag before being rudely interrupted, and the death's head in the left-hand corner (praised for decades as sublime symbolism) stands revealed as a medieval castle.

A work of art—any work of art, be it a painting or a piece of music—changes over the centuries, and so do the people who view it or listen to it. With paintings and literary masterpieces that have been continuously before the public through the

2

centuries, the change in public attitude has often been quite subtle and gradual; the Mona Lisa is a masterpiece to us in much the same way it was to those who viewed it centuries ago. But by far the major part of the output of Baroque composers has been hidden from view for two or three hundred years and more; this means that while it changed in relation to the music of other times and cultures, we ourselves changed without any reference to it except in a very limited way. Small wonder, then, that when the Baroque-music revival began to sweep across the world soon after World War II, so many embraced it enthusiastically for entirely the wrong reason—its so-called simplicity. It is only lately, and little by little, that the scholars and the new breed of performers have been wiping the dust off Baroque scores, and have brought new light and new insights to bear on Baroque performance. We now know that the much-admired simplicity only existed because we for our part failed to supply what performers were expected to supply—complexity. And we have become more aware of the difference in national styles (Italian Baroque, for example, as opposed to English or French or German Baroque); also we are now more aware of the differences within national styles (early Italian as opposed to late Italian Baroque, for instance).

Handel himself, that epitome of the Baroque, that very Italianate German Englishman, was acutely aware of the difference in national styles and performing practices. When he wrote his *Harpsichord Suite in D Minor*, the first measures of an "aria" were published as follows:

But when he republished it in England, he took English practice into account, changed the title to "Air in D Minor," and wrote out the ornamentation in this great detail:

Ideally then, any performer who wishes to play Handel correctly today has to be able to perform this same feat on his own. But how much art does it take, how many years of study, to turn eight simple quarter notes into more than forty smaller notes, not counting trills and sundry mordents? And when an almost infinite number of permutations seems possible, how does the performer make the right choice? Is there even such a thing as a "right" choice? Ah, for half an hour's quiet conversation with Quantz or C. P. E. Bach, or with old Bach, his father! Then it would not matter any more that for more than a century the Baroque tradition was totally lost and that for most of the twentieth century it has been almost completely misunderstood.

If we know anything at all about the Baroque ethos today, it is because musicologists have been able to reconstruct it, most painstakingly. The Beethoven tradition, in contrast, has been continuous; even today we can study with musicians who studied with musicians who studied with musicians who were around when Beethoven was a force to reckon with. It is like a laying-on of hands. They will say: "This measure is traditionally played slower," or "Here Beethoven himself ignored such-and-such a marking," and we accept it because it comes to us from someone who studied it with someone who learned it from someone who was Practically There. In spite of this continuity, in Beethoven's case it has been proven that memories have failed—notably Czerny's—and that tradition is often a liar. But what of Bach? And what of Handel? And who was around even earlier with Purcell? We have to turn to the chronicles of their peers, or of succeeding generations, and their mouths, as the Persian poet said, are stopped with dust.

This much is certain: In those rare cases where a Baroque composer wrote a melodic line that he did not wish anybody to alter or elaborate, he usually wrote a cautionary note, such as Come stà! ("as is," or "play as written"). But where the melodic line is spare, simple, and carries no cautionary notice, almost invariably the performer was expected to elaborate it. The composer in effect set up a very sketchy outline—a roadmap, shall we say, showing points from A to B; the musical traveler was expected to pick his own route. In a single measure, it is the musical equivalent of saying to a friend, "I don't care what you do at the Place de la Concorde, but be sure to meet me on the third level of the Eiffel Tower at 4:00 P.M." In an entire composition, it is like journeying from New York to San Francisco: the typical twentieth-century musician-motorist takes the superhighway as being the shortest route between given points; the true Baroque musician would take the scenic routes, putting in all manner of little side trips along the way. The variations would be endless. It would then be possible to go from New York to San Francisco a thousand times over, never covering exactly the same ground twice, and discovering fresh delights each time.

If this is so, you interject, what does one do with some of the works of J. S. Bach, or with Handel's "Air in D Minor," where the composer has worked out the ornamentation so carefully? What Bach and Handel are really saying is: "This is the general idea, friends; this is how I feel it could be done today. Tomorrow I may feel rather differently, and if you yourselves should come up with any good ideas, as I am sure you will, by all means let us have the pleasure of hearing them."

Three major problems arise in performing Baroque music today, and they concern the artist, the music, and the audience. How much preparation does an artist need? If we are to think in terms of perfection, it might take ten or fifteen years of intensive study before we could raise a generation of artists skilled enough to meet Baroque interpretative and technical standards. The danger is that in ten years we might acquire perfection—and lose our audience. Audiences are interested in Baroque music *now*, so it is today that our performers must begin, with whatever skills they have, adding to their expertise as they go along.

The second problem is the music. While the number of good editions keeps growing steadily, some Baroque masterworks are still only available in editions that are at best appalling. This adds yet another dimension to our already multidimensional Baroque performer: He must be technically proficient and knowledgeable, with the musicological sixth sense that enables him to distinguish the stylistically-correct edition from the run-of-the mill, so he can then come up with an inspired, seemingly-improvised performance once he has made his choice. The merits of various editions are discussed in later chapters in connection with individual works.

The third problem lies with the audience. Our audiences today seem eager for Baroque music, but are they ready to hear Baroque music the way it should be played? Having been educated to the greatness of Handel, they might applaud mightily should Handel suddenly appear with his favorite musicians and play a highly ornamented version of any of his instrumental or vocal works for us. But what would their reaction be if the local chamber orchestra tried the same approach? Might they say it sounded stilted, overdone, fussy, or pretentious? We don't know yet because an experiment of this sort has not yet been tried on a significant scale. Audience sophistication—or the lack of it—is a very real factor to take into account in programming. Brave and wise is the artist who goes beyond the current level of public taste and leads his audience on to a higher level of understanding through adventurous programming. Fortunately, there are a few such artists today; unfortunately, they are very, very few.

Simply stated, the artist's dilemma can be reduced to these terms: How much ornamentation should a performer use, and how much can the audience stand? Eighteenth-century audiences stood for increasingly larger doses until eventually even they became satiated and Baroque music faded away. But well beyond the time of C. P. E. Bach they were still clamoring for more. "The keyboard lacks the power to sustain long notes," he laments, "and to decrease or increase the volume of a tone or, to borrow an apt expression from painting, to shade. These conditions make it no small task to give a singing performance of an adagio without creating too much empty space and a consequent monotony due to a lack of sonority: or without making a silly caricature of it through an excessive use of rapid notes." And he adds: "Singers and performers on instruments which are not defective in this respect also do not dare to deliver an undecorated long note for fear of eliciting only bored yawns."

That was a problem that C. P. E. Bach, Quantz, and their fellow-musicians faced in the 1750s: performers were afraid that if they did not ornament profusely they would bore their audiences to death. The inference that is sometimes drawn—that performers in earlier decades of the Baroque era were ornamenting far less—does not necessarily hold true. Singers, for example, had become accustomed to coping with long and highly-ornamented vocal lines during the Renaissance; their technique and their flexibility carried over into the Baroque. Recorder players in the Renaissance, too, had become quite skillful, both in terms of pure technique and in the art of improvisation; the evolution of the more responsive, tonally better-focused Baroque recorders did not inhibit them in the least. Thus singing and recorder-playing had had the time needed for their practitioners to develop virtuoso techniques. The same holds true for cornetto-players, to a more limited extent; the early Baroque cornettists, although playing on wooden trumpets that had only a few holes and no keys, were more than a match for the upstart violinists who now sought to take their place.

It must be remembered that the violin was at a fairly early stage of its development. David D. Boyden believes that even the term *violino* did not become current in Italy until shortly after 1520, that three-stringed violins were being made by Andrea Amati at Cremona in the 1540s, and that Amati's first four-stringed violin was made in 1555—just 20 years before the date we have somewhat arbitrarily set as the beginning of the Baroque period.* Since Andrea Amati was one of the best violin makers of his time, it seems plausible to assume that most violins available in the early Baroque period were far from perfect, and that some of them may still have had only three strings. No wonder violin technique as we understand it was at a very elementary stage indeed.

If by some marvellous wrinkle in a time machine we were able to hear the same work being performed by both a cornetto player and a violinist at three widely-separated stages of the Baroque era (an unlikely series of events, since Baroque performances were generally given by composers interested in performing or promoting their own work, not the work of an earlier master), we might come up with the following scenario:

In 1575 the violinist, still unsure of his technique, would ornament very sparingly, even perfunctorily, while the cornetto player showed off his own rather spectacular brand of virtuosity.

By 1650 the contest would be more of a stand-off. Since the violin as an instrument had been greatly improved by then, and violin technique was much more secure, the cornettist would have to produce some dazzling high notes and extraordinary passage-work to defeat his rival.

By 1750 it would be "no contest"—no cornetto player could hope to compete successfully any longer with the dazzling array of ornaments a violinist could now put together.

Instrumental and technical developments were only two of several factors that controlled the development of Baroque style, particularly ornamentation. Nationality determined the social conditions that dictated the cultural environment. Consider the four great schools of Baroque music in the seventeenth and eighteenth centuries—the English, French, German, and Italian. In each of these countries, royal patronage was important. England had one great royal court that its composers could turn to; so had France, but in two centers—Paris and Versailles. The Germans had a multiplicity of smaller courts in addition to the court of the Emperor; the Italians, too, had many royal courts to which a composer could turn for patronage. Yet Italy had an additional advantage; since it was at one and the

* Boyden, *The History of Violin Playing from its Origins to 1761* (New York: Oxford University Press, 1965), pp. 19, 35.

same time not only a trading and banking society but a church-oriented society, vast wealth had been acquired by merchant princes as well as by the princes of the church. Members of both these classes competed with one another in sponsoring the arts, including music. No wonder that the arts, which had flowered so plentifully in Italy during the Renaissance, continued to flourish throughout the Baroque era!

Competition for royal appointments was extremely keen in Germany, as even the great J. S. Bach found out to his cost. Being a staunch Protestant, he could not turn to the wealthy Catholic Church for support; fortunately for him the Protestant tide ran strong in Germany and the Lutheran Church was more than willing to support church music at a grass-roots level. For much of his life, therefore, Bach felt he owed allegiance to three powerful forces—his pastor, the local town council, and God. He found the first two the hardest to please.

Now consider the situation of the composer in each of these four countries, from yet another point of view—that of performances. Because of the increasing permissiveness of the Catholic hierarchy in Italy (and perhaps because the Italian churches and cathedrals, with their high ceilings, their general spaciousness, and their feeling of airiness provided a better setting), a tradition of musical performances in a church setting grew up in Italy long before the time of Vivaldi. The performances at first were sacred in character, but it was not long before serious abstract secular music began to be performed. A general requirement (not rigidly enforced!) was that dance forms were forbidden. As a result, Italian composers began to develop the larger forms of music, and became expert at such forms as the trio sonata, the concerto grosso, the concerto for solo instrument(s) with orchestral accompaniment, and the sinfonia. J. S. Bach in his youth, seeking to improve his skills as a composer, began copying and transcribing the works of Vivaldi, Marcello and other Italian masters, taking the music apart and putting it together again. (See Bach's transcription and elaboration of a Vivaldi concerto, Appendix 1, p. 286.) The long, spun out phrases of the Brandenburg concertos, with their irresistible drive, and the various concertos Bach wrote for various instruments with orchestral accompaniment, are the direct result of the apprenticeship he served at long distance.

In France, as we have seen, the influence of the royal court was paramount; courtly dances therefore prevailed, either singly or strung together in a suite. Such was the dazzle of the French establishment that many of the courts of Germany adopted at least some of the customs of Versailles, and it was for practical as well as musical reasons that Bach, Telemann and other German composers reached out to Lully and to François Couperin le Grand until they themselves fully mastered the niceties of the French style.

Like the German composers to the north, French composers soon began to feel the lure of the larger Italian forms of musical composition; but unlike the Germans, the French as a group made a determined effort to stave off Italian influences as long as possible. Once Couperin had convinced himself of the true greatness of Corelli, French composers began to work actively towards a fusion of the two styles.

Meanwhile, across the Channel, English composers led by Handel and Geminiani absorbed the best that Italy, Germany, and France had to offer. Only the Italian

7

composers, of the four nationalistic schools we have named, were secure enough in their sense of leadership to feel no pressure to adapt their writing to alien ways.

In very general terms, this means that a musical or technical development in Italy took perhaps five years, perhaps ten, to become current in Germany and in England as well; and then it took another five to ten years to seep through into France. French developments got through to Germany and England within the same period of time; how quickly they crossed the Maritime Alps into Italy depended partly on chance.

The modern performer of Baroque music has to take these national "time-zones" into consideration; he cannot safely assume that a practice that was current in Venice or Naples in 1702 was necessarily known to the French at the same time, or vice versa. One must therefore be cautious when approaching the study of any new piece of Baroque music. But once the various possibilities have been explored, once the period of study is ended, enthusiasm should take over as performance time approaches.

A performer today has the advantage of hindsight, and with it the obligation to be historically and stylistically accurate—within reason. Thus we must seek to present small-scaled performances in small halls to secure the needed clarity and sense of balance; what we do not need to duplicate is the lack of adequate preparation, the use of defective instruments, and the out-of-tuneness that characterized eighteenth century performances, often through no fault of the performers themselves.

Which brings us to a very important question: What should a modern performance of Baroque music entail? Many performing groups today proudly proclaim that they are using "authentic instruments." Others qualify this further by claiming they use "authentic old instruments." Depending on the group, this can mean one of several things: (1) the instruments were made in the Baroque period and have not (or have) been altered since then; (2) the instruments have been made in our own time and approximate in varying degrees the authentic old instruments that have survived and have been reconstructed; (3) the instruments are frankly twentieth century adaptations of the old instruments. Beware!

Other performers make a fetish of pitch: "We play at old pitch!" has become a battle-cry, as well as a put-down of those presumed barbarians who dare to perform at modern pitch. But the definition of old pitch varies depending on the person one talks to: it could range from a semitone to a full tone-and-half below A = 440. Old pitch would also tend to produce a certain mellowness in the strings, or to take away a certain brilliance from the strings, depending on your point of view. Old pitch can be a plus under certain conditions; in itself, it does not impress.

Yet other groups claim they use "ornamentation"; on closer inquiry it turns out that in every slow movement they are using three trills and two mordents more than the ensemble that rehearses around the corner.

These various elements are important; singly or in combination they can contribute to the success of an evening of Baroque music-making. The most important elements are substance, style and spirit. Does the music belong? Is it well-edited? Has the continuo part been realized with a lively imagination? Are the string players using short, crisp bow strokes wherever these are called for? Is their vibrato firmly under control? Are they (and the wind players and singers if any) using crescendos and diminuendos on long notes—the famed Baroque practice of *messa di voce?* Is the ornamentation in keeping with the composer and the period in which the music was written? As for the spirit, is the music being performed with enthusiasm, elan, even a certain defiance and braggadocio? These should be at the very heart of Baroque music-making. The flashing eye, the flaring nostril, the exaggerated use of "body-English" were an integral part of the concert scene as composers, performers and audiences knew it two hundred and more years ago. They will cause our audiences to dissolve into laughter today, but these gestures were used then to incite performers as well as listeners to greater heights of fervor. Today we have to generate the same amount of excitement, without the bodily contortions.

With each work he plays, the present-day performer needs to ask himself: How much ornamentation is too much? How little is too little? If this question baffles us today, it also baffled the foremost practitioners in the late Baroque era. In their mid-eighteenth-century treatises Quantz, C. P. E. Bach, and Leopold Mozart all addressed themselves to it. C. P. E. insisted that the right balance could be found. "A golden mean," says he, "is difficult but not impossible to discover, particularly in view of the fact that our most usual (keyboard) sustaining devices, such as the trill and the mordent, are also well known to other instruments and the voice. Such embellishments must be full and so performed that the listener will believe that he is hearing only the original note. This requires a freedom of performance that rules out everything slavish and mechanical."

The proper use of ornamentation, then, is at the very heart of Baroque music-making. One must know the rules, but one must not play entirely by the book. Believability is a key word. Freedom is another. Formal ornaments must not be used as mere formulae. "Play from the soul," cries C. P. E., "not like a trained bird!"

Our Baroque performer therefore has to be flexible in his attitudes. The individual written note in the melodic line is no longer sacred; more often than not it is a guide to be filled in and elaborated, or even deviated from, at the performer's discretion. Further, the instrumentation itself is not sacrosanct. Ah, what a joy is this, and how different from the situation with later chamber music! If by chance you've formed a standard piano quartet, and planned an evening around Kasamovsky's dissonant *Quartet for Prepared Piano and Unprepared Strings,* consider what difficulties arise if any one member of your group does not show up: You may have to look for different music altogether. With Baroque music these difficulties largely disappear. You hand out a set of parts; who shows up determines who plays what. If it's a trio sonata for two violins and basso continuo (careful, that makes four players!) and the violinist does not show up, the flutist can take his place, with a minimum of transposition. If the cellist is missing, all is not lost; look for a bas-

9

soonist, or a bass recorder player (they're hungry to make music). If you cannot find either, drop the part! The keyboard has the bass line, anyway, and if the pianist or harpsichordist is absent, try it with flute, violin and cello. It will work!

Baroque musicians themselves seem to have had very few qualms about dropping a single part, and if J. S. Bach's own practice offers any criterion, they had equally few qualms about adding parts to a composition. His admirer Forkel says he was able, "if a single bass part was laid before him (and often it was a poorly figured one), immediately to play from it a trio or quartet; nay, he even went so far, when he was in a cheerful humor and in the full consciousness of his powers, as to add extempore to three single parts a fourth part, and thus to make a quartet of a trio."* Today this would be frowned on as tampering with the score.

So much for the music; what of the instruments? If you want to enjoy a new world of experience and aren't too finicky, do not rule out anything—not even a wash-tub bass. (Some very interesting recordings of baroque music have been made by an "electric ensemble.") With a piano, modern stringed instruments are fine. So is a modern flute, a modern oboe, a modern oboe d'amore. A recorder is less successful, because its tone is substantially weaker; a sonata for recorder and piano becomes a losing battle for the hapless wind player unless the pianist is sympathetic and plays down. *And* keeps his foot away from that pedal. A lute or, in a pinch, a guitar makes a good substitute for a harpsichord; but when all is said and done, the very best substitute for a harpsichord is another harpsichord.

Harpsichord prices vary depending on who makes them and how. A single-manual (that is, one-keyboard) instrument generally costs less than a double-manual or two-keyboard harpsichord of comparable quality. Concert instruments such as those used by leading harpsichordists are expensive, but they are not necessarily the most expensive. Of course these are custom-built instruments, made to the artist's specifications to meet his particular performing needs. Some have case walls only three-sixteenths of an inch thick. They may be over eight feet long and still weigh only around one hundred and sixty pounds or so. That is light indeed! A double manual with *handstops* (i.e., where the registers can be changed by hand) costs somewhat less than the same instrument with pedals. Remember, however, that though pedals are convenient because they free the hands, some of the greatest harpsichordists of our time scornfully reject the idea of a harpsichord equipped with pedals. "Historically unacceptable," they snap, pointing out that pedals did not come into use until very late in the Baroque period, even though Mace, in *Musick's Monument*, mentions that a London builder called John Hayward had devised such an instrument around 1660. These purists set the registration for each work before they begin, and they only make changes (if they make them at all) when the music comes to a halt, as at a double bar. This too must have been the way C. P. E. Bach performed until, almost a full century after Hayward's invention, he came across a similar invention by a German maker. He then praised it unreservedly: "The fine invention of our celebrated Holefeld [sic] which makes it possible to increase or decrease the registration by means of pedals, while playing, has made the harpsichord, particularly the single-manual kind, a much-improved instrument, and, fortunately, eliminated all difficulties connected with the performance of a piano. If only all harpsichords were similarly constructed as a tribute to good taste!"* Obviously C. P. E. Bach was enthralled once he saw the possibility of changing registration in the middle of a piece without having to take his hands off the keyboard; in Chapter 10 of our book we shall see how he put this new freedom to good use in a concerto. Since this was far from being standard practice, however, the purists still have a point.

If your budget cannot stand the strain of buying an already-completed harpsichord, consider buying a kit and building it yourself. Kits come in a wide range of prices; the cheaper ones will take you from sixty to a hundred hours to build, but more sophisticated kits may take from six hundred hours to a year to build. Can you do it? Even if you are sure you can, get a written agreement from each member of your family that they will not move parts around or "clean up" if you should put the work aside for a moment, a day, or a week. . . .

The early Baroque period was dominated by the harpsichord in combination with two other instruments, the recorder and the viola da gamba. Even today recorders and harpsichords make great music together; enough has been published for this combination to give you a lifetime of enjoyment. Once you have a good little recorder group going, you may want to add some other instruments. A gamba would take priority, but a cello can substitute if played softly. Then there are the delightful Baroque oboe, the oboe d'amore, and the oboe da caccia. But beware! Some replicas of ancient wind instruments are made to sound at modern pitch (A = 440); others are made to sound at old pitch (anywhere from a half tone to a full tone below). If you acquire a Baroque oboe at old pitch, you can tune the harpsichord down to match, and your string-player friends may oblige, too, though not without some grumbling (they lose brilliance). But recorders will not be able to join in unless they too have been built at the corresponding pitch.

Recorders are the easiest of all instruments to learn to play quickly; they come in seven sizes, with minor variations in length and bore. The little sopranino—high-pitched, brilliant, and a little hard to take unless the instrument has been voiced by an outstanding craftsman—is so tiny that finger-hole spacing becomes a major problem; if your fingers are at all broad, stay away from this one. It's chromatic, like the rest of the recorder family. You can use it in some consort music, a solo piece or two, and in some flashy concertos by Vivaldi.

The soprano recorder sounds a fourth below the sopranino. It generally plays the top line in a recorder consort, but aside from a couple of concertos there's not much authentic solo material available for it. The consort literature, however, is considerable. The soprano recorder's tone is sweeter and fuller than that of a sopranino.

The alto is *the* instrument of the Baroque period. Its solo literature is plentiful; consort music abounds. Bach used it in some of his cantatas; and he used it in the fourth Brandenburg concerto, magnificently. Telemann used it to dazzling effect, both in solos and duets. Handel wrote for it some of the most appealing sonatas in

---

* C. P. E. Bach, *Essay on the True Art of Playing Keyboard Instruments,* trans. and ed. William J. Mitchell (New York: W. W. Norton, 1949), pp. 368–369.

the recorder repertoire. Its tone can be mellow or strong, fluty or reedy, depending on the maker and his methods. As recorder players grow in skill, they tend to acquire more than one alto; some save one particular alto recorder for Bach, another for Handel, yet another for Telemann, depending entirely on the instrument's tonal characteristics and the feel of the music.

When buying a tenor see that is has double holes or double keys; you will not be able to play low C sharp on a tenor that has just one key. In choosing a bass, look for an instrument that speaks easily, from its lowest register all the way to the top. Keys help, including a split key for low F and F sharp. Until a few short years ago just about every bass recorder was made with a bassoon-style "crook" for the mouthpiece; more recently, "direct-blow" basses became available—you blow into these as you would into an alto. They have a strong, clear, flexible tone; the old jibe that you can only hear a bass in a consort when the bass stops playing no longer holds true.

The great bass starts on the C a fourth below the F of the bass. The contrabass is the granddaddy of them all; it starts a full octave below the low F of the bass recorder. Do not play these instruments unless you are strong of wind and limb. The chief drawback, however, lies in the great finger-stretch needed to produce the notes. Keys help, but not much.

Baroque flutes are much harder to come by than recorders, since too few are being made. The earliest flutes used in the Baroque period had just six holes, and the recorder held its own against the upstart *flauto traverso* until a D sharp key was added to the flute about 1660. By the time of J. S. Bach the flute had begun to gain the upper hand, but it was not till the late Baroque period that it supplanted the recorder entirely. Look for a flute that has good intonation, though you may never find one that is absolutely in tune.

Earlier wind instruments, such as the krummhorn, kortholt, or rauschpfeif, can bring fresh delight to the music lover who wants a change from the sweet recorder tone; a krummhorn in particular sounds like an angry hornet looking for a picnicker. Play one before you decide this is what you want. All these instruments use capped reeds (that is, reeds that are not touched directly by the lips) and require somewhat more care than does a recorder. Though they are basically Renaissance instruments, they can be used with or instead of recorders in early Baroque music. A simple rule of thumb: If the music goes beyond the range of any of these instruments, it's from the wrong period, so forget it.

Baroque oboe reeds resemble their modern counterparts. The tone is fat and languorous, somewhat lazier and less flexible than that of the oboe today. Buy extra reeds when you acquire your instrument, and the sooner you learn to make your own reeds the better. It is difficult and will take some practice but will make you independent and save you money.

Yet another woodwind instrument you might consider is the rankett or rackett, an early form of bassoon. You can tell a Renaissance rankett from a Baroque rankett because the earlier instrument is smaller and looks like a beer can with a bent straw stuck in it, while the Baroque rankett is larger and looks like a large coffee can with a straw stuck in it. Despite its relatively small size the tone is deep because the sounding tube is bored in such a way that it doubles back on itself. The Baroque rankett is often referred to as a *Wurst-fagott,* or "sausage bassoon."

The last instrument we will discuss is one of the most typical of the period—the viola da gamba. Here again, the viol family is large, but you need consider just four sizes. The soprano or descant is mostly a consort instrument; the alto (or treble) is used for both solo and consort work; the tenor gamba can be slightly larger or much larger than the alto, depending on where it was made; the bass has a wide range and a wider repertoire. With a good bass gamba in your hands, you can begin by playing the simpler continuo parts, and as your skill improves you can go on to the more difficult and rewarding solo literature.

There are very few reputable gamba makers in the world today, and each one has enough orders to keep him busy for years. The demand for even commercially-made instruments far outstrips the supply. The cheaper instruments are likely to be glorified soapboxes; on the other hand a high price in itself is no guarantee that the instrument is good. Try the gamba yourself if you can, or enlist the aid of a knowledgeable friend, or even appeal to the good nature of one of the established gamba players in the big city nearest you.

Not one of the instruments we have discussed is inordinately difficult to play. Even a beginner should be making music in an elementary way within a very few days. Where you go from there depends partly on how much time you devote to your instrument. You can ease off at any point you want or put in some intensive study and try to become, if not a virtuoso, then at least reasonably expert. This will involve more than just reading notes; you will have to study ornamentation and improvisation, and if you're a harpsichordist you will want to study thorough bass. Yes, there will be hours, weeks, months, even years of hard work; and what are the rewards? Through your fingers and your instrument, you will be able to bring a long-past era gloriously to life.

It is fair to warn you here that people who get involved in Baroque music become inveterate instrument collectors. One musician acquired ten harpsichords (he gave three to a son), one small spinet, two violins (one a Stainer), a violino piccolo, three violas, one little bass, two cellos, one viola da gamba, and a lute. Quite a collection for most people, but barely enough for the owner, a one-time cantor from Leipzig, Johann Sebastian Bach.

2

Beyond the Notes:
Ornamentation, Free Figuration,
Dynamics

The primary aim of all embellishments is to connect notes.
C. P. E. Bach, Essay, p. 84.

The roots of Baroque ornamentation can be found in the vocal music of the Renaissance; although it was written without frills, in practice it was very highly ornamented. The Baroque period saw a threefold development: it freed instrumental music from its dependence on vocal music, it named and codified the more common ornaments of the Renaissance, and it applied these ornaments to all music, instrumental as well as vocal. In *The Interpretation of Early Music*, Robert Donington lists more than one hundred and twenty-five signs that have been used for ornaments, one way or another, in early music;* only a handful, however, were used often enough to have become characteristic of Baroque music: the appoggiatura, the trill, the mordent, the turn—and that's about it. It follows therefore that anybody who learns these ornaments, and learns them thoroughly, is well on his way to achieving excellence in Baroque interpretation. Or is he?

It is true that the formulas for Baroque ornaments are easily learned. Even the exceptions—and they are many—can be mastered with time and patience. The characteristics of national schools can be noted. The idiosyncrasies of individual composers present no grave problem. But having learned all these, a more challenging task remains, because ornamentation goes beyond the business of tacking on artificial ornaments, like lights on a Christmas tree; ornamentation includes what I can only describe as free figuration—notes that fill in the contours of the melody as originally written, without distorting it, and give it a transcendental beauty. (Individual notes in the original melody can be moved up or down an octave, if such a move helps to create a smoother, more attractive, ornamented line.)

The first part of this chapter will therefore deal with basic Baroque ornaments; the second part will deal with figuration. Only the basic ornaments will be dealt with because the ground has been fully covered elsewhere; for example, the earnest student who wishes to find ornaments listed and described in profusion has only to turn to R. D. Donington's *The Interpretation of Early Music*, which was just mentioned; a section entitled "Index of Ornaments" (pages 573–580) forms a very useful

---

* Rev. ed. (New York: St. Martin, 1974).

dictionary of signs. If the player wants to take in all the rules, the exceptions, and the etceteras as they apply to the late Baroque period, he has only to turn to the books by C. P. E. Bach and Quantz. These should help him cope with almost any situation he is likely to encounter. As for the idiosyncrasies of the truly great, who made their own rules and often lived by them, he will find in this book a step-by-step presentation of how Bach, Corelli, Tartini, and others wanted some of their ornaments played. Finally, for figuration, we will look at formulas suggested by Quantz. Examples of free figuration in works by Handel, Vivaldi, Bach, Telemann, Corelli, Geminiani, Tartini, and other composers will be found in later chapters.

The Appoggiatura

The *appoggiatura* is a note that precedes a melodic note, steals some of its value, and is distinguished from it by the manner of writing—either it is written in small type, or with the stem up when normally a note would be written stem down, or both:

C. P. E. Bach as well as Quantz and other authorities stress the fact that the appoggiatura makes a double contribution: It improves the melody by linking notes smoothly together, and at the same time it livens up the harmony, since it is dissonant to the chord. It modifies, not just a single note, but the entire chord to which that note belongs.

The appoggiatura, says C. P. E., is louder than the tone that follows it, which is called a *release.* Both the appoggiatura and its release should always be connected (played legato) whether they are joined by a slur or not.

As for duration: In the early part of the Baroque period, an appoggiatura was almost always written as an eighth note, no matter what its actual length in performance. Later composers found it safer to write out its exact duration. C. P. E. Bach gives these written examples:

Here is a simple rule of thumb for length: If the release is duple length, the appoggiatura preempts half its value; if it is triple length (a dotted note), the appoggiatura takes two-thirds its value.

Tied and slurred notes present a rather more special problem. Here the appoggiatura not only takes over the prescribed time-value from its release but sometimes displaces it entirely, affecting the values of notes that follow:

Even more remarkable, when an appoggiatura and its release are followed by a rest, the rest may be wiped out entirely:

C. P. E. Bach   Quantz

Though this practice is attested to by C. P. E. Bach, Quantz, and others, modern performers can find it unsettling.

Short appoggiaturas can carry one or more tails—and lead to endless arguments. Play them quickly, when they fill in the interval of a third, says C. P. E., but in an *adagio* (a general term for a slow movement) play them as the first eighth of a triplet; they will sound more expressive.

Quantz distinguishes between accented and unaccented appoggiaturas. Accented ones occur on the beat. The unaccented (or in his phraseology, "passing") appoggiaturas fill in the gaps between notes that descend in thirds:

Using our rule of thumb, you would perform these this way:

According to Quantz you would be wrong. He in fact makes such appoggiaturas a part of the preceding note, and expresses them in notation as:

and in terms of actual sound demands that the dots be lengthened, and the sixteenths shortened, so the passage would come out sounding:

These appoggiaturas are part of the French style of playing, explains Quantz, hence the inequality.

One final point to remember: While the appoggiatura was one of the most popular Baroque ornaments and was freely written in by composers, it was often left to the performer to supply. So be guided by good sense, and if you feel a particular passage calls for an appoggiatura, use it. And is there any one type of music, you ask, where appoggiaturas might be most appropriate? Let's toss the question to C. P. E. Bach. Use very many in affettuoso passages, says he, because their pianissimo releases make such a passage very effective.

The oracle has spoken.

The Trill

Trills are the most difficult ornaments, says C. P. E. They are like salt, claims Tartini; use liberally, but beware!

The trouble with Baroque trills as they relate to us is mainly the trouble with us. The average musician sees them through the fog of history, dimly recognizes a sign that says "trill," and proceeds to execute it the way he plays the trills he knows best—early and late nineteenth-century trills and twentieth-century trills. How often do we not hear good violinists—not only performers but teachers as well—start a Bach trill on the main note itself!

In *The Interpretation of Early Music*, Donington gives various examples of Baroque trills, particularly those he interprets as starting on the upper auxiliary as an appoggiatura:

Despite the appoggiatura Donington's rendition should be regarded as essentially a trill on the principal note.

To help clear up some of the confusion and to do some exploring for ourselves, we will pick a group of articulate composers from 1600 to 1770, look through their theoretical writings or pedagogical instructions, and see what common ground we can find.

The sign *m* to denote a trill was used by the vast majority of Baroque composers, including Jacques Champion Chambonnières (born between 1601 and 1611, died 1672), first chamber clavichordist to Louis XIV; Gaspard le Roux (circa 1660–circa 1710); François Dieupart (died circa 1740), who played harpsichord under Handel's direction at a theater in London; Jean François Dandrieu (1682–1738); and finally C. P. E. Bach (1714–1788).

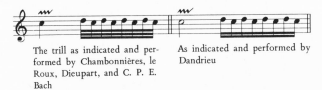

The trill as indicated and per-
formed by Chambonnières, le
Roux, Dieupart, and C. P. E.
Bach

As indicated and performed by
Dandrieu

Jean-Henri d'Anglebert (1635–1691) and Jean-Philippe Rameau (1683–1764) each used an *n* sign, with d'Anglebert spelling out his trill in thirty-seconds like Chambonnières and Rameau spelling it out in sixteenths like Dandrieu:

d'Anglebert

Rameau

J. S. Bach, too, used an *n* for a trill, but in working it out he came closer to Georg Muffat (1653–1704) and his son Gottlieb Muffat (1690–1770), both of whom indicated a trill by a *t*:

J. S. Bach

Georg Muffat

Gottlieb Muffat

Giuseppe Tartini (1692–1770) trilled like Chambonnières, Rameau, and C. P. E. Bach, but he was already using *tr* to denote a trill. In England a century earlier, Henry Purcell (born circa 1659, died 1695) trilled the same way, but he used a different sign altogether:

Tartini

Purcell

Though on paper some composers worked out their trills in thirty-seconds and others in sixteenths, this should not be taken to mean that a Chambonnières trill is to be played twice as fast as a trill by Dandrieu or Rameau. The composers merely showed the general shape of the ornament rather than the speed or intensity of the beats.

We see from the examples above that the standard Baroque trill—and this includes the Bach trill—does not start on its principal note but on the note above. In most cases the trill goes straight on through the full value of the note, but J. S. Bach himself, like the Muffats and a few other composers, prefers to cut the trill short, steady himself on the main note for a second, and then get on with other business at hand, much like a person cannily stepping off a somewhat unsteady escalator.

Another way to end the trill is to add what C. P. E. Bach calls a *suffix*—two small notes tacked on to the end. The suffix can be either written out in full, or indicated by a symbol. Since the symbol resembles the sign for a long mordent, it could cause confusion.

Written one of these three ways   Performed thus

A trill without a suffix is best played in a descending series of notes. Omit the suffix from consecutive trills, as well as from trills followed by short notes that are capable of replacing it.

The ascending trill is used mainly over long notes, especially, says C. P. E. Bach, at cadences and before fermatas.

Three symbols for an ascending trill (left) and how it is played (right). The first is most familiar to keyboard players.

The descending trill has more notes in it than other trills, and it was popular in the early Baroque. By C. P. E.'s time it was limited to repeated notes, descending progressions, and downward leaps of a third, where it neatly filled in the intervals:

Descending trill

The last trill we will consider elicited C. P. E.'s greatest praise—the short or half trill, or *Pralltriller*. He calls it "the least dispensable, the most attractive, . . . the most difficult embellishment." It has to be played with "exceeding speed"; it must "literally crackle." The short trill is used only with descending seconds. The notes must be short in themselves or have been shortened by an appoggiatura:

The short or half trill (Pralltriller)

Sometimes the symbol appears over a note that is made longer by a fermata:

Here you make the appoggiatura quite long, and "snap" the short trill quickly as your fingers come off the keys.

The Turn

This versatile ornament, which adds so much charm to music, revolves around the principal note and consists basically of the first four notes of the descending trill. Its interpretation depends largely on the tempo of the music:

Same turn at different tempos (C. P. E. Bach)

An accidental is generally indicated by the placement of a sharp above the turn symbol. A sharp to the left means that the note above the main note is sharpened, while a sharp on the right applies to the note below the main note:

In fast movements a turn may sometimes be used instead of a trill, but never on long notes: a turn would take up only part of a long note's value, causing an awkward gap in continuity. In a slow movement, strangely enough, the substitution works out quite well, because there the turn can be played slowly, and the pause on the main note (provided it is not too long) can heighten the pleasure of the resolution. In fast movements, a succession of trills can be more comfortably played as turns, and will be much easier on the ear.

A turn may substitute for a trill under certain conditions: in a slow tempo *(left)* or a fast tempo *(right)*.

Turns shown after notes, or between notes, are meant to be performed differently. C. P. E. Bach considers three cases:

(1) when the note is long

(2) when the sign appears over a tie

(3) when it appears after a dotted note

Readers are again referred to C. P. E. Bach's chapter on embellishments for a detailed discussion of the turn and other ornaments.

The Mordent

What we now call the *mordent* was called the *short mordent* in Baroque times. The actual Baroque mordent was long. Indicated as follows  , it would be played  and could be extended to without a change of sign.

The long mordent should be played only with long notes, but its symbol does appear over short notes in a slow tempo. The short mordent is indicated over notes of all sizes at all tempi:

written   played

To avoid confusion: The long mordent is written like an *m* with a vertical stroke through it; the short mordent, like an *n* with a similar stroke.

Short mordents add brilliance to leaps. They may be used effectively with ascending seconds, but not with descending seconds; there, an inverted mordent or halftrill is more appropriate:

written   could be played

C. P. E. Bach points out that the short mordent, of all ornaments, was interpolated most often in the bass by Baroque performers, especially on high notes that

are approached by step   or by leap

or when the following note dropped by an octave

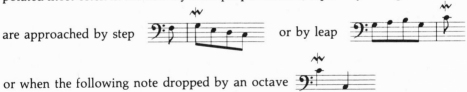

The brilliance and bite of a short mordent is enhanced if the interval between the two tones is changed to a half step.

Thus: 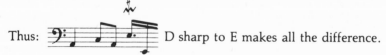 D sharp to E makes all the difference.

The Compound Appoggiatura

Be reassured, despite its name, there is nothing complex about the *compound appoggiatura*. It comes in just two ways:

The principal tone is preceded by the tones below and above it; play these notes quickly!

The note preceding the principal note is repeated, and a note just above the principal note is added. The ornament here is played more slowly.

The first type of compound appoggiatura can be found and used in all sorts of tempos, but the second should be reserved for slow passages only. C. P. E. says that with both types, Baroque performers played the notes of the appoggiatura more softly than the principal note.

C. P. E. Bach particularly recommends use of the compound appoggiatura—in slow tempos—when it is placed between two notes an augmented second apart, as it then makes the dissonance more acceptable.

Extraordinarily simple? The Baroque masters must have found it so, too, which is why they came up with a complication—what do you do when a note is repeated and then descends, or when it goes up by step and then descends?

You use the *dotted compound appoggiatura*, of course, at points we have marked with an asterisk.

The dotted compound appoggiatura steals as much time as is necessary from the note it modifies; the notes we have marked with an asterisk in these examples above are both reduced to thirty-seconds.

How is a dotted compound appoggiatura notated?
It can reveal its true nature right away:

or it can appear as a simple ascending appoggiatura:

You break up the simple appoggiatura by introducing a second, short appoggiatura above the principal note and dotting the first appoggiatura:

The ornament takes as much value as is necessary from the succeeding F, so the passage will be played as follows:

C. P. E. states that the dotted note should be emphasized and the others played softly. "The second note is connected as rapidly as possible with the principal tone and all three are slurred."*

Points to remember:

The dotted compound appoggiatura is never used in quick movements but is effective in affettuoso passages.

The note that follows the ornament—the "release"—gives up as much of its own value as necessary.

"The slower the tempo," says C. P. E., "and the more expressive the melody, the longer the dot must be held." And he gives this example:

In the 1787 edition of *Essay on the True Art* C. P. E. gives "right" and "wrong" examples of the notation of a dotted compound appoggiatura that is played as follows:

* *Essay*, p. 135.

23

The wrong notation is given as a dotted sixteenth followed by a thirty-second:

The "right" notation is given as an eighth followed by a thirty-second. Note that the eighth is undotted:

and if you check back a few lines you will find that the eighth is also undotted in the example where Bach shows how these notes are actually played! Perhaps this is a variant from the normal, and can be accepted as such. It could be a misprint, however; notation and execution would then be:

The Slide

The *slide* may consist of two or three notes, and the two-note slide may be dotted or undotted.

Four ways to show a two-note slide: (1) as small sixteenths, (2) as small thirty-seconds, (3) as large thirty-seconds, and (4) by a special symbol.

Three ways to look at a three-note slide: (1) in small notation, (2) C. P. E. Bach's own symbol, (3) as it is played.

The manner of notating and playing the dotted two-note slide may best be learned by studying some of the examples C. P. E. gives:

written   played

The smooth working-out of the ornament in the preceding examples should not blind us to its versatility. For example, here's how it can be used:

written   played   *p*   *f*

Finally, the ornament can be worked out differently in two or more identical situations:

(1) Written so;   (2) play it this way—   (3) or this!

Free Ornamentation

J. J. Quantz, in a remarkable series of tables, has given us a fine insight into the infinite variety possible in free ornamentation. Most often he takes not phrases but two- and three-note fragments, varying them in a number of imaginative ways. To save you time we have condensed some of these tables within the following pages.

Quantz did not claim that his examples would make us great ornamentors overnight. Rather their purpose was to make his younger contemporaries aware of the very great possibilities and by freeing their imagination make it that much easier for them to attempt the art of ornamentation.

For a start, let us look at some of the variants that Quantz got out of a single note—C above middle C repeated three times:

Johann Joachim Quantz *On Playing the Flute*, trans. Edward R. Reilly (New York: Schirmer Books, 1966), p. 140.

Play these and all succeeding examples over and over until the sound of each segment is firmly in your ear.

25

These are only some of the variants that Quantz has come up with. Variant 1 seems no better than the original; in fact the thrice-repeated ornament on a single note only points up the banality of certain types of ornamentation. To our ears, either of these alternatives would sound better: a turn on the first quarter note only or no turn on the first quarter note and turns on the other two. Variants 2 and 3 display melodic as well as rhythmic variety. In variant 4 the syncopated leap to G is masterly. And even though the appoggiaturas that follow bring us relentlessly back to C, the hold of the three repeated Cs has been broken. Note too that since there is a rest in this measure the appoggiatura on D can become a quarter note, and the quarter rest will be displaced entirely. Variant 5 would sound bright in a fast passage, and it could be played very affettuoso in slower tempos; variant 6, on the other hand, would work best in a slow tempo. Both variants 7 and 8 sound like the ending to a concerto; variant 9 has the greatest rhythmic variety of all. Variant 10 combines triplets with straight sixteenths and a quarter. It is safe, and far better than nothing.

At this point you will find it useful to work out a few variants of your own on paper. Melodic fluidity is important—the part must sing. Any leaps must lie within the implied harmony. But leaps should be the exception; if you move by step, you ensure smoothness. And how about rhythmic vitality? Are all your variants basically the same, or are you allowing for a change of pace? If this seems like rough going, do not despair—you will get some more practice in a moment.

Now here is another three-note fragment that Quantz is going to work on:

Try it on your own. Although at first glance this example seems more promising than the three repeated Cs, you may actually find it more restrictive. Now compare your efforts with these selected variants by Quantz:

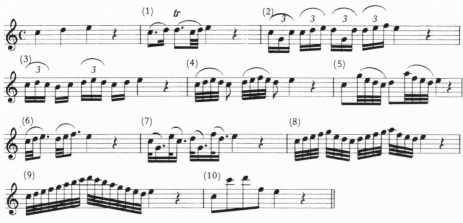

Quantz, *On Playing the Flute*, p. 141.

You may have found variant 10 the most satisfying, though it is easy to imagine contexts in which any of the others would work well indeed.

The very next three-note segment turns back on itself; work on it awhile, and again compare your efforts with Quantz's:

Quantz, *On Playing the Flute*, p. 147

Let us compare notes now on how well we think Quantz has done in each case. For a start, variant 4 seems weaker than variant 3, and variant 3 seems weaker than variant 2. Why? In fact, why does variant 4 look like the weakest variant in the whole set? Not because it runs through the tones of the tonic triad; so do many of the others. Nor could it be a combination of that and rhythmic sameness; look at variant 13. But then, variant 13 soars up to high C, and that in itself would be a high point in any grand opera. Yes, there we have it! In variant 4 we hear no dramatic first leap, no smoothly flowing line—just insipid movement in thirds. What do you think would happen if you introduced a slide on the first C and the second E in variant 4? Magic! Notice too how variants 1, 2, 3, 5, and 13 succeed in varying degrees, depending on how free and untrammeled the sequence of notes appears to be.

We move on now to a sequence of two notes only:

Here are some of the possibilities, as Quantz has worked them out:

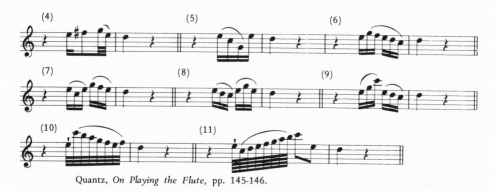

Quantz, *On Playing the Flute*, pp. 145-146.

The previous examples dealt with the descent of a major second. Now here are two variants for a descending minor third:

Based on Quantz, *On Playing the Flute*, p. 147, ii and kk.

In variant 11 of the previous set, we were introduced to sixty-fourths for the first time. In variant 2 above, we have not only sixty-fourths but one-hundred-and-twenty-eighths. If these seem to you like miniscule subdivisions, smaller ones are yet to come. These busy little notes came to be a characteristic feature of performance in the late Baroque period; if you are going to play late Baroque music (and who isn't?) you might as well get used to seeing and playing them. For example, in his *L'Art du Violon* (Paris, 1798) Cartier reproduced a Nardini violin sonata with the original melodic line supplemented by an elaboration. In this sample measure

Original melody as written:

Ornamented version as played:

there are six beams in the figuration before the trill; you're playing two-hundred-and-fifty-sixths, and, as if matters aren't complicated enough, there are double stops thrown in throughout the movement.*

* Caution: Do not add up the very small notes used in baroque ornamentation and expect to come up with a mathematically correct total. The notes are only meant to convey a visual image of the general shape of the figuration.

As a final example we take a dramatic two-note downward leap of a seventh, which in this working out Quantz transforms into a leap of a sixth followed by a minor second:

Quantz, *On Playing the Flute*, p. 149.

Yes, you *are* looking at a G sharp in variant 1, an F natural in variant 2, and an F sharp in variant 3.

We come now to a unique document from the Baroque era—a master lesson by Quantz. In a chapter on playing the adagio (which, as we have previously mentioned, is a coverall name for any Baroque slow movement) he not only weaves the embellishments he has shown us into a simple air, but he also analyzes all thirty-two measures of it in extraordinary detail. C. P. E. Bach, Muffat, and others have spoken of dynamics in relation to performance, it is true; yet the Quantz effort is perhaps the only instance in all of Baroque literature where a note-by-note analysis of dynamics has been offered by a Baroque master.

And yet its importance has been largely overlooked, perhaps because in Quantz's book the music and its analysis appear on different pages. Much is lost when one has to flip pages back and forth; the analysis then seems as dry as it is fussy. This defect is overcome when the analysis is placed directly beneath each relevant measure, as we shall do here now. Further, we are numbering the notes in each measure consecutively, making identification easy; the analysis now comes to life.

Here then is Quantz's air, plain and ornamented, with his own performance notes beneath each measure. Since Edward R. Reilly's translation of Quantz's *On Playing the Flute* cannot be bettered, we have followed it closely; please note that he uses the terms *weak* and *strong* deliberately; they should by no means be confused with piano and forte but instead treated as shades.

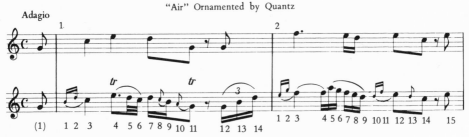

Pick-up note (1) crescendo. *Measure 1:* Notes 1, 2 weak, 3 stronger, crescendo; 4 with trill, strong, decrescendo; 5, 6 weak; 7 strong, 8 weak, 9 strong, 10 and 11 weak; 12 weak, 13 and 14 stronger.
Measure 2: 1, 2 weak, 3 crescendo to 4; 5, 6, weak; 7, 8, 9 stronger; 10, 11 weak; 12 strong, 13 weak, 14 strong and decrescendo, 15 crescendo.

Measure 3: 1 crescendo, 2, 3 weak; 4 crescendo, 5, 6, 7, weak; 8 strong, 9 weak, 10 strong, 11 weak, 12 strong, 13 weak.

Measure 4: 1 strong, 2 crescendo, 3 and 4 weak, 5 crescendo, 6 weak, 7 crescendo, 8 decrescendo, 9 crescendo, 10–13 weak.

Measure 5: 1 crescendo, 2, 3, weak; 4 strong, 5 and 6 weak, 7 strong, 8 and 9 weak, 10 with trill strong, 11 and 12 weak, 13 strong, 14 strong*, 15–17 weak, 18 strong.

Measure 6: 1 strong, 2 weak, 3–5 decrescendo, 6 strong, 7 weak, 8–10 decrescendo.

  *In this group of notes, and in other small-note groupings in later measures, the note values do not always add up correctly. They should therefore be treated as mere indications of relative value. Here, to be mathematically correct, either the D would have to be a dotted thirty-second, or the two following notes would have to be sixty-fourths.

Measure 6 (cont'd.): 1 strong, 2 weak, 3–5 crescendo, 6–8 decrescendo, 9 crescendo.

Measure 7: 1 still crescendo, 2–5 weak, 6, 7 strong and with hard attack, 8–11 weak, 12 strong and with hard attack, 13 weak, 14 with trill crescendo, 15 weak, 16 crescendo, 17–20 crescendo, 21–25 crescendo.

Measure 8: 1 weak and crescendo, 2, 3, weak; 4 strong, 5 and 6 weak, 7 strong, 8 and 9 weak, 10 with trill, 11 weak, 12 crescendo, 13 strong.
Measure 9: 1 with trill, strong and decrescendo; 2, 3 weak, 4 strong, 5–7 weak, 8 crescendo, 9 with trill decrescendo, 10 crescendo, 11–15 decrescendo.

Measure 10: 1, 2 crescendo, 3 strong, 4–6 weak, 7 strong, 8 weak, 9 crescendo, 10 with trill decrescendo, 11 short and strong, 12–14 weak.
Measure 11: Trill on 1 strong, 2 and 3 weak, 4 strong, 5 crescendo, 6 weak, 7 strong, 8 crescendo, 9 weak, strong trill on 10, 11 and 12 weak, 13 strong, 14 crescendo, 15–17 decrescendo.

Measure 12: 1 weak, 2 crescendo, 3 weak, 4 crescendo, 5–8 weak, 9–12 strong, 13 with trill strong, 14 weak.
Measure 13: 1–3 crescendo, 4 and 5 weak, 6 strong, 7 weak, 8 strong and decrescendo.

Measure 14: 1 strong, 2—4 weak, 5—9 strong, 10—12 weak, 13 strong, 14 weak, 15 strong, 16 crescendo, 17—19 weak.
Measure 15: 1 crescendo, 2 weak, 3—6 strong, 7—13 weak "and flattering,"

Measure 15 (cont'd.): trill on 15 strong, 16—19 very weak. Quantz omits mention of note 14.
Measure 16: 1—7 strong, 8 decrescendo. *Measure 17:* Entire measure very weak.

Measure 18: Crescendo up to and including last eighth note; the turn weak.
Measure 19: 1 strong, 2 and 3 weak, 4 strong, 5 and 6 weak, 7 crescendo, 8—10 weak, 11 and 12 crescendo.

Measure 20: 1 crescendo, 2—5 decrescendo, 6—7 strong, 8—11 weak, 12 strong, 13 strong, 14—16 weak, 17—19 strong, 20 weak, 21 and 22 to be played as fast as the trill that follows on 23. Make a crescendo and decrescendo while trilling,

allowing yourself roughly the same time as four slow eighth notes. 27 and 28 piano and diminuendo. After the fermata, the first note crescendo, the others decrescendo.

Measure 21: 1 strong, 2 and 3 weak, 4—6 strong, 7—9 weak, 10—16 strong (16 should be trilled, said Quantz, but music as written shows no trill). 17 crescendo, decrescendo to end of measure.
Measure 22: 2—4 and 8—10 weak, 11 strong, 12 weak, 13 and 15 strong, 16 crescendo.

Measure 23: 1—4 strong, 5 weak and crescendo to 6, 7—12 weak and crescendo.
Measure 24: 2—4 strong, 5 weak and crescendo through 6, 7—9 weak. 10—15 strong, 16—21 weak, 22 strong, 23 weak.

Measure 25: Strong trill on 2, says Quantz (but not shown in music): 3 and 4 also strong, 5—15 strong, 16 weak.
Measure 26: 1 crescendo, 2 and 3 weak, 4—7 strong, 8 and 9 weak, 10—12 strong, 13 weak.

Measure 27: 1–7 weak, 8–16 strong, 9–13 crescendo, 14–15 weak and crescendo through 16 and up to 3 of measure 28.
Measure 28: 4–6 decrescendo, 7–8 crescendo, 9–11 strong, 12–14 weak, crescendo.

Measure 29: 2–4 weak, 5 and 6 crescendo, 7–9 strong, 10 strong, 11 crescendo, 12 weak.
Measure 30: .1–3 strong, 4–11 weak, 12–13 weak, 14–17 strong, 18 weak.

Measures 31 and 32: 1–8 weak and flattering.* Triplet groups strong and sustained. Strong and sustained playing to the end with diminuendo on the final note.

*According to Quantz, the passions expressed in music change frequently in fast as well as in slow movements. He says "the performer must therefore seek to transport himself into each of these passions, and to express it suitably . . . . Flattery is expressed with slurred notes that ascend or descend by step, and also with syncopated notes, in which the first half of the note must be sounded softly, and the second reinforced by chest and lip action . . . . Flattery requires appoggiaturas, slurred notes, and a tender expression." Quantz, *Essay,* Chapter 12, sections 24 and 26, pp. 133–134.

Quantz, *On Playing the Flute;* pp. 169–172, 176–178.

The full implications of Quantz's suggested dynamics will be discussed later. Our immediate study in this chapter is ornamentation, and the remarks here will be directed solely at this aspect of the Quantz example. Its most striking feature is that, while it has been freely and profusely ornamented, the outline of the music is adhered to. At almost every major point of beat the original version and the ornamented version coincide. Where they do not, it is either because of an appoggiatura or a run. This type of working-out is safe and unobjectionable.

So far we have drawn largely on the vast resources of both Quantz and C. P. E. Bach. In the following chapters we will examine yet other examples of Baroque ornamentation, some of them from the finest sources possible: Corelli by Corelli, for example; Corelli by his pupil Geminiani; Vivaldi by Vivaldi; Vivaldi by his star pupil Pisendel; and Vivaldi by J. S. Bach.

You may be tempted to study the present chapter awhile, but I would urge you to go on because your perspective will change. It is the sense of perspective and its application that produces the best results, not just the accumulation of knowledge.

We need to remind ourselves constantly that the composer must be placed in his proper milieu. If he lived in the early period of the Baroque, we should ornament his music sparingly. But this is an obvious oversimplification, because if the same early-Baroque composer had left us two works—one for the recorder, the other for the violin—the music for recorder would be ornamented much more heavily than music for the violin. The recorder in the Baroque period was already an old instrument; its technique was well established, and virtuosos abounded. The violin, on the other hand, was very new and was not yet quite trusted by many composers; since its technique was in the early painful stages of development, most players could not cope with passages of any great difficulty. Early Baroque violin pieces can generally be played in the first position, and if you are writing a cadenza, avoid giving notes to the then-unreliable G string.

It is important to remember, in dealing with ornamentation of instrumental music by individual composers and national schools, that the Italians generally were about ten years ahead of German composers, and the Germans perhaps ten years ahead of the French. So as a rule of thumb, when playing an Italian, a German, and a French composition all written around the same year, you would ornament the Italian work most of all, the German somewhat less, and the French the least. This rule of thumb applies to instrumental music only; early French songs should be profusely ornamented.

Again there would be exceptions, depending on the genius of the composer. While much technical progress in violin playing originated in Italy and is reflected in the works of Italian composers, Germans led the way with experiments in other areas of violin playing, such as *scordatura* (changing the tuning of the open strings) and multiple stops.

Finally, how rigidly does one observe the precepts of C. P. E. Bach and Quantz? They should not be applied thoughtlessly to the music of the early Baroque. C. P. E. and Quantz did what any good theorist would do: they cast a backward look and hoped to exert a forward influence. In other words, they crystallized the thinking of the previous fifty years or so, and we can surmise that their findings and rules and regulations will be particularly valid for the period from 1730 to 1760. As their books were published, their influence—already great by virtue of their stature as soloists and composers and their position at the court of Frederick the

Great—spread further . . . up to a point. The future was beyond their control; they had come towards the end of a period and were bucking the still-rising tide. So although their pleas for restraint were soon reinforced by Leopold Mozart, from 1775 to 1800 they were quoted with approval by pedants, while they were more and more ignored by performers influenced by Tartini and his elaborate ornamentation. Ornamentation by this time would actually become grotesque, and the revulsion against it would set in. The Baroque period would die, killed by its own excesses; classic simplicity would prevail.

3

Working from a Figured Bass: Hints from C. P. E. Bach

A great deal of the challenge of Baroque music lies in the manner in which the continuo part has to be performed. Though the word *accompaniment* will be used later, and was in fact generally used by both C. P. E. Bach and Quantz, we will avoid it for now as it seems to imply a slavish subordination, or at least subordination. But the term *basso continuo* or *figured bass* implies foundation; it supports the entire structure of the composition, principal part most of all; and the principal part is tied to the figured bass and illuminated by it even as the bass is tied to the principal part.

A *figured bass* consists essentially of a bass line with numbers written above or below it. It is a shorthand that tells us what harmony the composer had in mind at that particular moment in his composition. One can learn the figures and their meanings with a minimum of fuss, and with practice one can develop into a correct, competent, and perhaps not too pedestrian continuo player. If that is your goal, R. O. Morris's very slim two-volume set, *Figured Harmony at the Keyboard*, (New York: Oxford, 1932) will give you the information you need as well as a great deal of practice at the keyboard. It will thus give you facility in translating a figured bass into sound, but because it contains no historical notations whatever, you will not gain a sense of differing national or individual styles unless you also go through one of the two major essays by twentieth-century scholars. The first is Hermann Keller's *Thoroughbass Method*, available from W. W. Norton in an inexpensive paperback edition; the other is F. T. Arnold's monumental *The Art of Accompaniment from a Thorough Bass*, published by Oxford in 1931 and now available in an inexpensive paperback reprint from Dover. Any time that you expend on these works will be well spent; you will gain facility as well as historical perspective.

Naturally the role of the figured bass changed considerably during the one hundred and seventy-five years or so that the Baroque period lasted. At first it stood for a fairly routine, completely continuous accompaniment to be played from the beginning of a composition to its end. Hence the term *thorough*, in the sense of "through." Later it became more sophisticated and more inventive. By the early eighteenth century, composers like Padre Vivaldi had begun to explore yet another dimension of figured bass—its use as an orchestral device. They specified, for example, when it should not be used, thus exploiting its absence as well as its presence as a source of orchestral color.

Many attempts were made in the Baroque period itself to set down the ground rules for thorough bass. But it stands to reason that Michael Praetorius writing in 1619, or Schütz in 1623, would have a point of view rather different from Niedt in 1700, Heinichen in 1728, or Mattheson in the 1730s. In the search of a major broad-based original source, where should one go? To the court of Frederick the Great of Prussia and those two familiar figures—C. P. E. Bach and Johann Joachim Quantz. In their role as performers, composers, and teachers, both had been exposed to the music of many nations and many periods, and had developed an international point of view; both wrote masterly treatises that encompassed thorough bass, Bach from the viewpoint of the keyboard musician, Quantz from that of the soloist; their treatises are available in excellent English translations. In this chapter we will rely more heavily on the writings of Bach than of Quantz.

Fingering

It is no accident that C. P. E. Bach's *Essay on the True Art of Playing Keyboard Instruments* begins with a chapter on fingering. Harpsichordists of the early Baroque differed from those of the later period almost as much as the latter differ from us. "My deceased father told me," says C. P. E. almost casually, "that in his youth he used to hear great men who employed their thumbs only when large stretches made it necessary. Because he lived at a time when a gradual but striking change in musical taste was taking place, he was obliged to devise a far more comprehensive fingering and especially to enlarge the role of the thumbs and use them as nature intended; for among their other good services, they must be employed chiefly in the difficult tonalities. Hereby, they rose from their former uselessness to the rank of principal finger."[*] Add this, then, to Johann Sebastian's roster of achievements: he not only exalted the human spirit—he freed the human hand.

The principles of fingering that J. S. Bach discovered and established, and that C. P. E. extended and codified, while representing a tremendous advance over previous systems, contain elements that will certainly seem odd to keyboard players today unless their purpose is understood. A summary of these principles is presented here. However, we strongly urge you to read C. P. E. Bach's chapter on fingering in its entirety, and try out the various fingerings at the keyboard.

Because of the shape of our hand and the shape of the keyboard, says C. P. E. Bach, short raised keys (black keys on the piano) "belong essentially" to the three longest fingers. Hence Rule 1: "Raised keys are seldom taken by the little finger and only out of necessity by the thumb." (The term *raised keys* will be used here to prevent confusion since with most harpsichord keyboards the short raised keys that represent sharps and flats are not black but white.

He regards the change of fingers as "the most important element in our study." Five fingers in close position can play just five notes, but the range can be extended by two means—turning the thumb, and crossing the fingers.

[*] C. P. E. Bach, *Essay*, p. 42.

One should avoid turning the thumb under the little finger, and crossing the little finger over the thumb; crossing the third finger over the second, or the second over the third. One should also avoid crossing the fourth finger over the fifth. (This last rule has an exception).

In stepwise passages the little finger should be held in reserve; it is to be used only when a run begins or ends with it.

In ascending passages the right thumb is to be used after one or more raised keys; and it should be used before them in descending. The reverse procedure is followed for the left thumb.

With a flexible thumb came complexity in playing: "Because our forerunners rarely used the thumb, it got in the way. Hence, they often found that they had too many fingers . . . Today, despite improvements in the use of the fingers, we find, at times, that we have too few of them."*

Example 52 contains some right-hand fingerings: (1) a "more usual" fingering for the scale of C, (2) a usable fingering for the scale of G with an added chromatic passage and (3) a "more usual" fingering for the same passage:

C. P. E. Bach, *Essay*, (1) p. 46, (2) and (3) p. 49.

If fingers 3 over 4 bothers you, consider the advantages; with practice your fingers will ripple smoothly over the keys without the thumb clunking down now and then. Furthermore, while fingers 3 and 4 are chasing one another over the keyboard, 1 and 2 are available to hold down a note or two, depending on the tempo. These examples demonstrate how rewarding a study of the Baroque system of fingering can be. There will be an initial period of hesitancy, of course, but perseverance will bring rewards, and soon you will find your fingers scuttling around the keyboard with all the agility of a crab on the beach.

Thorough Bass

C. P. E. devotes 113 pages to discussing the intricacies of thorough bass. Anyone who wants to play continuo will obviously have to go through that material several times to derive maximum benefit from it. Here we can only provide a very brief summary of Bach's main findings, including definitions, and the main rules, but leaving out exceptions and elaborations.†

The triad, consisting of a basic tone, a fifth, and a third, is the "most perfect" consonant chord; most works begin with a triad, and all works end with one.

Add an octave, and the triad becomes the common chord. The fifth must

* C. P. E. Bach, *Essay*, p. 73.
† Ibid., pp. 198–311.

always be perfect. A major or minor third determines whether the chord is major or minor.

Either the fifth, the octave or the third may appear in the upper voice.

You play the common chord when you have any of the following under or over a non-passing bass-note: (1) nothing at all; (2) an accidental; (3) the figures 8, 5, or 3 alone or in combination with each other.

You are allowed to omit the octave of the bass, and double either the third or the fifth.

You are safest when you use the upper voices in contrary motion to the bass; you then avoid consecutive and hidden fifths and octaves.

The prohibition of such fifths and octaves is absolute (almost!) where the upper voice and the bass are concerned. But they can be tolerated in inner voices or between any inner voice and the bass.

The beginner should set limits for himself within which to play: the left hand within the confines of the bass clef, and the right hand stays between Middle C and fifth-line F on the G clef.

Master a few major and minor common chords at a time, learning them in their three positions (octave, fifth, or third on top).

In spite of the limits set for each hand, you must practice these chords over the entire keyboard. Eventually you will be playing major and minor triads on each degree of the chromatic scale, making twenty-four chords in all. Your goal is to be able to play any common chord without the slightest hesitation, in any one of its three possible positions.

Intervals must be practiced until they can be recognized instantly.

If two successive chords have tones in common, these tones should be retained in the same voice.

When a bass rises or falls a second, the upper voices must move in contrary motion.

After you have mastered contrary motion, you can look for situations where parallel motion would be preferable.

In a final cadence, the octave or third is the best note to use in the upper voice; never use the fifth.

The chord of the sixth (first inversion) is usually indicated by 6 alone. Its use makes for good voice leading.

This chord however, is not useful in two-part accompaniment, where one of the voices would have to be omitted.

You must train yourself to look ahead, since these chords can be realized in various ways, and you will want to adapt the chord you are playing to what is yet to come.

In diminished or augmented triads, the octave is omitted in three-part accompaniment.

Unisons

The remainder of C. P. E. Bach's chapter on thorough bass is devoted to more complex situations and chords and should be studied in context. But much sound advice is contained in his chapter on accompaniment (pp. 313–429). The very first point concerns the proper use of unison accompaniment. (The word *unison* is not used in its narrow sense but includes accompaniment in octaves.) If the other performers are playing in unison, says C. P. E., "it is only natural that the accompanist too should follow the unisons and give up his chords. Such passages usually carry the indication, *unisoni* or *all 'unisono.'*" If the ripieno parts are in unison with the bass, however, and the principal part has either a long held note or a different melody altogether, the case is different. Do the ripieno parts include "the essential intervals, especially the dissonances and resolutions of the underlying harmony"? Then the accompanist merely plays in unison with the ripieno. If it is felt, however, that the unison ripieno parts imply a harmony that needs reinforcing, then the accompanist must supply the chords as needed.

A melody in the bass has its own set of rules. If it is accompanied at the unison without octave doublings, the harpsichordist should accompany it with the left hand at the unison, without chords. In general, brilliant bass passages should be accompanied at the unison. Where there is no ripieno, and a brilliant bass solo or aria is accompanied by harpsichord alone, a chordal accompaniment is usually provided.

We have seen that unison playing sometimes includes doubling at the octave. When a composer wants the accompanist to play the left hand alone without octave duplication, the indication in the score is *t.s., tasto,* or *tasto solo.* "Italians do not use either of these accompaniments," says C. P. E. Bach sadly. He attributes this to Italian keyboard practice, against which composers rebel: "They [Italian composers] do not care to have the tinkling sounds of their keyboardists in such places;" and he adds bitingly "the more so because it is known that they can play scarcely any chord without rolling it." C. P. E. speculates that emphasis on chord playing has led Italians to believe that the harpsichord is "unfitted for the accompaniment of the most beautiful, affettuoso passages." And he draws the conclusion: "Hence in Italian works, delicate passages usually carry the direction *senza cembalo* over the bass as a kind of warning. Whole arias sometimes have this indication, which is laughable to the singers of that country when they are shown the words in their own scores."*

German practice differed greatly from that of the Italian. German composers used *tasto solo* ". . . To great advantage . . . . when the bass and principal part move in thirds and sixths with no additional voices. The piece may be for two or more parts." This accompaniment is particularly useful when the bass is marked *piano* and the thirds and sixths lie close together. In such a situation the double basses are silent while the other bass instruments play softly in the notated register along with the keyboard."† But if similar situations arise in symphonies and concertos in which the basses are doubled and the thirds and sixths widely separated, the harpsichordist should play in unison, and if possible should double the bass in the lower octave.

* C. P. E. Bach, *Essay,* p. 316
† Ibid., p. 317.

Pedal Points

Tasto Solo is used where a pedal point occurs. Should you find strange and complicated figurings in the continuo part, they will become clearer if you disregard the bass. "When this is done, the strange signatures [figures] turn out to be indications of nothing more than the ordinary progressions of thorough bass." C. P. E. strongly recommends that the figures be ignored and the organ point played by itself: "To play the organ point *tasto solo* removes the necessity of scanning unusual signatures and successions of towering figures." To avoid crossing parts, the organ point would have to be played in divided accompaniment: "This is an excessive demand." A little earlier he remarked: "Assuming that the right hand could accompany all organ points, gratitude would never compensate for the expended anxiety and trouble."*

Appoggiaturas

Embellishments such as appoggiaturas affect the manner in which a figured bass is realized. Where the principal part is ornamented, the harpsichordist must be careful not to obscure such ornaments and their resolution by throwing up a wall of sound. "Accompaniments must be so contrived that they clarify or at least do not obscure the various refinements of melodies whether these consist of chromatic intervals, retarded and anticipated resolutions, or, above all, syncopations, especially in slow pieces of an affective nature."† The careful accompanist will not hesitate to insert a rest or to drop a particular note in a chord if this will favor the soloist. "Clarity is attained through rests, and obscurity can be avoided by thinning the chords."

The importance that C. P. E. Bach attaches to appoggiaturas can be gauged by the fact that he devotes forty pages to discussing their treatment. "When the principal part of solos or other pieces requiring a delicate accompaniment has many appoggiaturas in a slow tempo, the accompanist, in order to avoid an obscuring of the melody, should not play all of the ornaments," he advises. He suggests that those ornaments that cannot easily be omitted by the accompanist should be modified by partial rests in the right hand: "A momentary withholding of the accompaniment gives the soloist an opportunity to introduce the appoggiaturas alone. This modification, brought about by rests, is increased in effectiveness when the bass maintains a uniform pattern throughout the passage. *The beauty and charm of appoggiaturas are most clearly perceptible when performed in this manner*"‡ (italics ours).

Performance

Correct realization in itself is not enough to make a good accompanist, says C. P. E.; he must be able to make "intelligent adjustments" regarding volume and

---

* C. P. E. Bach, *Essay*, p. 319.

† Ibid., p. 326.

‡ Ibid., p. 341.

chord placing. And he insists: "It is required of the accompanist that he fit to each piece a correct performance of its harmony in the proper volume and with a suitable distribution of tones" (*Essay*, p. 367).

Proper volume depends on context. A harpsichordist playing continuo during a forte in an orchestral passage will certainly have to use *volles werk* but when playing forte against a recorder or baroque flute in low register, an eight-foot and a four-foot register, and sometimes even a single eight-foot register using the loud lower manual, may suffice. This is stating the problem in its broadest terms. On another level, the texture of the accompaniment itself has to be refined as the number of players decreases. "The fewer the parts in a piece, the finer must be its accompaniment." The accompanist should avoid "gratuitous passage work and bustling noise" so that the principal part might be free to embellish. The appeal has to be made to intelligent listeners; they should be allowed to hear "an unadorned steadiness and noble simplicity in a flowing accompaniment which does not interfere with the brilliance of the principal part." But the accompanist merely bides his time: "Should the opportunity arise and the nature of a piece permit it, when the principal part pauses or performs plain notes the accompanist may open the draft on his damped fire" (*Essay*, p. 368).

In his discussion of performance practice C. P. E. deals first with the question of volume. He finds the problems involved in using a single-manual instrument "most perplexing"; the only way to create a forte or a piano is to increase or decrease the number of parts one is playing. He praises Hohlfeld's invention of pedals, which allows the registration to be increased or decreased while playing, without interruption. While single-manuals now being built in the United States generally do not have pedals, some imported instruments have a knee lever for the four-foot set of strings, and even a second lever for another eight-foot set. The four-foot set and second eight-foot set can thus be used at will, without the slightest disruption in the playing.

With two-manual instruments the problems are largely resolved. Forte and fortissimo are played on the lower manual. To play fortissimo both manuals are coupled; further, the left hand duplicates all the tones of consonant chords and the consonant tones of dissonant chords. C. P. E. recommends that the two hands play fairly close together, leaving no space between them. He also warns that the lowest register must be avoided; otherwise "the rumbling low notes will create a miserable blur" (*Essay*, p. 369. This precaution nowadays need only apply to those instruments that have short bodies and short wound strings in the bass; instruments with bodies that are light and long enough do not need to use wound strings, and the tone on bass strings is satisfactorily full.)

To play mezzo forte, C. P. E. suggests playing the left hand on the lower manual and the right hand on the upper; where the dynamic indication is piano, both hands use the upper manual. To achieve a pianissimo, both hands reduce the number of parts.

Not only must the wishes of the performer of the principal part be considered, but the accompanist must also be aware of the constant need for adjustment. Does the singer have more power in the top tones? The accompanist must take this into account; further, when the soloist is growling in the depths, the accompanist must be careful not to cover the voice. Is the flutist playing in the flute's lowest register? Once again, since these tones are weak, the accompanist must beware of playing too loudly.

A special situation arises when the player of the principal part has a long held note and performs the *messa di voce*, that finely graded swelling of tone from pianissimo to fortissimo to pianissimo again that is one of the hallmarks of late Baroque style. "The accompanist must follow with the greatest exactness," writes C. P. E. "Every means available to him must be employed to attain a forte and piano. His increase and decrease must coincide with that of the principal part; nothing more, nothing less."*

It is important from the start to seek a sustained singing style in accompaniment. Unless the bass is specifically marked staccato, any chords above it should be played as smoothly as possible. "Tones that already lie in a preceding chord and can be carried over to a following one are held. Such an execution, when associated with flowing progressions in the best distribution, gives the accompaniment a singing effect. It is indispensable with legato notes."

Pizzicato in an orchestral setting calls for special treatment. When the pizzicato occurs in the bass part as well as in other parts, the harpsichordist does not play. If only the bass line is marked pizzicato, and there are no figures written in, the harpsichordist uses his left hand alone, playing staccato. If figures are written in, he plays the left hand staccato and adds staccato chords in the right hand. If a *coll'arco* ("with the bow") follows a pizzicato, or such passages alternate, the harpsichordist has to make this distinction absolutely clear in his playing.

Part of C. P. E.'s chapter on performance consists of advice on how to attack certain notes more loudly to hold an ensemble together, to make sure an attack comes in time, or to signal the soloist that an extended cadenza is expected of him. This was required practice in the old days when soloist and continuo players might not have gotten together until a few minutes before the performance. That a great many performances were given without benefit of prior rehearsal becomes clear from this passage: "It is sometimes necessary and not really improper for the accompanist to *discuss a piece with the performer of the principal part before its performance* and let him decide on the liberties that are to be taken in the accompaniment. Some want the accompaniment to be greatly restricted; others not. Since opinion varies so greatly and it is up to the principal part to decide, the safest procedure is to seek a preliminary understanding."

Especially valuable is C. P. E.'s advice on how to end a piece. With rare exceptions, twentieth-century performers tend to slow down in the last measure or two to give a feeling of finality; the eighteenth century, however, had its own set of conventions.

Basically, there are just two types of situations:

1. Where a piece ends with a closing trill
2. Where it ends without a trill

* C. P. E. Bach, *Essay*, pp. 371–372.

When should closing trills be extended? According to C. P. E., "if a piece has reprises, the extension of trill and accompanying bass note takes place only at the end of the final repetition. By this means weight is added to the conclusion and the audience is made to feel that the piece is about over." (*Essay*, p. 375.)

But if a passage is brilliant, the closing trill must be played in tempo:

The same holds true when a passage is reflective:

Yet another example, in a slower tempo:

There is also no ritard if the trill appears over a moving bass

unless the last of the moving bass notes is the fifth of the key, as in the example below:

45

in such an instance, says C. P. E., the last of the moving bass notes "should be held until it is observed that the principal part or the other executants are ready to conclude their trill."

Again, if only the fifth of the key is repeated in the upper or lower octave of the bass after the trill begins, as happens here—

—it is held until the principal part or the other players are ready to end their trill.

So much for situations involving closing trills. But what if pieces end without a trill, as in the two examples given below?

"If a piece ends without a closing trill," says C. P. E. Bach categorically, "it should be played in tempo without holding back."

Our audiences today might find it difficult to accept such an ending; perhaps even more than in Baroque times, they have to be "made to feel that the piece is about over." If therefore conductors and other artists decide for themselves that in a given situation they want to make a slight ritard, peace be on their heads! The matter need not give rise to passionate argument, since neither a major nor a minor crime will have been committed.

Cadenzas

C. P. E.'s treatment of cadenzas contains cautionary material that applies equally well to conductors and to continuo players. The trill was a puzzle to the incompetent then as now—when does one come in? There were soloists in those days with a puckish sense of humor, as this warning points out: "Some principal performers take satisfaction out of playing a long trill on the fifth, leading the accompanist to enter with his resolution of the six-four chord, after which they continue with elaborations which often do not harmonize with the resolution. The accompanist should contain himself in the face of so bold a stroke, in the assurance that no justifiable criticism can be directed at him. . . ."[*] It almost sounds like a prank that Quantz might have tried to pull on C. P. E. at a concert before Frederick the Great!

[*] C. P. E. Bach, *Essay*, p. 382.

Refinements of Accompanying

While there is no question about the soloist's right to elaborate the main part, C. P. E. raises the question of what then happens to the continuo? To accompany with discretion, says C. P. E., means "to make modifications in accord with certain liberties that are taken at times by the principal performer. . . . the principal performer in introducing embellishments sometimes substitutes one . . . series of signatures for the other. The accompanist must modify his harmony accordingly. In addition to such substitutions, the accompanist must be attentive and give way when embellishments, introduced into the principal part, lead to a later entrance of chords than actually denoted by the signatures." (*Essay*, pp. 387–88).

The harpsichordist is granted considerably more freedom in the treatment of transitional passages, particularly when the principal part is silent. Pointing out the "enticing challenge to inventiveness," C. P. E. Bach cautions that it must accord with the "affect and content of the piece." Providing this is done, the harpsichordist, in C. P. E.'s view, can make radical changes in the written music: "So much the better if part of a preceding phrase can be reintroduced, even if this requires a modification of the bass and a revision of the transition. Rational sovereignty must be granted to the accompanist in this case, so long as the principal part is not thereby hampered." (*Essay*, p. 401).

One of the enlivening devices that both soloist and accompanist can use is imitation. When to use it and how much depends on context and circumstances. In regard to the music itself, "Imitation is often used in passages which are varied on their repetition" (*Essay*, p. 403). However, there are problems involved in its use. For example, how can imitation be used without obscuring one part or the other? A more serious problem concerns the relative skills of the performers: "Leader and follower must stand in close rapport and be familiar with each other's powers and inventiveness." An accompanist who leads an imitation "must know how dependable his follower is in the ways of variation. If he lacks full confidence in the ability of the latter he must deny himself the delights of variation and play the notes simply." If an inept soloist insists on playing unsatisfactory imitations, the harpsichordist should stick to the written notes, not only to "free himself of complicity," but to make sure the poor variation is heard only once (*Essay*, pp. 403–405).

Where the soloist is capable, however, the accompanist may excite him. Once they get going, "the brilliant and the plain must be judiciously alternated." Whenever one partner has the imitation, the other must remain subdued, for "it is just as wrong for both to be noisy at the same time as it is for both to fall asleep."

C. P. E. Bach has very valuable, detailed advice to offer, and his book is absolutely essential for Baroque music performers. However, if you are a complete beginner as a continuo player you may find it most useful at this point to pick up *Thoroughbass Method* by Hermann Keller, which gives you excerpts from Praetorius, Telemann, Mattheson, Heinichen, Quantz, Mattei, J. S. Bach, and C. P. E. Bach; it also puts you to work. The rest is practice.

4

The Music of
George Frideric Handel

Handel's surviving output of vocal and instrumental chamber music could by itself earn him a respected place among Baroque composers. Many of his works can be counted amongst the glories of the period. Choose your instrument and take your pick—flute, recorder, oboe, violin, cello, gamba, voice, or harpsichord, and you may come up with a winner. In our survey here we can give you only a taste of the Handelian repertoire; we will study a representative recorder sonata and a group of violin sonatas; the principles that we derive can be applied to other chamber works as well. (A vocal work is discussed at length in chapter 10). We will discuss Baroque techniques and Handel's own idiom. We'll try to make music Handel's way—up to a point.

You will need to refer to three basic books: C. P. E. Bach's, Quantz's, and David D. Boyden's *The History of Violin Playing from Its Origins to 1761*, which has also been mentioned earlier. These will be adequate for most purposes.

The lure of playing Baroque chamber music is that a performance is so full of glorious uncertainties. You depart from the prepared text; you become increasingly venturesome. In this chapter we will begin to try out some ornamentation, a little at a time. Accept nothing as final. Write out several versions of any one passage; when you have achieved what you consider the ultimate version, don't throw the earlier ones away—tomorrow you may prefer one of them. You could combine bits and pieces of several versions to give an entirely fresh reading to the work; experimenting is part of Baroque music making.

A Recorder Sonata:
Comparing Editions and Recordings

Handel's recorder sonatas are ideal for trying out your skills. With the rest of his chamber music, they have been described as "domestic" and "suitable for amateur performance." That's damning them with faint praise. The truth is that though any recorder player just beyond the beginner level can play them with some satisfaction, they still present a strong artistic challenge to the virtuoso performer. The level of difficulty is determined by how much ornamentation you put in.

We have chosen for study the *Sonata for Recorder and Basso Continuo in F, opus 1 no. 11*, the fourth and final recorder sonata of a set. Here is the first movement as Handel wrote it, with melodic line for recorder and a single line for figured bass. Look this over before you begin to play so you will be prepared to work with it later.

Now you are ready to play the music over just as it is, stark and unvarnished. If you are a keyboard player, be conscious of the figuring under the bass line and try to imagine the harmony, but don't fill it in yet—not until we have looked at a number of editions to see how they present the bass. If we can discover the good and weak points in these realizations, it will help us fashion a better performance. Here is what five editors have come up with:

Editor: Schwedler

Larghetto

Editor: Bergmann and Edgar Hunt. Published by Schott (edition
no. 10050). Reproduced by permission.

Larghetto (Grave)

Editor: Hilleman. Copyright 1950 by Schott. Reproduced by permission.

Editor: Mönkemeyer. Published by Moeck (edition no. 2012). Reproduced by permission.

Editor: Woehl. Published by Peters.

The Schwedler edition is least satisfactory. The realization of the bass moves in clumps of heavy chords like a late nineteenth-century work rather than with the linear freedom of the music of Handel and his contemporaries. The wind part has also been overedited and chopped up by slurs, tonguing marks, and breath marks. It is a creature of the editor's own time rather than of Handel's. It serves a purpose, however, as an example of what we should avoid.

Bergmann's realization for Edgar Hunt is much better. It should be, since it is based on Handel's own transcription of the recorder sonata into an organ concerto (opus 4 no. 5). Yet Bergmann and Hunt have fallen into a trap: with the organ as solo instrument, the quarter notes in measure 1 are not too objectionable. They have less justification, however, with the much weaker recorder as soloist. The top continuo line also partially duplicates the solo line in measures 3, 5, 7, and 8. But a more serious objection is that there are too many blocks of notes on the printed page. They compel your attention; you will be so busy playing what the editor has written that you'll have little time or opportunity to depart from it. A good harpsichord realization is never the final word; instead it provides a starting point for the player. Within limits set by the composer through the figured bass, you must feel free to move spontaneously in any direction, depending on what the recorder player is doing. Harpsichord "accompaniment" is hence more than accompaniment in the orthodox sense of the term. True, a first-rate artist at the piano can be vastly inspirational in a joint recital; but a good harpsichordist accompanying a sonata can be more than inspirational—he or she is expected to be quite creative as well.

That is what makes the realizations by Mönkemeyer, Hillemann, and Woehl so acceptable. You will notice that although all three versions are quite distinct from one another, each of them still bears the unmistakable stamp of George Frideric Handel.

The performance of the melodic line is considerably easier than the realization of the continuo part. The most important consideration for the soloist is choosing the right tempo. Schwedler suggests a metronome marking of $\quarternote = 60$, a tempo so slow as to be painful. It is the slowness of his tempo, in fact, that causes him to put in two breath marks in the middle of the very first phrase (in measure 3 and between measures 4 and 5). The only way the movement could be played at this tempo is with a wealth of ornamentation, and the simplicity of this movement and dignity of the theme preclude that. A tempo between $\quarternote = 76$ and $\quarternote = 84$ lets the music flow naturally; you should be able to play it at this pace with only one quick breath, as indicated in measure 3 of the Schwedler edition. If you feel yourself running out of air, take a quick breath after the high B flat in measure 6. By continually working towards better breath control, you should eventually be able to play the entire passage in one breath.

Let's go back to measure 1. Whatever edition you are using (we prefer the Mönkemeyer), the harpsichordist should roll the first chord and avoid playing the second-space A in the right hand, the recorder's first note; the entry of the recorder should be quiet and undisturbed. The harpsichordist may want to roll the initial chord in measure 3, always bearing in mind that not all chords need be rolled.

The recorder player should make a crescendo and diminuendo in measures 2 and 4, and in measures 3 and 4 he can break up the quarter notes as follows:

Granted, this is timid. But it is better to begin the piece with simple ornamentation and to add more as we go along. For example, in measure 6 motion in eighth notes from G to C and in measure 7 a mordent on A will both be appropriate.

If you now feel you can do much better, go ahead. Put this book down for now and write out half a dozen variations of your own ornamentation.

We are fortunate in that three of the greatest recorder virtuosos of our time have recorded this sonata. Franz Brueggen, Bernard Krainis, and Hans-Martin Linde are names to conjure with; it would be a privilege to hear any one of them play in recital; thanks to modern recordings, we can not only hear them, we can compare them; the results are startling. If we were comparing three performances of a Romantic violin concerto without knowing who the artists were, we might make statements like: "It has to be Heifetz; listen to the drive and the cool perfection of his technique"; "It's Menuhin; I'd know that warm tone anywhere"; or "It's Francescatti; such musicianship!" Unless they made cuts or used differing versions, their performances would match, note for note. But with Krainis, Linde, and Brueggen the music is recognizable Handel, but the notes vary widely, and they are tempered, elaborated on, and transformed by the soul of each artist.

See for yourself: on page 55, Handel's own unornamented melodic line for the first movement of the sonata in F is again reproduced. Immediately above it, for ease of comparison, you'll find the same music as it is played by these three virtuosos, somewhat freely transcribed from their recordings. To prevent personal predilections from clouding the discussion, we will not yet reveal which soloist is playing a given line. Play the lines over, have a friend play them for you, and try to figure out why certain passages are worked out the way they are.

A word of caution is necessary here: two of the versions given are based on recordings of the actual Handel sonata opus 1 no. 11, for recorder and basso continuo. The third is Handel's *Concerto in F for Recorder and Strings*, which is based on the organ concerto (opus 4 no. 5) that Handel transcribed from his original recorder sonata (opus 1 no 11). The reconversion of the organ concerto into a recorder concerto means only that strings and recorder alternate, with the strings playing the music straight and the recorder ornamenting as it goes. Please note that ours is a rough-and-ready transcription that does not do full justice to the rhythmic finesse displayed by the soloists.

Let's call our three mystery lines X, Y, and Z. Each reflects Handel's characteristics as seen through the player's own personality; each is legitimate, each believable in our own time. We feel that some recorder virtuosos in the Baroque period might have played as sparingly ornamented versions as these (witness the

[played by strings

[played by strings - - - - - - - - - - - - -]

writing of C. P. E. Bach). But there were countless other performers who ornamented so lavishly it was difficult to hear the notes for the mordents.

A few points will bear mention. In each case ornamentation is introduced gradually. The first four measures are absolutely untouched. In measure 5 X sticks his toe in the water (an appoggiatura to the third quarter note) and is ready to dive bravely into the briny in measure 6, where he splits the third quarter note in two. If one may be permitted to mix metaphors somewhat, in diving in this way he not only bridges the gap from C to A but also introduces a new rhythmic figure—a dotted eighth followed by a sixteenth—that Handel reserved for measure 8. In measure 9 Y makes an elegant entrance, and Z counters with a flourish. Measure 10 is a standoff, and in measures 11 and 12 X seems to stake out a claim as the most conservative of the three. In measure 17 X plays both quarter notes staccato (why he does so is a good question); in the same measure Y is still very imaginative: remember this is Baroque music and permutations are permissible. Would you like to play Y's measure 17 followed by X's measure 18? Good combination! In measures 19, 20, and 21 Z becomes very restrained. In fact, in none of the preceding measures has he been really adventurous, moving always by step and giving a solid, safe, almost pedestrian performance. Let's do some more minor switching: if we take the third beat of Z's measure 22 and substitute it for X's beat 3, is this an improvement? X has the field to himself in measures 24 and 25. But in measures 26, 27 and 28 all three either stick closely to Handel's original or move with limited freedom. The same characteristics are seen in measures 31 through 35. In this last measure Y prepares intelligently for the downward leap from fifth line F to second space A in measure 36; he makes the leap believable. In the hands of a less competent player it looks as if either Handel or his copyist or his first printer had made an error and substituted one note for another. In measures 36 through 39 Y's beautifully-turned phrases are a joy to the ear; in measure 42 he begins to soar upwards again, and in measure 43 he touches high F, a brilliant and unexpected climax to a movement at a point where Handel had written the F an octave below. What makes Y's sally particularly exciting is that he breaks through the bounds Handel had set himself - an upper limit that X and Z honor to the last.

Now we'll identify our soloists. X is Brueggen, Y is Krainis, Z is Linde, placed on the staff in alphabetical order. If you acquire any of their recordings of the Handel sonatas, you will get a close-up view of some of the problems of ornamentation —and of the different ways they can be met. You will see, too, that these three artists leave fast movements virtually untouched. The slow movements, however, are invariably ornamented.

The competent player will find nothing frightening in the range of Handel's recorder sonatas; his highest written note is D in the third space above the treble staff, a note that even beginners can play with ease. Obviously, then, it is not the difficulty of the notes, but what one puts between them that makes or breaks a piece. Courage is of the essence. An occasional daring leap is worth fifteen stepwise progressions. "Float like a butterfly, sting like a bee" is advice that applies to Baroque music as much as it does to boxing. Many worthy recorder players lack confidence in themselves and wind up stinging like butterflies!

The Violin Sonatas

Even more cautious are the orthodox violinists. When they refuse to ornament and insist on sticking closely to the printed note, Handel's violin sonatas come out sounding like glorified first-position pieces. From the time they started playing they were told by their teachers to follow the markings: "Upbow here, downbow there: observe the bowings!" Trained to play only what they see before their eyes, the vast majority of violinists are baffled by the peculiar needs of Baroque music; some are openly hostile to it. Yet, the very first violinists cut their teeth on Baroque music; and such violinists of the first rank as Corelli, Vivaldi, Veracini and Tartini embellished and improvised like fiends when necessary. How are the mighty fallen!

Equally ironic is the fact that quite a few violinists of star quality will not open their recital programs without first genuflecting before the Baroque altar. They will play a work by Locatelli or Loeillet, or a sonata by Handel or Tartini, using full bow, a warm vibrato, and never a trace of original ornamentation, and the purblind audience will applaud as though Veracini himself stood bowing before us. It must be true, must it not, that every society gets the artists it deserves! If audiences rebelled, if they insisted that any violinist or conductor who performed Baroque music should get into the spirit of Baroque music making, if they refused to applaud sloppy performances, if they hissed down a performer who played Baroque music "straight"—if audiences observed all these "ifs," standards of performance would rise. The knowledgeable Baroque revival is taking shape around us; as a matter of fact it now takes a determined effort of the will to maintain one's ignorance.

Does it make sense that the same brilliant artist who can toss off Bach's *Chaconne in D Minor* cannot cope stylistically with a simple sonata by Handel?

Can one declaim Shakespeare and be thrown by Lovelace? Shouldn't a wise teacher make sure that his pupil wait to tackle the Bach *Chaconne* until after he has learned to embroider a Handel sonata? Wouldn't that be a good way to arrive at an understanding, not only of the delicacy and finesse of Handel, but also of the grandeur and splendor of Bach?

What should a violinist do? What any self-respecting recorder player does: study the period, the design of the piece, and ornamentation. Then he should pick up his instrument and drop his inhibitions. He should team up with good recorder players and harpsichordists. He should consort with gambists.

Handel's recorder sonata, opus 1 no. 11, is also often played as a sonata for violin and basso continuo. A violinist who wants to familiarize himself with Baroque style can start with it, trying some of the ornamentation worked out by Krainis, Brueggen, and Linde. He should practice this in secret, with his door closed, windows shut, blinds down, shades drawn, with a mute on the bridge playing on a backless practice violin lest he be discovered and disgraced by that other violinist living down the hall. But once he has the flair and the feeling, he can go proudly out into the musical world and sin no more.

The aspiring violinist exploring Baroque music will move easily from Handel's opus 1 no. 11 to the six sonatas in opus 1 written specifically for the violin. Though these sonatas were published when Handel was about forty-six years old and an established writer of virtuoso operatic music, they do not contain any difficulties beyond the ability of the patient and persistent amateur. They can even be played almost entirely in the first position if necessary, though we would not recommend it. The highest note is the E on the third ledger line above the treble staff, and it occurs in about four measures in the *Sonata in A*, opus 1 no. 3. The same high E occurs again in yet another *Sonata in A*, opus 1 no. 14. The second movement of this particular sonata, marked Allegro, is peppered with double and triple stops, as is the final Allegro; here you will also find yourself playing thirty-seconds at a fairly brisk tempo. So if your bow arm needs a little oiling or your left-hand fingers are not as fleet as they could be, opus 1 no. 14 is not yet the sonata for you; on the other hand you might consider it just the challenge you need to do some serious work to improve your technique.

Violins in Handel's time were rather different from what they are now, so any authenticity you strive for will have to be tempered by realistic considerations. Very few old violins exist in unaltered condition, with short necks and short fingerboards. A few modern violins may be found that have been altered to conform with Baroque measurements; if you find one of these, consider yourself lucky. The bow situation is better. Good modern replicas of old bows exist, and they need not be expensive. Beware, however, of the so-called Bach bow, in which the stick is greatly arched and the hair tension is regulated by the thumb. This bow is not authentic but was specially designed to conform to a theory. The old-time violin bow closely resembles a gamba bow; it is slender and has a very gentle arch. It may surprise you by its short length. In 1720, just eleven years before Handel's sonatas were published, the longest bow in use was called the "sonata bow." According to Sir John Hawkins, it measured twenty-four inches tip to tip. That makes it a full inch shorter than our present-day half-size bow, and its construction made it even lighter than that bow.

If you want to approach the Handelian sound and style, begin by bowing more lightly than you normally do. Play fast sixteenths with a short sharp wrist motion rather than with a forearm movement and bow longer notes détaché—not just not slurred but *really* détaché, with space between the notes. You will also have to eliminate much of your vibrato. Because some of these ideas are so contrary to current violinistic thinking, we will repeat these admonitions, exhortations, and sermons throughout the balance of this chapter. Take time out here to look at chapter 7 and Geminiani's bowings, in particular. After you have read through it all and played a great deal of Handel, consult David D. Boyden's *History of Violin Playing* for a comprehensive discussion of the techniques involved.

Finding a reliable score is not easy; you may have trouble locating a first-class edition of the Handel violin sonatas. More than a dozen editions exist, and almost all are uniformly bad. One of the better ones, which is published by Peters, is based on the Urtext, but it has been edited by Walther Davisson and Gunther Rämin. The editors of string music never seem to be aware how much they change or even destroy the character of a composition by changing the bowing. One characteristic of Baroque string music is its use of the basic violin stroke, which is clean, crisp, short, and non-legato. When a Baroque composer like Handel wanted a slur, he meant it as a special effect and wrote it in as such. Davisson and Rämin, like the legion of editors before them, slur just about everything in sight; they water down the melodic line and soup up the keyboard part. It would be uncharitable to wish a plague on the houses of all editors, but a mild touch of the flu, maybe?

It is really important to learn a piece from a good edition. Even though the Bärenreiter edition of the Handel violin sonatas is more expensive than the others, it is worth acquiring. The violin part comes printed above the realized bass, but the continuo part has to be purchased separately. The great advantage of this edition is that you get the music the way Handel wrote it and that the keyboard part has been tastefully realized. All dynamic, expression, and metronome markings tacked on by previous editors have been removed. And every now and then in slow movements, immediately below Handel's own violin line, you will find some of the ornamentation and embellishments worked out.

Let's look briefly at the *Sonata in G Minor*, opus 1 no. 10. The tempo for the first movement is andante, and the time signature shows four quarter notes to the bar. The solo part has plenty of running sixteenths, subdividing on occasion into thirty-seconds and very fleetingly into sixty-fourths. Obviously, if the solo line were considered by itself, a tempo of $\flat$ = 60 might seem a little too precipitous; on the other hand we do not want to take it so slowly that it turns into an Adagio Calamitoso. You be the judge; try $\flat$ = 48, and if it works out comfortably, you're ahead. If it doesn't, adjust the tempo to suit.

Not much need be done here by way of ornamentation if the tempo has been chosen correctly. But if you find the tempo dragging, by all means look on it as an invitation to ornament. You may also, depending on the situation, want to try out a mordent or what we now call an inverted mordent in some measures where

Handel has a dotted eighth followed by a sixteenth (refer to the guidelines in chapter 2). A trill would also be in order on the dotted eighth in measure 20 preceding the final chord.

The allegro should not be taken too fast. Look ahead to measures 30 and 31 and you will see storm warnings hoisted; ♩ = 104 is about right. Take a leaf out of Menuhin's book, and give the impression of playing faster than you actually are by the judicious use of rhythmic accentuation. You don't need much ornamentation, and beware of introducing any but a minimal vibrato on the tied half-notes in measures 3, 4, and 5—it would not be in style. Instead, even if you feel the tempo does not allow it, try using the *messa di voce,* the crescendo and diminuendo that Baroque musicians made on notes that lasted half a measure or more. Use light, crisp bow-strokes from the wrist on all sixteenths; use détachés on eighth notes.

The movement begins forte—a mellow, jolly forte rather than the forte of a massed chorus in *Judas Maccabaeus.* Play softly in measure 8, forte in measure 9, piano again in measure 10, forte in measures 11 into 14, and piano from the last beat of measure 14 to the double bar. And—contrary to opinion that prevailed a few years ago—you should use nuances and shadings within all these levels of dynamics. You will still find musicians of the old school who believe you should play in sharply-contrasted terraces of sound, the forte to remain forte from first note to last, the piano to stay piano all the way to the next forte. The newer school suggests that this is fine for harpsichordists, who are hampered by the tonal limitations of their instruments, but that string and wind players and singers should be allowed to exploit their dynamic range within reason. The latter approach is preferable, but shun for now the too-sweeping crescendos, dramatic diminuendos, and languishing ritards one associates with a much-later period in music history.

From measure 19 on keep the bow strokes short and crisp, slur little, and at night you'll sleep the sleep of the just.

The short Adagio that follows can be played with lyricism. A suggested tempo is ♩ = 48. Use the whole bow freely; if you feel like experimenting with a Geminiani-type bowing (see chapter 7) this is a good place to start. Again, avoid a broad vibrato; the vibrato was used in Baroque music only where expressly specified. Leopold Mozart recommended that it be restricted to a closing note or to sustained tones. (But there were rebel violinists then as now. "Some performers," complains Leopold, "tremble so much on each note you'd think they had the palsy.") So instead of relying on vibrato to color your playing, try to work out the best ornamentation possible. The Bärenreiter edition provides a challenge in the form of an ornamented version immediately below Handel's own melodic line. It has been skillfully done, but regard it only as a guide, not as the final word on the matter. Above all, beware of the slurred bowing.

The concluding Allegro is spirited, and it is taken considerably faster than the Allegro we came across previously. A metronome marking of ♩. = 98 seems close to a desirable tempo, but choose the marking that seems suitable from your own and your harpsichordist's point of view. If you can find a tempo that's comfortable and within the limits of your technique, you can make it seem faster than a tempo that lets you just scrape through.

We also recommend Handel's *Sonata in F*, opus 1 no. 12. The problems are similar to opus 1 no. 10. The bass in the Bärenreiter edition has been worked out in musicianly fashion, and enough ornamentation has been provided on a separate line to make your experience worthwhile. Play all repeats in this and other Handel sonatas; they give a feeling of symmetry to the music that will be most rewarding. What's more, this is spacious music written for more gracious times; take the time to play it in a relaxed manner.

The remaining three violin sonatas are also worth trying. Opus 1 no. 13, in D, begins with a truly delightful Affettuoso. Since the writing is already quite detailed, ornamenting it further depends entirely on your personal taste and the tempo at which you are playing. In the final measure of the first movement of this and later sonatas, Hinnenthal (the editor) provides a cadenza for the violinist. Accept nothing at face value, but keep trying to improve on the suggested ornamentation wherever possible. Continue to write things down and to play them over several times until you can clearly visualize the sound of a given passage. If you then put it aside for a while, you may come up with a better version the next time you play it.

In the *Sonata in A*, opus 1 no. 14, beware of taking the Adagio too slowly and the Allegro too fast. How you cope with the opening chords in the Allegro will determine the pace of the entire movement; it will therefore be worth your time to spend five minutes smoothing out these particular difficulties, as you will then be able to breeze through the rest of the movement (chords were often arpeggiated—see the end of chapter 7). Hinnenthal has ornamented the Largo; use his working out as a guide. Be very careful with the final Allegro. The tempo here is not set by the double stops in the first two measures, or by the easy slurred thirty-seconds in measures 5, 6, and 7 but by the thirty-seconds in bars 43 through 56. Bowing here is tricky and should be carefully worked out so that you may avoid hours of frustration later.

The final sonata, opus 1 no. 15, in E, has no comparable difficulties, and on this sunny note we leave the Handel violin sonatas, with one final exhortation: Writing out ornamentation may not be everybody's favorite way of spending a relaxing Sunday afternoon, but there are compensations and rewards for those who persist. Having read this far you are ready to profit by this task.

5

The Music of
Padre Antonio Vivaldi

Perhaps you have felt, with Luigi Dallapiccola, that Vivaldi wrote "not four hundred violin concertos, but the same concerto four hundred times over." Perhaps you are tired of hearing the "Four Seasons" performed year in and year out. So a Russo-Irish violin virtuoso is going to play all four of them in Carnegie Hall next week, you yawn; what else is new?

The Four Seasons: Winter

What could be new is O'Violinsky's manner of playing the Four Seasons. Take *Winter*, for example. At first, all goes predictably. The very first movement, Allegro Non Molto, under a young and zealous conductor, is more molto than non. The icy shivers in the strings are expertly executed. At measure 12 the frigid moaning of the horrid wind sends a chill down your spine. By measure 22 you too feel the need to run and stamp your feet every moment. The movement ends as expected in a flurry of flapping arms and chattering teeth, followed by a long held note—Aaaah! So far so good.

In the second movement, complacency is shattered. So familiar is this music that you hear in your mind's ear the cantilena of the solo violin, even before the conductor has raised his baton and musicians have laid bow to string. Nor is there anything in O'Violinsky's countenance to signal that tonight his performance is going to be anything other than it normally is—extraordinary. As his bow starts its sure descent, the violins begin their plucked figurations, the violas hold on to their high D, and the low strings and harpsichord growl out their measured eighth notes. The first measure you know. You thought you knew the second, but it comes out somehow different, and yet unchanged. And so on for measures 3 and 4, and all the rest. The outlines have changed, and yet the music has stayed the same. It is like seeing a well-loved and long-known friend suddenly under a different sky, against a different light, and sensing a change; but where is the change? In the beloved, or in ourselves? In both? Is there a change at all?

If we sense the change, without knowing immediately and precisely what has been changed, then O'Violinsky has done a masterly job of ornamentation. He has followed C. P. E. Bach's dictum that music should be ornamented so skillfully that it seems as if only the main notes are being heard. Let us see, then, if we can follow

O'Violinsky's lead, and perhaps even improve on it. From the examples of elaboration and ornamentation that have come down to us from Italian virtuosos such as Corelli and Tartini we know that the effect to be aimed at in Italian Baroque music is smoothness, rather than the bite imparted to French music by incessant use of devices like the mordent. Certainly, in the context of the adagio from *Winter*, we will attempt nothing that will obscure the lines of the melody, or detract from the mood of calmness that must prevail.

Measure 1, for example, calls for very little change—perhaps just a mordent on the third beat. In measure 2 we can introduce a mordent on the third sixteenth, the better to point up our arrival on D and the upward leap of a fifth to A. The bare repetition of the A can be avoided by discreet use of smaller note values. In measures 3 and 4 we will keep the descending leaps of a seventh, but will break up if possible the steady upward march of the sixteenths. In measures 5 and 6 we will vary the pattern not only of the tied notes but also of the three sixteenths as well. In measure 7 we can take advantage of the downward stepwise march of the sixteenths to introduce alternate half-trills. In measure 9 the original theme is repeated a fourth lower, and we can now begin filling in more extensively. The upward and downward leaps of a fifth, even when filled in by running sixty-fourths, are now in no danger of being obscured. By using smaller note-values in this part of the movement, we not only achieve a heightening of tension without changing the calmness of the tempo, but we also provide the variety implicit in Baroque music. In the second half of measure 15 we begin to prepare for the end of the movement; we leave the downward leap of a fifth (F to B flat) unchanged, but we cut the eighth rest in half to make room for a second bold upward leap of a fifth (F to C immediately resolving to B flat). Then the slower sixteenth notes lead naturally to a suspension (E flat to D) preparing for the final long and so-peaceful trill.

Here then, for the pleasing of a breathless world, is one form of the slow movement of Vivaldi's *Winter* concerto as we would like to hear it played. Bear in mind that this is not the sacred final word but is only intended to be a starting point, to provoke you and other hot-blooded violinists into developing figurations of your own. The top line is Vivaldi's; the second line, our own elaboration.

Vivaldi, *The Four Seasons, Winter Concerto,* opus 8 no. 4, with suggested elaboration by V. Rangel-Ribeiro.

The Four Seasons: Other Slow Movements

The slow movements of the three remaining *Seasons* present problems of a markedly different nature. The second movement of *Summer,* for example, features an adagio cantilena in the solo violin that alternates with presto sixteenth-note passages played by the orchestral strings on a single tone.

Vivaldi, *Summer Concerto,* op. 8 no. 2, Adagio

Notice the eighth rests used in measures 1, 2, and 3—what an air of mystery they lend to the solo! Equally important is the distinction Vivaldi makes in orchestral tone color: violins only to accompany the plaintive solo violin; snarling violas, cellos, and basses thrown in with basso continuo to reproduce the *tuoni fieri* (sounds of the beasts). The continuo player must be cautioned against filling in those rests or disturbing the carefully planned orchestral distinction between high and low strings. In fact it would be best if the harpsichordist refrained from playing at all at this point. Perhaps the best way of driving this lesson home is by reproducing the violin and piano reduction (edited by Newell Jenkins and Fritz Kübart) and published by Eulenburg as part of their "Educational Series."

The keyboard player using the piano reduction in this edition should: (1) omit completely the pianissimo low octaves in the left hand in measures 1 through 6 and elsewhere and substitute an eighth rest in their place; (2) ignore the spurious ottava bassa indication in measures 16, 17, 19, 20, and 21; and (3) omit the low G at the very end of the piece. It is a quite unnecessary way of telling the audience that the movement is over.

Incidentally, in this same piano reduction the key signature of two flats is mysteriously left out in the right hand from measure 16 through to the end. That should produce some rather interesting effects if the player lets his mind wander for just a little while! There is another disturbing omission: nowhere is the original sonnet printed, nor are individual lines of the poem sprinkled throughout the musical text, as is customary.

One simple and logical way to treat the Adagio is to take the rhythmic pattern used by *ripieno* (orchestral) violins 1 and 2 and adapt the rhythm to the melody, something like this:

An idea that looks good on paper, however, may turn out less well in actual performance, and this effort at ornamentation could be a case in point. Do you agree?

The third concerto, *Autumn*, has a larghetto interlude sandwiched in towards the end of its opening Allegro. The entire movement represents a celebration; noses begin to light up as the liquor flows. By measure 41 the tipsy revelers are beginning to stagger around the ballroom:

Vivaldi, *Autumn Concerto*, op. 8 no. 3, Allegro

By measure 89 the drunks are falling asleep, and the tempo drops to a larghetto:

The text printed above measure 89 reads: "The drunkard who sleeps," so any elaborate ornamentation at this point would be out of place. What could Vivaldi have had in mind? I believe that at this point Vivaldi's intentions are best served if we preserve the stark lines of the solo violin part. Since Vivaldi was a realist, however, and a bit of a jester to boot, we can introduce a grace note in measures 90, 91, and 92 to represent a series of somewhat loud and unexpected hiccups:

At measure 98 the melody begins to descend in whole notes, a half step at a time, until it comes to rest on a C that lasts five full measures. The principal violin makes a messa di voce in each measure; the viola makes two in each. Rely on the accompanying strings to sustain interest at this point; the sixteenths should be slurred, the eighths, staccato. Your own tone should be crystal clear and have almost no vibrato.

Now follows one of Vivaldi's loveliest slow movements. Dazzling in its simplicity and shimmering translucent harmonies, it is, in fact, one of the loveliest slow movements in all violin solo literature.

Vivaldi, *Autumn,* op. 8 no. 3, Adagio.

Although a messa di voce on the top line is a must, the strong temptation to ornament further must be resisted staunchly. Ornamentation in Baroque music may be freely used when one part of the structure stands out as the melody and the remaining parts are clearly accompaniment. Ornamentation is considered undesirable, however, when the entire structure is harmonic and the melodic line is very closely tied to it.

The Largo of the *Spring* concerto is fascinating. Here once again Vivaldi paints a pastoral scene with charm and wry humor. A goatherd is lulled to sleep by the murmuring of fronds and plants; by his side lies his faithful dog, barking loudly. Only the first and second violins are used to portray the sighing of the leaves in the wind;

"Largo and pianissimo throughout," the composer cautions the violinists. From the viola players, who portray the barking dog, Vivaldi demands a far different kind of sound: "This should always be played very loudly and in a rasping manner!" he commands. The cellos, basses, and harpsichord are silent.

If we look at the melody as pure melody, the possibilities of ornamentation are very wide. The pastoral nature of the scene, however, and the calmness of the music entrusted to the violins suggest that the ornamentation be kept simple and smoothly flowing. As for the violas, many conductors tend to ignore Vivaldi's instructions and instead instruct the violas to play mezzo forte; this writer believes that the violas should be asked to play *molto forte e strappato* (very loudly and in a wrenching manner) throughout, since Vivaldi obviously wanted to carry his little joke to the extreme.

Vivaldi, *Spring Concerto*, opus 8 no. 4: Largo

A note about the mordents used in our elaboration: Use our standard mordent (the Baroque short mordent) in ascending passages and the inverted mordent in descending passages. You will then prevent the needless weakening of a later note through anticipation.

For the most part Vivaldi's slow movements rely on a smooth, very cantabile application of the bow for their effectiveness. In contrast, his fast movements, where he uses eighths, sixteenths, and smaller note values in profusion, call for a short crisp bow stroke, using the top quarter of the bow. More pressure and a faster stroke take care of the fortes; a smaller, slower stroke takes care of piano, pianissimo, and echo effects. It is imperative that string players uniformly observe this rule of using only the top seven or eight inches of bow where this type of bowing is required. Subtle dynamic changes and contrasts are more difficult to achieve if the middle or the lower third of the bow is used.

A Chamber Sonata for Violin and Basso Continuo

Vivaldi's *Sonata in G Minor* for violin and basso continuo (number 102 in the Hortus Musicus Series) makes a good starting point for a study of his chamber sonatas. The manuscript of the sonata has no tempo indication for any of the movements, but Walter Upmeyer has made a wise choice of tempos. The opening sixteen-measure section begins like an operatic recitative:

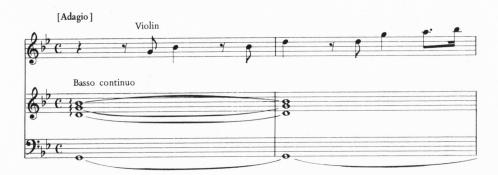

After the harpsichordist's initial rolled chord this introductory section will sound much more convincing if the violinist plays in an improvisatory manner rather than in strict, mechanical time. Give a little more weight to the first eighth note, for example. Pause infinitesimally on the eighth rest on the fourth beat of the same measure; break up the last eighth note (B flat) in this measure, going through C to the quarter-note D in measure 2. Again hesitate slightly at the rest on the second beat; then move decisively to scale the heights. The passage should now look like this:

As the movement draws to a close, you will feel the need for more filling in (in measures 13, 14, and 15). The concluding measure, however, should be left very much the way you found it, except that you should play a half trill on the dotted eighth note on the second beat. The passage should now look like this:

This movement begins like an introspective recitative. Therefore begin it mezzo forte and increase the intensity somewhat as the melody soars, but be careful to remain on the softer side of forte. From measure 13 you have a note-for-note repeat—which you will vary, of course—of a passage beginning with a pick-up note in measure 9. But the dynamics have changed: you are now in piano. The tonality has also changed, and with it the mood, which is now more somber. Suggest to your friend at the keyboard that instead of repeating the accompaniment slavishly, as is the case in the piano reduction of this edition, he be prepared to experiment.

The allegro would be a simple piece of fiddling in 3/8 were it not for the double stops. They are introduced casually enough in measure 3, but rapidly acquire a significance of their own. Measures 25 through 37, and to a lesser extent measures 71 to 90, will need some careful working out to keep the two voices in the violin part distinct and convincing.

We go on to a brief Largo that has a rather awkward feel to it; a five-measure phrase with a pick up, repeated, leads to a six-measure phrase with a pick-up, also repeated. The entire movement cries out for ornamentation. Make sense of the first phrase and of the piece by judicious filling out and ornamenting; the same technique should be applied to the second phrase; make the repeat as ornate as you please.

The Allegro should be played crisply, with the endless running sixteenths coming cleanly through. The final movement is a lively Siciliana in 12/8.

Do not allow the brisk tempo to restrict you to the simplest type of ornamentation—much can be done without detracting from the pastoral quality of the music.

A Virtuoso Piccolo Concerto

Next we will examine a virtuoso work—the Concerto in C, F VI no. 4, for piccolo, strings, and harpsichord. Franco Colombo publishes an edition by the flutist

Samuel Baron, with a piano reduction by W. R. Smith. Be prepared for fireworks; sixteenths (sometimes in triplets) run through almost the whole opening Allegro. There is wry humor in Quantz's recommendation on avoiding disaster in such quick passage work: "All the fingers must be raised equally and not too high." The wonder is that there is time to raise them at all. Quantz's chapter, "Of the Manner of Playing the Allegro," contains other useful hints that have specific application in this context. In the following passage, for example:

Edited by Samuel Baron, © 1962. Reduction for flute and piano (edition no. NY2279). All excerpts reproduced by permission.

one can see the practical application of the following rule: "If . . . after quick notes several slow singing ones follow, the player's fire must be moderated immediately, and the slow notes executed with the requisite sentiment, so that they do not become boring." This implies a "fire" (that is, an increase of intensity) in measure 25 and a decrease in measure 26; an increase in measure 27, a decrease in measure 28, and so on in measures 29 and 30; throughout all this the flute tone should range from piano to no more than mezzo forte so that when the forte bursts on us in measure 32 it comes in at a different dynamic level altogether. It is clear at a glance that Baron's crescendo and diminuendo marks meet Quantz's requirements measure by measure. It is a pity, therefore, that these marks have not been shown in parentheses, not only to distinguish them from Vivaldi's own scanty markings but so that a true understanding could be gained of the extent of Baron's own musicianly contribution.

Measures 98 through 100 present another study in dynamic subtlety:

Even though the tempo is allegro, the performer is expected to do some shading. Trills such as occur in measures 98 and 99 should be played "happily and quickly." But there's more to it still; according to Quantz, "in passage-work where the principal notes ascend and the passing descend, the former must be held slightly and stressed, and must be sounded with more force than the latter, since the melody lies in the former" (Quantz, p. 132). Quarter notes such as those in measures 99 and 100 "must be played in a singing and sustained manner" (Quantz, p. 133).

At measure 102 Vivaldi takes us into an orchestral ritornello that leads to a rather enigmatic passage beginning at measure 112; leaping eighth notes replace the arpeggiated and running sixteenths we have become accustomed to:

What does one make of this passage? Did Vivaldi actually want these bare eighths here, or is he again leaving room for elaboration? In my view this passage requires filling in. Keep some of the eighths, but intersperse them with sixteenths; use mordents wherever appropriate, remembering to keep all endings clean.

The Largo is only 26 measures long, including repeats; yet for every one of these measures the piccolo soars high above a static orchestra, with no place to hide. Samuel Baron provides two lines for the soloist; the first is Vivaldi's own, the sec-

ond an ornamented version for repeats. If you are bold you can take Baron's ornamented line as your starting point and work up something even more elaborate
to play the second time around:

The first section of this movement, as well as the movement itself, ends in a long
held note; at this point you should avail yourself of the messa di voce to ensure a
correct interpretation:

Quantz has left these specific recommendations on how a "messa di voce" should be played on a Baroque, one-keyed flute: "If you must hold a long note for either a whole or a half bar, which the Italians call *messa di voce,* you must first tip it gently with the tongue, scarcely exhaling; then you begin pianissimo, allow the strength of the tone to swell to the middle of the note, and from there diminish it to the end of the note in the same fashion, making a vibrato* with the finger on the nearest open hole" (*On Playing the Flute,* pp. 165–166).

A little later he says that each singing note, whether it is a quarter, eighth or sixteenth, must "have its own Piano and Forte, to the extent that the time permits." Because of the nature of the flute, however, this procedure can lead to fluctuations in pitch; Quantz prescribes techniques to correct the situation:

> If you wish to produce a long note softly and then increase its strength, you must first withdraw the lips, or turn the flute outwards, as much as is necessary for the note to remain in tune with other instruments. And when you blow more strongly, advance the lips or turn the flute inwards; otherwise the note will be first too low, then too high. If, however, you wish to end the same note softly again, you must again withdraw the lips in the same proportion, or turn the flute outwards [*On Playing the Flute,* pp. 57–58].

And there you have it—a messa di voce that is true in pitch from beginning to end, with a vibrato to boot.

The "Pisendel Concerto"

For a final glimpse at Vivaldi's own performance practice, we will look at the *Concerto in A Major* (the "Pisendel Concerto") for violin and string orchestra. The work was written for Johann Georg Pisendel, a young virtuoso protégé of the Elector of Saxony, while Pisendel was visiting Vivaldi in Venice and studying with him. It includes a cadenza by Vivaldi and first-movement embellishments that the editor Ludwig Landshoff believes were worked out by Pisendel himself under Vivaldi's watchful eye.

The examples here are taken from a reduction for violin and keyboard edited by Landshoff for Peters.

---

* This is not a true vibrato in the modern sense but rather a kind of pulsation.

The first set of embellishments in the Allegro begins at measure 66:

Not quite thirty measures later, a second group of embellishments is noted; this set, however, represents, not rhythmic changes, but changes in phrasing and in direction; in measure 96 there is a change that involves a flashier bowing:

The slow movement, a Siciliano, has no variance by other helpful hands. But the Allegro third movement in 3/8 time presents its surprises, the first at measure 50. Note in particular the more intricate bowing and the syncopated rhythm demanded in measures 50 and 51:

Beginning with measure 120 Pisendel changed some solo violin passages that were originally in double stops to a fluid single line and left in the double stops in other places—altogether a happy solution. The double stops continue through measure 139; then at measure 143 we are faced with:

At this point, we have not one but two ornamented versions of an allegro passage, and both of them probably carry Vivaldi's express approval; either one can be played at the performer's fancy. We are getting to the end of the movement now, and the triplet sixteenths by themselves will no longer suffice. Thirty-seconds were introduced fleetingly in measures 132 and 136 through 140; they come in again strongly at measure 172,

and moments later we arrive at Vivaldi's cadenza. All thirty-nine measures of it are written out in full, possibly to serve as an example to young Pisendel as much as to curb undisciplined performers who would destroy the unity of the work with overly long and irrelevant passages. In terms of technical difficulty and virtuoso display it cannot match the great cadenzas of the nineteenth century; in fact it is completely different, soaring to the heights and ignoring completely the lowest register of the violin, which in those days was much less sonorous than it is today. Not the least

praiseworthy of its qualities, however, is the manner in which Vivaldi brings us
back to earth in the eight measures preceding the final tutti:

We have it all here: descent from the heights, longer note values, rhythmic variety,
diversity in bowing, and inevitability; after a quick tutti section we reach the end.

6

The Challenge of Johann Sebastian Bach

This chapter includes a plea for freedom and an appeal for restraint. Through the decades Bach's music has become encrusted with a whole system of traditions and sacred myths. His high priests are legion; their followers, fanatical. Witness the child who instinctively inserts a Baroque short mordent or half-trill at a cadential point in a minuet and is promptly stopped by the teacher. "Bach *always* set down all the notes," the teacher says. "You never *never* NEVER tamper with Bach!" And sometimes, in a tone of desperation: "Do you think *you* can add *anything* to *Bach?*" The situation becomes really laughable when the child has been playing a minuet from the *Anna Magdalena Notebook;* the work turns out to be not by Bach himself but by unknown composer X, and the short mordent is perfectly acceptable anyway.

Not all ignorance exists at this basic level. Even quite knowledgeable musicians—eminent pianists among them—believe that Bach took care of the ornamentation at all times. When he wrote in the French style, the reasoning goes, he used the type of shorthand symbols favored by the French school; when he wrote in the Italian style, he wrote out the ornamentation in full, taking no chances with the performer. And that was that. It is rarely acknowledged that there are many pieces that the performer can ornament. For Bach wrote in the Italian style in two ways: sometimes he wrote out the florid passages as in the slow movement of the *Italian Concerto* for harpsichord, and sometimes he set down only enough notes to make a complete melody, leaving the elaboration to the performer. Yes, we have proof, and we will share it with the world. The problem is how to do the elaboration. Determining the national influence and style is not enough; whether it is French, German, or Italian, the architecture, the grandeur, the logic, and the musical accents must be indubitably Bach. Only by a thorough study of his idiom can we find clues for elaborating in a given situation.

Italian Concerto

To get a good idea of Bach's conception of Italian florid writing, we will look at that extraordinary example he has left us—the Andante of the *Italian Concerto.*

Here, to the rhythm of a relentless bass, the right hand of the harpsichordist is launched upon an endless tide of figuration; now rising, now falling, now eddying for a moment, the waves of sixteenths and thirty-seconds sweep on until they have worked out their logic and their destiny:

Much can be learned here by reversing the process of composition—by taking the Andante as Bach wrote it and working back, simplifying it progressively down to the bare bones. Then we could build it up again through more and more complex stages until the final Bach version or its approximation is reached. We will leave the notes of the left hand as written and take out the ornamentation in the right hand. It takes only a few minutes of wrestling with this exercise to convince oneself of the absolute logic of Bach's florid writing; no simplified version can even approach the magic of the original:

Notice the difference in rhythmic feel between the bass as it occurs in the original, and when we deliberately break it down into three units of two eighth notes each. It becomes chopped up, overly accented, and the overall impression of smoothly flowing unity is lost.

Now that we have simplified an elaborate movement, let us see how we can ornament another famous Bach slow movement, the Sarabande from the *English Suite No. 2:*

On the face of it, this movement as written is complete. Perfect. Variation is undesirable or unthinkable, depending on your training. Probably ninety-nine out of a hundred recitalists who have played the suite in the past one hundred years have performed the Sarabande this way, and the repeats have been exact note-for-note duplications of what was played seconds earlier. What a travesty of Bach is this, and if it continues, may the audience demand its money back at the box office! Variation and embellishment *are* not only possible, they are desirable and are in fact implied. Heresy? Let's take a second look at the music.

Measure 1 is perhaps best left as it is. We will do something about the bare repeated sixths in measure 2 but we'll leave measures 3 and 4 undisturbed. Measures 5 and 6 look much more promising. What can be done about the twelve successive eighth notes clumping along? We can fill them in with sixteenths and get some rhythmic variety. Perhaps we can try to achieve melodic variety too. Remember that we have come across this step-wise filling-in before when dealing with Vivaldi, whom Bach admired and whose concertos he transcribed. We should be prepared, however, to have the same type of figuration sound completely different in the two composers; while Vivaldi's harmonies tend towards simplistic sweetness, Bach's harmonies are far more varied and rely heavily on the use of dissonance. Measures 9 and 10 present a situation similar to measures 5 and 6, but measures 11 and 12 can be left more or less as they are. Here is a comparison of the right hand of the two versions of the entire section, with Bach's original above and the ornamented version below; the Henle edition is our source:

Before we begin hurling brickbats at the perpetrator of the ornamented version, let's consider it dispassionately. By stretching generosity to its limits, we might even find some virtues in it. It is certainly busier than the Bach original; but is *busyness* a virtue in itself? Well, maybe not. Is it *smoother*, perhaps? Uh, yes. Melodically, does it stay true to the Bach original? Ye-es, though the D in measure 6 is anticipated by the D ornament in measure 5 and measure 9 is a mess! In this measure Bach's entire melodic curve, in fact his entire sequence of notes, has been covered in the course of just two beats; furthermore, to hide his own ineptness the embellisher has now repeated his first group of four sixteenths, causing the high G to be played twice and robbing the measure of whatever architectural tension the original possessed! All right then, let's grant you this: you don't like it as much as the Bach original, and you certainly would not play it instead of the original the first time around, right? Would you then consider playing it as the repeat? No? Bach would disapprove of such tampering, you object, and besides what would the critics say? What *could* the critics say, when Bach himself wrote the alternative?

Yes, in both the second and the third English suites, Bach provided a Sarabande and "the agréments to the same Sarabande"; agréments, as Robert Donington explains in *Grove's Dictionary of Music and Musicians*, are "a sample playing-version to suggest suitable embellishments, but not to exclude others invented by the performer." Now here are the first four measures of the Sarabande from the *English Suite No. 3* in two versions; the first version, which seems to be plain, has two half-trills indicated by symbols in measures 3 and 4:

In his proposed agréments to the same four measures, Bach combines Italian-style ornamentation (but fully written out!) with French-style symbols; when the symbols indicated in each measure are played, the new version that results is far more complex, both rhythmically and lineally, than Bach's original:

Bach's *agréments* added

Now that you see the way Bach varies his own music, you may feel less inhibited about ornamenting it yourself. Even if you do not succeed, you have much to gain in making the effort.

Sonatas for Violin and Harpsichord

Intriguing problems arise in Bach's *Six Sonatas for Violin and Harpsichord*, BWV 1014–1019. Our preferred edition is the set edited by the late Rudolf Gerber and published by Bärenreiter (BA 5118 and BA 5119 in their catalogue). The text should be thoroughly checked, however, against the Urtext in the *Neue Bach-Ausgabe** (BA 5012 in the Bärenreiter edition) for reasons which will become apparent.

These sonatas illustrate the danger of blindly following a tradition. A few years ago musicians playing through these works would find the keyboard part encrusted with chords, while the violinist played in the ponderous style then considered "scholarly"—a far cry from the enlightened scholarliness we know today. Then suddenly a few musicologists and musicians became aware of the fact that Bach's writing here was consciously different—that he had written what appeared to be trio sonatas for two instead of four musicians. The violinist and the harpsichordist's right hand played the two melodic lines and the harpsichordist's left hand replaced the basso continuo. The gamba that normally played along was left out entirely.

It now appears that even this view of the sonatas was too simplistic. Today the very basis of the sonatas is being questioned. Gerber spotlighted the unusual setting of the works, and Hans Eppstein, the editor of the prestigious new Henle edition, has taken the reasoning a step further: some movements are in two-part writing, some in three-part writing, and others could have been written with even a small chamber group in mind. This becomes plausible when we consider that the sonatas date from Bach's years at Cöthen, when he wrote the Brandenburg concertos.

The first sonata, in B Minor, opens with four measures of solo harpsichord that seem to challenge the violinist to use double stops in the popular North German style of imitation. Such imitation was a basic formula for composition and performance in Baroque times. If we were in the audience at a first reading of this Bach sonata (around 1720), we would have looked at each other with knowing smiles and nodded, and somebody nearby would have whispered "Double stops for the violin coming up, like Biber." "Or Walter," you might have interposed. "Exactly!"

* A revised edition of the complete works begun in 1954.

The example shows the original cembalo part. The tempo is adagio. The violin is silent. Bach is at the keyboard. From the very first beat his right hand is playing firmly and consistently in thirds. In measure 3, he goes up to B above the staff, and then for a measure and a half, he comes down inexorably by step; in measure 4 the violinist prepares himself; as measure 5 approaches one senses the imminent entry:

All excerpts from the first three sonatas copyright © 1958 by Bärenreiter. Reproduced by permission.

Will the violin enter playing double stops like Walter and Biber? Instead it enters with a clean held F sharp and goes on from there with a fluid single melodic line of its own:

A marvelous way for the violinist to heighten the drama of the moment is to start the F sharp pianissimo and go immediately into a messa di voce. Similar situations (but of a shorter duration) where a messa di voce is appropriate occur in later measures (7–8, 9–10, 12, 13, 20, 26, 31, 32, and the final measure, 36). Other measures involve the use of double stops; the violinist who can pull off an effective messa di voce while playing double stops should do so without hesitation.

The harpsichord part in the first movement is straightforward and calls for no particular comment. In the Allegro, however, the part as it is printed in Bärenreiter's practical "performing" edition (BA 5118) has much that is amiss. Here is how measures 1 through 5 appear on page 6 of that volume:

The perceptive reader, knowing that Bach has been using a deliberately thinned-out texture, will question the use of the figured bass in these measures, particularly since the chords obscure the imitative harpsichord entry in measure 5. A quick reference to the Neue Bach-Ausgabe (Bärenreiter BA 5012) shows Bach's original:

Notice that Bach himself allotted the harpsichordist's right hand four entire measures of rest, that the figuring is shown in brackets as being suggested by someone other than Bach, and that the imitation between the harpsichordist's right hand and the violin becomes instantly clear once the intrusive chords are left out. True, the Bärenreiter "practical edition" shows the figures in brackets and the realized notes in small type; yet so great is the awe with which people regard the printed note that many performers will play the realized chords unquestioningly merely because editor Gerber or an assistant put them there. A similar procedure was followed in measures 102–105. Indeed we are faced here with the type of situation C. P. E. Bach warned us about, in which a composer pointedly precludes figured chords and a too-zealous harpsichordist or editor supplies them. If further corroboration is needed, let me point out that the entire texture of Bach's harpsichord writing in this movement is strictly two-part, without a single chord being interpolated; hence the three-part writing introduced into these eight measures by the editor goes directly against the composer's intentions and should be rejected by the conscientious performer.

If you disregard the added notes in smaller type, you will find that the manner in which the sonatas have been laid out on the printed page in the Bärenreiter edition will help to clarify your thinking. The three staves—one for the violin and two for the harpsichord—are given equal prominence, and rightly so. Not only are the violin and the harpsichord equal partners in the musical enterprise, but the harpsichordist's two hands generally carry equal weight. With one notable exception the writing is linear and contrapuntal rather than chordal; the rests and silences in both hands are deliberate and carefully reasoned. The editor has recognized this, for example, in the final Allegro of the sixth sonata, BWV 1019; it is strange that he should have been so afraid of allowing small silences elsewhere.

The second sonata, BWV 1015, demands unusual coloration. The violin plays in a low part of its register against a long low held A in the harpsichord. In measure 1 both parts are marked *dolce*. Yet *dolce* is a descriptive term one associates more readily with a bowed string instrument than with a harpsichord; looking once again at the opening measures one can see that the low held A would suit a gamba or a cello far better than it does a harpsichord.

In the Allegro, let the harpsichordist beware once again of insidious chords for the right hand (set in small notes in the Bärenreiter edition):

It is so easy to accept the chords written in here for keyboard as "part of the tradition of those times"—so easy to go along with those countless performers and listeners who have become imbued with this false tradition and expect continuous clatter from the harpsichordist. A glance at the *Neue Bach-Ausgabe*, however, will remind us that Bach was only partly bound by tradition, that he was also a strong original thinker and innovator, and that amongst the flashes of vision he continually had, could be included moments like these:

Play this over several times, relishing the silences as much as the sounds and the transparency of it all; relish above all the clean crispness of the harpsichord's imitative right-hand entry in measure 6 and contrast this with the turgid sound of a realized figured bass.

Try the messa di voce with those long held notes for violin in measures 12–14, 34–37, 47–49. The arpeggiated passages for violin beginning at measure 74 could be started as straight sixteenths and then played in triplet sixteenths from measures 79–91. (For arpeggiation possibilities, see chapter 7 on Geminiani.) Again, ignore the unnecessary keyboard chords in 93–98.

In the Andante un poco, as happens sometimes when a composer tries to be precise, his very preciseness can give rise to the danger of imprecision. How andante is andante? How little is poco? If you ornament heavily, the pace will be slower; if you only ornament a little, you'll play it faster.

The harpsichord's bass line is marked staccato sempre. We can accept this at face value and just play the left hand staccato. Or, if we have a two-manual instrument, we can play the left hand on one eight-foot set of strings using the buff stop and play the right hand on the other manual. The two melodic lines will then stand out, and the accompaniment will sound pizzicato and muted. This may well be what Bach had in mind; try it both ways and decide for yourself.

The concluding Presto has repeats, so be prepared to ornament at least the second time around. Leave out the chords supplied in measures 1–6 and play the bass line alone.

The third sonata holds a few surprises. The Adagio has a very florid violin line, worked out in thirty-seconds. What's more, out of all twenty-five movements of the six sonatas only this first movement of the third sonata has a keyboard part that strongly resembles writing for winds:

For the rest of this unusual movement the violin is firmly established as soloist and the keyboard serves as accompanist—an intelligent, musicianly accompanist, to be sure, but an accompanist nonetheless.

How different is the role of the keyboard in the next movement.

The keyboard part runs on for 26 measures without a break; a quarter rest in the right hand occurs at the beginning of measure 27; the next break, which is also a quarter rest for the right hand, comes on the last pulse of measure 110, and a three-and-a-half measure rest begins in the second half of measure 125. The left hand only has rests in measures 58, 59, and 60.

The question is: how can the harpsichordist (or pianist) get through all these notes without making them sound like so much mechanical nattering? If we first decide how the notes should be played and then how fast to play them, we will resolve the difficulties. First, feel two beats to a measure; second, play all the quarter notes staccato; third, dwell, but really dwell, on half notes; play them tenuto, and hold them for full value, when they are followed by a quarter note; fourth, when a half note, two tied quarter notes, or a half note tied to a quarter note or to an eighth is followed by eighth notes, hold it for almost (but not quite) its full value; and lastly, the violinist and keyboard player should both adhere faithfully to these points, or their phrasing will not be consistent.

Try these measures on the harpsichord:

On the keyboard, the left hand will play a continual staccato, while the right hand plays measures 1–3 as follows:

In measures 9, 10, and 11, however, hold the half note for a fraction less than its true value because it is followed by eighths; at the same time the violinist should hold the half notes for their full value:

Notice that the harpsichordist's left hand holds the half notes for their full value in measures 13 and 14 even though the right hand cuts the tied notes slightly short.

In measures 17–21, the violinist should also cut his half notes slightly short. Further, if the keyboard player has decided to use a short trill on the half notes beginning in measure 9, the violinist can use a short trill in measures 17, 18, and 19 and a long trill in measures 20 and 21, and the harpsichordist should match this with a long trill in measure 21. Mordents, or short trills, can be used effectively on the dotted notes in measure 23. The style for the entire movement has now been fully set and should be carried through to the end.

As acquaintance with the music grows, however, the performers may well ask themselves, "Must we be tied to this endless succession of eighths, quarters, and half notes, or can we at some point branch out on our own?" The violinist leading into measure 111 and the following measures may well wonder:

Why not, in one mad impulse, try something like this?

The ineptness or inadequacy of such an attempt might become clear just seconds after we play it or set it down on paper. And if realization comes slowly, we can hasten the process by asking ourselves: is the experimental ornamentation in keeping with the character of the music? Is it Bach-like and believable? Does it blend in?

Discouraging answers should not lead us to give up immediately. It is important that we persist. If we are still unsuccessful after repeated tries, we still have gained, because we then will be able to play Bach's original line with a deeper understanding and greater conviction than ever before.

In this type of situation we should remember that if one partner lays down such a challenge, the other will have to match it at the first available opportunity. Both players should bear in mind the following wise provisos laid down by C. P. E. (1) if one partner has the technique and musical skill to engage in such a duel, and the other does not, the first should refrain from issuing the challenge, and (2) if one partner does issue the musical challenge, and it is poorly done, the second should refrain from imitating it; it is bad enough that such a musical crime should have been perpetrated once, without its being committed all over again.

Since you will be ornamenting, you might prefer ♩ = 88 as your tempo; again, choose the pace that best suits what you will be doing with the music.

The violinist should remember to use the favorite Baroque device of messa di voce wherever feasible. Because of the rapid pace it may not prove very practical on notes that last only half a measure; however, one should be able to use the device very effectively in measures 35, 37, 39–40, 47–48, and wherever a note is held for a full measure or more.

The third movement has special significance from the rhythmic point of view. Many musicologists believe that the rhythm of two against three or three against two should not be played as such in Baroque music, and they go so far as to urge that wherever this situation occurs, the 2 be stretched to fit the pattern of the triplet so that a disturbing clash of rhythms might not occur. You will find this point of view challenged in the epilogue, where the subject is dealt with at length, particularly as it pertains to Bach; for now, suffice it to point out that Bach has the two rhythms follow one another in the violin part in measures 7 and 8:

It is not long before Bach actively pits the two rhythms against each other. Here is measure 24, as Bach has it (*left*) and as some musicologists and musicians insist it be performed (*right*):

Similar juxtapositions arise in measures 26, 27, 36, 44, 48, and 52; I recommend that you play the rhythms as Bach wrote them. The violinist should use messa di voce in measures 22, 25, 34, and 47. There are some double stops in this movement; we have not encountered them since the first movement of the first sonata.

In sonatas 4 through 6 Bach breaks away from some of the patterns he set up in the first three. In the Largo of *Sonata No. 4*, BWV 1017, a quite bare violin part is set against a keyboard part that comes closer to being pure accompaniment than anything else we have encountered so far. The movement is in two parts, and each one is repeated, so be prepared to ornament not just the first time around but with variants the second time as well. In the next movement Bach abandons the soloist-accompanist relationship and once again has some very felicitous three-part writing, the harpsichordist taking two parts against the violinist's one. Bach has pitted the two melodic lines played by the violinist and the harpsichord's right hand against a bass that is not only very active but a full participant in all the complex figurations and imitative passage work. The movement has phenomenal vitality and busyness, and the balances will have to be even more carefully worked out than usual.

The third movement, an Adagio, has no dynamic marking in the first measure:

All excerpts from sonatas 4 through 6 copyright © 1960 by Bärenreiter. Reproduced by permission.

Normally in an Adagio one would presume that the opening is quiet; in measure 5, however, where the violinist repeats the theme, the marking is piano. We must assume that this marking contradicts the beginning dynamic, which would then be forte. In measure 5 the sensitive harpsichordist should be able to match the diminution in the violinist's tone by moving on to a quieter register.

Once again we have here the clash of rhythms. Not only must we keep them distinct, but we will have to accentuate their differences because the dotted eighth followed by a sixteenth in the violin part must be played as a double-dotted eighth followed by a thirty-second.

Note that the violin part, which is very spare and austere in measures 1 through 4, repeats the same passage more softly in the next four measures. Since the violin part dwells on the same rhythmic figures for fifty-six measures, if you are ever going to try to ornament Bach's music, you might as well start here.

The fifth sonata begins with no tempo indication of any kind. However, the second movement is an Allegro so it is reasonable to assume that the first movement should be played at a slow tempo. The beginning is worth examining closely, particularly because it will show what a grave injustice is done to Bach by throwing in figured chords indiscriminately.

Here are the first three measures as they appear in both the *Neue Bach-Ausgabe* and in BA 5119, Bärenreiter's practical edition:

You will notice that there are three voices in the harpsichord, and there is a fourth in the violin part. Silences—as represented by rests—are important, as in a conversation among friends. The value of the rests and the danger of supplying chords can best be seen by writing out each voice in the first ten measures on a separate line; the violin enters in measure 6 with "Mmmmmmm, but . . ." In measure 8, the top two voices in the harpsichord fall silent, deferring to violin and bass; the violinist has an appeggiatura followed by a trill. C. P. E. Bach suggests in an analogous situation that the harpsichordist avoid intruding upon the ornamentation of the solo voice; obviously J. S. Bach intended that the violin part at this point be allowed to stand by itself.

Alas! He fell victim to the industriousness of editors and of professional chord suppliers. They abhor a vacuum; so not only does the middle of measure 8, which was left so marvelously empty by Bach, get filled in with sound, but the quarter rest in measure 9 is also obliterated and the same "service" is performed again diligently in measures 16-17. And in 44-45, and 48-49, and 52-53, and 57-59, and 87-88.

(Above) the first ten measures of Bach's Sonata 5, BWV 1018, transcribed into open score; *(below)* measures 8-9 in open score with editorial additions. The added notes (shown in brackets) get in the way of Bach's very clear part-writing.

In the next movement, an Allegro, the chord suppliers get to work right away adding chords in measures 1–4, after which Bach gives them no scope whatever.

The next movement is an Upside-down Adagio in which the harpsichord has the thirty-second note filigree and the violin plays rather square-looking double stops:

Adagio

Let the violinist not be lulled into thinking that the double stops are a humdrum exercise to be disposed of routinely. Bach wants them endowed with life, and a little careful thought and attention to moving parts will show where the emphasis should lie. That Bach intends this to be serious part playing becomes clear at measure 11, when the two parts in the violin are for the first time made distinct by rests. By measure 23, with the end of the movement in sight, the interplay of the double stops increases in subtlety:

A sprightly Vivace in 3/8 time ends the sonata; beware of an interpolated figured bass in measures 1–5 and 111–116. Otherwise it is plain sailing with no repeats.

The last sonata of the set is the most enigmatic; Bach gave some extraordinary thought to it. The first movement is an Allegro, a switch from the normal pattern. We can presume a forte beginning because of the tempo and bright nature of the music. The texture is generally light and fast moving until the editor throws in a figured bass from measure 22 through the first beat of measure 27. Ignore all notes written in these measures for the harpsichordist's right hand. The same holds true for measures 1–3 of the Largo. In this movement you will find close imitation between the two instruments; if one ornaments, the other should follow.

So far was Bach from thinking of the harpsichord as a vehicle for figured bass in this sonata that the third movement (surprise!) is an Allegro for harpsichord alone. Since it is in two sections with repeats, we strongly urge you to ornament it at least the second time around. The fourth movement is an Adagio that is rather fully worked out. The fifth movement is a blazing Allegro in 6/8; the pace here should be tempered by the knowledge that there are six sixteenths to the beat and crispness of articulation has to be maintained throughout. There are intimations here of the fourth and fifth Brandenburg concertos, and this impression is heightened when all three parts come rushing to a fermata in measure 71. But it is a false alarm; after a half-measure rest, the harpsichord picks up the tempo, the violin enters in measure 74, and the two instruments scurry along, largely in thirds and sixths, until Bach with his irrefutable logic demands that the movement should end. Two alternate movements to this sonata are included in an appendix.

The *Sonata in E Minor*, BWV 1023, is a work that was long considered to be of doubtful authenticity, but it is now believed to be by Bach and is included in the

Neue Bach-Ausgabe. The performing edition is Bärenreiter's BA 5121, and like the sonatas discussed above, it too has been provided with a gamba part. Unfortunately, in the words of the preface, "No attempt has been made to distinguish the editor's additions from original markings; both are printed only in the customary form." It is hard to reconcile this attitude with modern publishing practice. Since the text of the performing edition closely matches the *Neue Bach Ausgabe* (except for the realized figured bass and the treatment of the pedal point in the first movement), the performer who wants to distinguish between the original markings and the editorial additions will have to write to the Sachsische Landesbibliothek at Dresden, Germany; the Sonata's call number in that library is 2405 R/1.

Although this sonata, like the other sonatas we have been discussing is presumed to have been written around 1720, when Bach was thirty-five years old, it is markedly different from the others. To begin with, the first movement consists entirely of rapid violinistic fireworks over a twenty-nine-measure pedal point:

If you remember C. P. E. Bach's insistence that a pedal point not be notated with a figured bass, and if it is so notated, it should be ignored, you will be surprised to learn from the editor of the practical edition, BA 5121, that "the pedal point in the first movement has been broken up to suit it to the harpsichord." You might personally think it was a master stroke of Bach to have set off masterly fiddling against twenty-nine measures of pure drone; now along comes an authoritative edition that invites your harpsichordist to strum along with chords for the entire twenty-nine measures plus a beat, the reasoning probably being that as long as you've got somebody sitting there at the keyboard, he might as well earn his keep. But since you have a gamba or cello to help sustain that endless E, please play the work without the supplementary harpsichord harmonies. The tempo is allegro, and as long as the harpsichordist marks the beginning of each measure by repeating the long-held E, that may be all the accent the bass part needs.

The prelude leads directly into an Adagio ma non tanto in 3/4. The remaining movements are an Allemanda and a Gigue, which can use some variants in its repeats.

Works for Solo Violin

Before considering Bach's other chamber works let's review the discussion to this point. If you have attempted the ornamentation of some Bach movements or if you have even begun to admit that ornamentation is possible, we have made some progress! Those performers who fear that their attempts at ornamenting are too wild or daring for such an austere and conservative composer, are laboring under a misconception; Bach was daring beyond belief. What should be done, for example, with the following simplified passage for violin, to get it to match the original elaboration by the composer?

If we were told the original was by Vivaldi, we would not hesitate to try mordents here and there, a filling-in of intermediate notes, and trills and turns as needed. But if we *knew* the original was by Bach, we would inhibit ourselves into thinking small even though Bach invariably thought big, in endless sweeping curves and impassioned workings-out. This is how Bach elaborated this bare outline; it is the opening Grave of the second of his *Six Sonatas and Partitas for Solo Violin* (BWV 1003):

We can see immediately, even without playing the notes, that Bach's ornamentation, far from being austere or conservative, was extraordinarily fluid and imaginative when he chose to write out a passage in full. Fortunately for us numerous examples exist of Bach's very florid writing for the violin. We refer the interested reader to the Neue Bach Ausgabe, Series VI, vol. 1, which contains Bach's complete works for violin excluding the concertos. (This is BA 5012 in the Bärenreiter edition.) We refer you particularly to the following works for unaccompanied violin: the Adagio from the *Sonata No. 1 in D Minor*, BWV 1001 (p. 3), the Grave from the *Sonata No. 2 in E Minor*, BWV 1003 (pp. 20–21), the celebrated Ciaccona or Chaconne from the *Partita No. 2 in D Minor*, BWV 1004 (pp. 35–41). You may also want to study the Andante from the *Sonata No. 1 for Violin and Harpsichord, in D Major*, BWV 1014 (pp. 92–93). Bach's keyboard music and keyboard concertos will yield other examples, as will the cantatas, passions, and other vocal and choral works. Painstaking study of these examples will make it possible for you to ornament Bach's works with a greater degree of freedom and feeling for Bach's musical idiom than would otherwise be possible.

The monumental Sonatas and Partitas are amongst the most revered works in all musical literature; alas! they are also amongst the most abused. We present-day musicians recognize that they are complete in themselves; yet when Mendelssohn and Schumann introduced them to the musical public in the nineteenth century, how were they presented? These great composers were nobody's fools; they led musical taste in their time and considered themselves to be the scourge of musical Philistines. Yet they could not bear to see the sonatas and partitas as they were, and provided them with keyboard accompaniments the way missionaries in Hawaii draped grass skirts on the Hawaiians.

The technical and interpretative problems inherent in the unaccompanied sonatas and partitas lie outside the scope of this book. Absolute technical mastery is a must; so is breadth of vision. The late violinist Joseph Szigeti recommended that violinists first "look out for works that can serve as stepping stones towards this supreme challenge, such as the Sonatas by Biber (1644–1704) and Pisendel (1687–1755)." To us it is significant that Szigeti should have regarded Pisendel's music as providing a stepping-stone to Bach, since (as we have seen in an earlier chapter), Pisendel's teacher Vivaldi through his violin concertos strongly influenced Bach's own development as a composer. Szigeti, however, goes a step further by suggesting that Bach was influenced by Pisendel himself: "A glance at Pisendel's *Solo Sonata in A Minor*—Pisendel was about thirty years of age when Bach started writing his sonatas—will bear out my supposition that Bach was familiar with the great Dresden Concertmaster's playing style and with the Solo Sonatas."*

The pieces of the puzzle now fall into place: Vivaldi influenced Bach; he also influenced Pisendel who influenced Bach and Quantz as well. Quantz taught Frederick the Great, who employed C. P. E. Bach. C. P. E. was taught by his father, J. S. Bach, and was hence indirectly influenced by Pisendel and Vivaldi (not to mention Rameau, Couperin, and Legrenzi). There was so much influence and counterinfluence in the Baroque period that it was almost incestuous.

* Szigeti: *Szigeti on the Violin* (New York: Dover, 1979), p. 126.

Works for Flute

Publishers generally divide Bach's works for accompanied flute into two groups—the three sonatas for flute and keyboard alone and the three sonatas for flute and basso continuo. In the Peters, Breitkopf & Härtel, and G. Schirmer editions the first three sonatas form volume 1 of the set and the last three, volume 2. A recent G. Schirmer issue, however, with the keyboard part realized by Louis Moyse, includes an unnumbered *Sonata in A Minor* for flute alone and a *Sonata No. 7 in G Minor* for flute and basso continuo. Schmieder describes this as "Jugendwerk," a youthful work that is not as important as his more mature writing. Only four of these sonatas are available in Bärenreiter's performing edition No. 4402—sonatas 1, 3, 5 and 6.

Two other works for flute are also available in print: the *Trio Sonata in G for Flute, Violin, and Basso Continuo* (BWV 1038) and the *Trio Sonata in G for Two Flutes and Basso Continuo,* (BWV 1039). The *Trio Sonata in B Flat for Two Alto Recorders and Basso Continuo* was edited by Waldemar Woehl and published by Peters; it is Mr. Woehl's own transcription of the *Trio Sonata in G for Two Flutes and Basso Continuo.* Two more transcriptions of this work exist—one for gamba and harpsichord, and the other (of movements 1, 2, and 4 only) for organ alone. Both are by Bach himself.

There are significant differences in the major editions. In the 1970s the available Breitkopf & Härtel scores were not Urtexts, and they are the least satisfactory of the editions mentioned. Over the last few years, however, Breitkopf has been revising its published music, and perhaps we shall soon have a set of the flute sonatas worthy of the house that published the original Bach Gesellschaft and many other worthwhile works. Where the Peters editions are designated as Urtext, they correspond closely to the *Neue Bach-Ausgabe* published by Bärenreiter, with some significant differences; keyboard players who are accustomed to thinking of themselves as "accompanists" (or even as "antagonists"!) and nothing else may prefer the Peters scores for typographical reasons—Peters publishes the keyboard part in bold type, with the flute line shown in small type above it. Bärenreiter, however, prints three lines of equal weight, which is the way the music was written, and the way it should be looked at.

Sonata No. 1 in B Minor, BWV 1030, presents a puzzle in the first movement. The time signature is 4/4, the indication andante. Yet because the harpsichord right hand is written almost entirely in running sixteenths with thirty-seconds and triplet sixteenths thrown in, a true andante beat based on four quarter notes to the bar will begin to sound like allegro con brio. Does one then subdivide each beat? You may want to play it in a not-too-slow four before you begin to subdivide; that way, you will arrive at a tempo that sits comfortably with the music, while if you start out too slowly and are satisfied you may never know what you have missed.

The harpsichordist produces a continuous stream of music from beginning to end of the 119-measure movement; the flutist too plays long phrases. It is thus important to take great care to set the right pace, or the performance will sound out of breath. The flutist should aim at smooth playing. Depending on the tempo, however, the first eighth note in measure 1, 5, and wherever this ♪ ♩ pattern occurs should have a slight accent and a staccato lift.

Let the harpsichordist consider his articulation carefully, it can breathe life into the music. The rule regarding two-note slurs should be applied, and other ornaments should be crisp. In left-hand phrases like ♪ ♫♩ (measures 2 and 3) the first eighth is played staccato, the second gets the accent, and the third is shortened; in situations such as ♪ ♩ the eighth is generally staccato and the quarter is accented and played for its full value (measures 7 and 8); when several eighth notes in the left hand are separated from each other by eighth rests, they should be played mezzo staccato (measure 9); and, finally, disjunct as well as repeated eighths in the left hand (measures 10 and 11) should be played staccato. The last rule will apply to both hands in measures 59–62, 102, 105, and wherever similar situations arise. A keyboard part played in this manner will give the entire performance a light and airy quality.

A glance at the next movement reveals why you should not take the first movement too slowly; the second movement is marked Largo e dolce and it contains carefully worked out ornamentation that ensures a truly slow tempo. Be sure to vary the ornaments when you repeat it—Bach put a lot of effort into showing how he wanted the passages played the first time.

Spitta's rhapsodic praise for this particular sonata has thrown the others into the shadows—an unjust fate! They merit study, even though they are built on a smaller and far simpler scale. The *Sonata No. 2 in E flat*, for example, makes few technical demands on the flutist, and although the keyboard part is busy, the problems are technical rather than interpretative. The sonata consists of two fast movements with a Siciliano in a slow 6/8 sandwiched in between them.

Sonata No. 3 in A has a fascination all its own. While the second and third movements exist complete in manuscript, only a fragment of the first movement is extant. Peters, Breitkopf and Härtel and G. Schirmer all print the sonata in two-movement form—a Largo e dolce followed by an Allegro; that is the form in which musicians and audiences commonly know it. Bärenreiter has been more adventurous; it took the fragment of the original first movement and completed the forty-six missing measures. Ignore the notes in small type written in for the harpsichordist's right hand in measures 9–11, 13–16, and 25–27, and the right-hand passage from the second beat in measure 91 through the sixteenth-note chord in measure 94; there should be a sixteenth rest there instead. (This same movement has also been completed by Samuel Baron and is published by Oxford University Press).

We now come to the three sonatas for flute and basso continuo. Peters presents the most usable edition of the *Sonata in C* (no. 4 in the set). In the opening Andante, treat Kurt Soldan's meticulous bass realization as a take-off point; it can be livened up. A subito Presto begins in measure 10 against an unfigured pedal point in the bass; in every performing edition we have seen, the editors have added chords for the harpsichordist from the start of the Presto through the first half of measure 25. Omit the chords and let the pedal point stand by itself, supported only by the gamba; begin to play chords only in the second half of measure 25, where the pedal point ends and Bach resumes the figuring.

In *Sonata No. 5 in E Minor* the continuo realization of the Adagio ma non tanto by Max Schneider for Bärenreiter gives the keyboard player more scope than Waldemar Woehl's busy version for Peters. There are also different slurrings in the flute parts. Look carefully before you decide which one you prefer; you might even incorporate some features from both.

The *Sonata No. 6 in E* is edited by Max Schneider and Hans-Peter Schmitz for Bärenreiter and by Kurt Soldan for Peters. Soldan slurs three sixteenths in measure 3 because Bach slurred a similar figure at the end of measure 4; he slurs notes on the third beat of measure 9 because Bach slurred a similar figure in measure 11. But one may ask why, in each instance, did Bach leave the first set of notes unslurred and slur the second? Schmitz, who edited the flute parts for Bärenreiter, has these cautionary remarks: "In passages where signs of articulation are given, similar passages without them may be articulated in the same way but do not absolutely require to be. Above all, *the player should guard against any desire to improve on Bach by making the articulation of analogous passages agree where the composer has made them differ*" (Italics mine).

The ornamentation in the opening slow movement is extensively worked out. In the final movement, Allegro assai, the advantage lies with Bärenreiter because of the manner in which the flute part is edited. But try playing the last movement this way: the first time around, use Max Schneider's harpsichord realization, and at the repeats, switch to Woehl's. Interesting? You will see the matter of repeats in a new light. A repeat in romantic music is a note-for-note instant replay; in Baroque music, a repeat opens the door to the unexpected.

Works for Two Instruments and Continuo

Bach also wrote four trio sonatas for two melody instruments and basso continuo (Peters 4203a and b, an urtext expertly put together by Ludwig Landshoff). The first sonata, for two violins and basso continuo, presents quite a musical challenge. The first violin plays a high G messa di voce for just over a measure, adagio and softly, and in the very next measure immediately jumps into sixteenths, thirty-seconds and sixty-fourths; the second violin enters in measure 3, playing in imitation at the fifth. Meanwhile the harpsichordist, coming in after an eighth rest, begins to weave a marvelous web of sound—Landshoff outdid himself with this continuo setting. At measure 4 the two violinists indulge in the kind of intricate interplay found in the *Concerto for 2 Violins in D Minor*. Constant, concentrated attentiveness on the part of the violinists is absolutely necessary if the performance is to be convincing. There are no dynamic markings in the score, but the range is from piano to forte; because the intensity of each part varies from measure to measure, each performer must be ready to yield the right of way.

The second movement pits the two violins against each other more boldly. Instead of subtle nuances, the lines are clearly drawn. Where violin 1 has whole notes descending by half step (use messa di voce) violin 2 has a strongly rhythmic passage in eighths, quarter notes and half notes—and a good deal of syncopation. The entire movement should be played robustly without let-up until measure 121, when the gamba begins a long held G as a pedal point and the harpsichordist falls silent on the second beat. The "tasto solo" marking here means that the harpsichordist should use the left hand alone in unison with the gamba's pedal point; yet rests are indicated for both hands until the harpsichordist is brought in again at measure 130, and all four musicians play through to the end.

Ornamentation is definitely called for in the largo that follows. Here is the theme as it is written and normally played by the first violin:

It is hard to believe that Bach wanted this line to remain unadorned in actual performance. One might instinctively come up with something a little more elaborate:

Do not be satisfied too easily; keep varying the elaboration and you may achieve interesting results. Since the movement is canonic, anything the first violin does should be promptly imitated by the second; if it is not done, the mismatch will be obvious. The concluding movement is a Gigue in a fast 12/8.

If the second trio sonata sounds familiar, perhaps you know it in its other form—as a sonata for viola da gamba and obligato harpsichord. A glance at the first two measures of the trio sonata explains how Bach managed this feat:

Ignore the realized continuo part for the moment and concentrate on the top three staves. Together they represent a complete musical entity; the harpsichord does a lot of filling in within the framework of the three top lines. Bach transcribed the work into a true trio sonata for two instruments only, simply by treating the harpsichordist as an individual with a split personality—the left hand represented one musician, the right hand another. This is how it looks:

In summary, one should not be afraid to ornament the music of Bach, but the project must be approached with extra care. A thorough study must be made of Bach's idiom so that the strong individuality of the music is maintained. The artist must determine the manner in which Bach was writing at that particular moment. If the melody is written out in the florid Italian style, then Bach has already done most of the ornamenting himself; the artist can however legitimately change some of the ornamentation the first time around and is at perfect liberty to make further changes on the repeats. If the writing is spare, is it deliberately spare to provide a contrast between two florid sections? If so, the line may be very discreetly ornamented, but the outline should be left alone. If the melodic line is spare because Bach was writing in true Italian style—with the ornamentation left to the will of the performer—then the artist has the *obligation* to ornament. The only requirements are that the ornamentation should be so Bach-like in nature and grow so naturally out of the original that the listener accepts it with delight. Of course, the danger is that if it should not measure up to Bach, the performer will be held accountable. It is a hard choice for an artist, but one that must be faced.

116

7

Corelli, Geminiani, and The Art of Playing on the Violin

It is curious that the course of Baroque music was set less by men like Bach and Handel, whom we now regard as giants of their time, than it was by four Italian composer-violinist-teachers: Corelli (1653–1713), Vivaldi (1678–1741), Geminiani (1687–1762), and Tartini (1692–1770). Through their teaching skill, their unusually challenging music, and the international renown of their many pupils, they channeled Baroque music irresistibly in the direction of ever-greater complexity. Vivaldi has already been discussed in chapter 5; this chapter treats Corelli and Geminiani. Corelli made major advances possible in Baroque violin playing and ornamentation twenty years earlier than Vivaldi, and Corelli's pupil Geminiani so far surpassed his master that violin playing was never the same again. Chapter 13 deals with the final leap forward made possible by Leopold Mozart and by Tartini (with a little help from the devil).

Corelli's 12 Sonatas, Opus 5

Arcangelo Corelli's impact on the Baroque period can be gauged by studying the violin works that preceded his as well as those that were written later. There were, of course, significant violinist-composers before Corelli; but few became widely known outside the boundaries of their own countries. And suddenly, there stood Corelli. His fame first outgrew Bologna, then Rome, then Italy, and then it spread through France to Holland and England, where he was celebrated by poet and musician alike.

The presses of Amsterdam and London vied to publish his music. Composers wrote and published sonatas "in imitation of Signor Corelli." Even Couperin in Paris was impelled, first to imitation under an assumed name, and finally, in the *Parnassus or the Apotheosis of Corelli*, to paying open tribute. When Telemann and Handel were young men in Germany, they studied Corelli's compositions; Bach too copied Corelli's music and used parts of it in his own work.

His impact as a composer in his own time was great; in our own century Corelli's influence is felt in a far different way. While Bach, Handel, and Vivaldi are played continually, Corelli is played very little; yet Corelli's hand firmly controls the performances of Bach, Handel, Vivaldi, and other Baroque composers given by any fine modern orchestra or string ensemble. The next time you go to a concert and admire the precision and unity of bowing of the strings, remember it was Corelli who started it all. "Corelli regarded it as essential to the ensemble of the band," said the music historian Charles Burney, "that their bows should all move exactly together, all up, all down; so that at his rehearsals, which constantly preceded every public performance of his concertos, he would immediately stop the band if he discovered one irregular bow."

Corelli's preoccupation with bowing did not end with rehearsal technique. The last "sonata" of his *12 Sonatas, opus 5* written in 1700, consisted of twenty-three variations on *La Follia*; for the first time Europe's violin teachers had on hand a work that could have been subtitled *The Art of Bowing*. No violin method worthy of the name had been published before this date, and none would be commercially available until Geminiani's *Art of Playing on the Violin* was published in London in 1751. Today the *La Follia* variations are so commonly available that there is no need to spend time on them here. Far more important to us, from the piont of view of performance and ornamentation, is the reissue of the early eighteenth-century Roger edition of the first six sonatas of Opus 5 carrying ornaments "as Mr. Corelli himself plays them." Though for a while the authenticity of the ornaments in this edition (which is reprinted by Augener) was questioned, it has become increasingly clear as the result of research by William C. Smith and other authorities that they are Corelli's own; further, Roger, the publisher, boldly offered the originals for inspection, and he also offered to show correspondence with Corelli that would establish their genuineness.

The date of publication is important. Hare and Walsh of London advertised the set in 1711; since they regularly pirated Roger's editions, Roger had probably published the sonatas a little earlier. If the ornamentation had not been genuine, Corelli could have challenged the claim himself; as far as we can tell he did not.

The ornamented versions now available in the Augener edition therefore represent an invaluable document regarding the state of the art of ornamentation in Corelli's lifetime, and it can safely be used to guide us in ornamenting other works by Corelli and by his generation.

Here are the first nine measures of the first sonata in opus 5:

These measures are puzzling to twentieth-century violinists. What can an artist do with such mediocre stuff? Thirty years ago an editor or teacher would mark the first two measures piano and espressivo, ask for a crescendo in measure 1 and a decrescendo in measure 2, suggest a strong vibrato throughout, and let it go at that. Is that good enough now?

Our more perceptive artists today instinctively feel the need to ornament the first two measures. Would they ornament as much as Corelli? That is rather doubtful, because here is what Corelli did:

Corelli's graces

Visually the greatest change takes place in measure 2. But part of the change in measure 1 is not indicated in the printed version—the crescendo-diminuendo (the messa di voce) on the tied half note. Measure 1 is played somewhat strictly in time, but measure 2 would have a strong rubato; you could slow down on the last four thirty-seconds before the indicated trill on the second beat, and you would certainly slow down markedly on the last four thirty-seconds preceding the fourth beat. These thirty-seconds do not represent real time values; Corelli uses them to indicate notes of much shorter duration.

The arpeggiated sixteenths in measures 3–9 can be played straight for now, although considerable variation is possible even here.

Corelli's ornamentation is quite elaborate. It may even remind you of the Handel aria that became an air, which was quoted in the first chapter, but there are subtle yet significant differences. Corelli was born thirty-two years before Handel; by the time Handel came of age, ornamentation had become both more elaborate and more artificial. Handel's ornaments move skittishly about, and he is forced to define the general outline by trilling on or otherwise emphasizing the main melodic notes; Corelli on the other hand begins with the main melodic note and then moves in very smooth curves through other notes to the next high point, a half measure or more away.

We must surmise, particularly because of the shortness of the introduction, that the method of playing was very free, somewhat after the manner of an operatic recitative. The harpsichordist in this situation cannot even dream of part playing. Instead he should come in with quick, crisply articulated arpeggiated chords, except on final chords following a ritard; here the arpeggiation can be quite slow and deliberate.

The remainder of the movement has the same smooth flow of the opening measures. Aside from the need for a messa di voce on the half notes in measures 14 and 15, what can be deduced about Corelli's manner of ornamenting?

It is interesting to discover that Corelli does not ornament every beat in an adagio; in measures 11 and 12, he leaves the first two beats unchanged. On the third beat of measure 11 ♩ changes to ♪♫ ; this gives him a dramatic upward leap of an octave; on the first beat of measure 13, he changes ♪♪ to ♩♫ , making it possible to fill in the interval of a third by step.

It seems that in a slow tempo Corelli is inclined to leave untouched any cluster of notes that meets two conditions: (1) the notes move by step, and (2) none of them is a quarter note or larger.

A few measures of the Adagio from the same sonata illustrate further points:

First, the use of half notes in this type of movement should not mislead the performer into choosing an unusually slow tempo. It merely means three beats to the measure, so treat the music as though it were in 3/4, with each half note equal to a quarter note and each eighth to a sixteenth.

In measures 1, 3, and 4, Corelli fills in melodic intervals of a third and instead moves by step; faced with dramatic leaps of a sixth, a fifth, or a fourth, however, he sometimes leaves them untouched.

Armed with these few skimpy pointers (or should we say assumptions?), perhaps you should get your rough manuscript pad out again and see how you can elaborate the opening movement of the second sonata. Here is Corelli's original line and figured bass. Good luck!

Take your time over this musical exercise; work it over and over again until you have several alternate versions for each measure. When you feel you have enough material, compare your efforts with Corelli's own elaboration.

Based on our previous experience, we would expect Corelli to leave measures 9 and those that follow almost untouched. Yet he breaks up measures 9, 10, 19 and 21, proving that one can rarely lay down absolute rules for the music of this period. Again, the thirty-seconds represent notes of much smaller value:

It is unwise to jump to any firm conclusions yet, but you may find it instructive to make tentative assumptions based on the work we have done. You can review them later after you have analyzed the six sonatas for which Corelli's ornamentation exists. It seems that Corelli uses the most elaborate ornamentation when he is moving away from a long note by step; that he changes things hardly, if at all, when small notes move by a leap of more than a third; that there exists some correlation between the amount and complexity of figuring in the bass and the shape of the melodic line above it. Would you agree that the more complex the bass is, the simpler the ornamented line?

In the third sonata there is a different problem; what is one to do when faced with a long tied or dotted note followed by a repeated note, in slow tempo?

Corelli's solution is to hold the long note as long as possible and then immediately go into a turn, a trill, a scale passage, or a combination of the three in such a way that the repeated note seems to be obliterated but has in reality been worked into the design.

It is fortunate that the Augener edition of these Corelli sonatas is readily available.* We will not spend more time on them except to point out, in the beginning of the fourth sonata, how the skilled composer or performer can take certain motivic elements or rhythmic patterns and weave them into the elaboration. For example, in measures 1 and 2, the bracketed figure appears only once in the solo violin part, but in "Corelli's graces" it appears

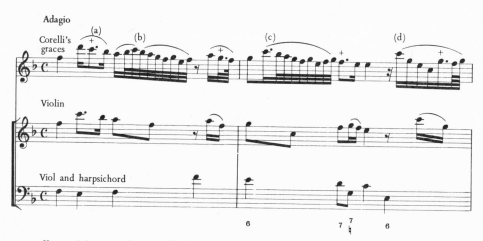

partially at (a), completely filled in at (b) and (c), included without the B flat in the arpeggio, trill, and turn at (d) (the A appears in the trill).

* That edition number is 4936c.

126

In measures 7 and 8 Corelli takes two similar three-note figures and repeats them freely:

No rule tells us when and how often such a device can be used; let good taste be your guide.

Geminiani as Ornamenter

Corelli's outstanding pupil was Francesco Geminiani, an Italian violinist and composer two years younger than J. S. Bach. When he arrived in London in 1714 he established himself as a virtuoso, and his performances of Corelli's music aroused great interest. Fortunately for us, the historian Sir John Hawkins came across Geminiani's own ornamentation of Corelli's *Sonata* opus 5 no. 9, and published it.* We are thus able to compare Corelli's original with Geminiani's version in some detail, even though space limitations do not allow us to quote the sonata in its entirety.

Corelli's version is on the upper staff and Geminiani's elaboration below. Play or read the Corelli up to the double bar several times before playing the Geminiani. Then study the Geminiani version carefully and play the Corelli again immediately afterward. When the two versions have been thoroughly assimilated, the serious student will profit immeasurably if he then goes a step further and makes his own elaboration of the sonata.

* This version is reproduced in *Hawkin's General History of the Science and Practice of Music*, vol. 2 (New York: Dover, 1963), pp. 904–907.

In measure 1 Corelli has slurred the sixteenths D and C sharp; Geminiani, having introduced a D at the beginning of the measure, avoids repeating it, and slips in a D sharp as part of the third beat. In measure 2 Geminiani's and Corelli's lines move in opposite directions for the first two quarters. So far Corelli has confined his melody within the narrow space of an octave (first line E to fourth space E). Geminiani has pushed both boundaries slightly outwards, from a low D sharp to fifth line F sharp. He also introduces an eighth rest towards the end of this same measure. In measure 3 Geminiani soars to a high B where Corelli merely writes a pedestrian repeated fourth-line D natural. In measure 4 Geminiani has an E sharp. Since we have learned to expect a certain adventurousness from Geminiani, the remainder of this section needs no comment.

The preceding remarks are not to be construed as pitting Geminiani's musicianship against Corelli's. Corelli's melodic line was deliberately printed plain to give performers like Geminiani a free hand. The amount of freedom depends on the skill of the performer; his success depends on his imagination and sense of historical perspective, factors we have touched on repeatedly in these pages.

The end of the Largo poses an interesting problem. What does one do in such a situation—ease up on the ornamentation or increase it? There can be no set rule; it depends on the inner logic of your workings out. Geminiani here prefers no respite until the very end, and he relies on the final trill and ritard to bring a feeling of repose:

The next movement is a Giga, taken in a brisk allegro. Even in a fast movement like this Geminiani takes considerable liberties, while maintaining the spirit of the movement:

One way of performing this Giga would be to keep Corelli's original first measure the first time around and to play Geminiani's very charming variant on the repeat.

Six measures from the end Corelli begins to pull back on the driving triplet rhythm, but Geminiani will have none of it:

In that measure Corelli's first triplet drops to low D, which makes the double stop E and B much more logical than it is in Geminiani's version. As an artistic challenge rather than a dreary exercise, see if you can work out an alternative ending to this hot-blooded and exuberant Giga.

The quiet eight-measure Adagio that follows is ornamented by Geminiani with restraint:

Modern performers are needlessly chary of ornamenting fast movements, taking comfort in the belief that Baroque performers, too, let fast movements go relatively unornamented. We have already seen that they are mistaken in this belief. Here are two more examples to drive home the point; both are taken from Geminiani's ornamentation of Corelli's concluding Allegro (Tempo di Gavotta).

If you feel like breaking these chords in the twentieth-century manner, go ahead and do it. On page 144, however, Geminiani's own special manner of dealing with chords is presented.

The Art of Playing Baroque Violin

Although increasing numbers of violinists are becoming interested in the music of the Baroque period, relatively few go so far as to seek out old instruments in their original condition; even fewer try to relearn to play the violin in the Baroque manner. And yet an excellent Baroque violin method is readily available; it is the first major violin method to have been published anywhere: Geminiani's *The Art of Playing on the Violin*, originally published in England in 1751. Two centuries later, a facsimile was published in New York by the Oxford University Press. The editor was musicologist David D. Boyden. On a quick examination of the original he was struck by a curious anomaly: The main body of the text, printed in the front of the book, was entirely in English, but the other section—the musical examples—had captions in Italian. This led him to examine the possibility that the musical plates had been engraved in Italy before Geminiani emigrated to England around 1713 or 1714. "In view of the advanced technique implied in the examples, such a possibility is unlikely," he concluded, adding: "besides, such mature pedagogy could hardly be expected from a man not more than 27."

This line of reasoning carried two implications: (1) If the musical examples were prepared before Geminiani left Italy, the actual author of the method could have been somebody else; (2) conversely, if Geminiani is really the author, the method must have been prepared after his arrival in England. A closer scrutiny of the material has since convinced Boyden that the work was in fact prepared after Geminiani's arrival in England; the Italian captions to the musical examples, he points out, are a carryover from a long-established practice, and the music plates in fact carry the imprint of the English engraver Philips.

One intriguing question remains. Corelli in his music does not go higher than the fifth position. Alessandro Scarlatti, at the Court of Naples during the same period, composes works where the orchestral violin parts go up the eighth position. Vivaldi, by at least one contemporary account, was already playing close to the fifteenth position, and not just on the E string, by 1715.* Why then does the Geminiani method stop short at the seventh position, thirty-eight years later?

The limits of left-hand violin technique, 1701-1751.

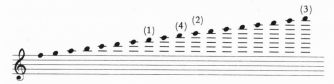

(1) Corelli's limit, 1701-1702: fifth position; (2) state of the art in Naples, 1701-1702: eighth position; (3) Vivaldi in actual performance, 1715: fifteenth position; and (4) Geminiani, *The Art of Playing on the Violin*, seventh position.

The Geminiani Method

Geminiani's method itself is one of the most succinct ever devised. It has three objectives—for the left hand, the development of good intonation and a thorough knowledge of the fingerboard through seven positions; for the right hand, sensitive control over the bow, flexibility in technique, and the development of a finely con-

---

* The Baron von Uffenbach, a visiting amateur violinist, went to the opera in Venice on February 4, 1715, where according to his account Vivaldi "added an improvised cadenza that quite confounded me, for such playing has not been heard before and can never be equalled. He placed his fingers but a hair's breadth from the bridge so that there was hardly room for the bow. He played this *on all four strings*, with imitations and at unbelievable speed. Everyone was astonished, but I cannot say that it captivated me, because it was more skillfully executed than it was pleasant to hear" (italics mine). Marc Pincherle, *Vivaldi* (New York: W. W. Norton, 1962), p. 41.

trolled tone; and for the total musician, an awareness of the intention of music and the harnessing of technique to that intention—expressiveness is a key word.

An excerpt from his short and very relevant preface tells us both what his method is about and, very pointedly, what it excludes:

> But as the imitating the Cock, Cuckoo, Owl and other Birds; of the Drum, French Horn, Tromba-Marina, and the like; and also sudden Shifts of the Hand from one Extremity of the Finger-board to the other, accompanied with Contortions of the Head and Body, and all other such Tricks rather belong to the Professors of Legerdemain and Posture-masters than to the Art of Musick, the Lovers of that Art are not to expect to find any thing of that Sort in this Book. But I flatter myself they will find in it whatever is Necessary for the Institution of a just and regular Performer on the Violin.

Thus with one blow from his mighty bow arm Geminiani has felled an entire corps of English country fiddlers, decimated a battalion of French nature-imitating composers, and bloodied the head of Padre Antonio Vivaldi, who as composer and performer could have provoked the attack all on his own.

On the positive side Geminiani's remarks are equally succinct and pertinent:

"The Intention of Musick," he declares, "is not only to please the Ear, but to express Sentiments, strike the Imagination, affect the Mind, command the Passions."

He continues: "The Art of Playing the Violin consists in giving that Instrument a Tone that shall in a Manner rival the most perfect human Voice; and in executing every piece with Exactness, Propriety, and Delicacy of Expression according to the true Intention of Musick."

How does one accomplish all these tasks? Geminiani believes they can be accomplished in two ways—by varying the rapidity or duration of ornaments such as the *beat* (or mordent) and by varying the pressure of bow on string to achieve the messa di voce, crescendo, diminuendo, forte, piano, and subtle dynamic nuances.

The basis of the Geminiani method consists in learning one thing at a time and learning it well. First, he wants the fingerboard marked with all the tones and semitones of the diatonic scale; he claims twenty-three of them within the compass of the instrument—three octaves and a note.

Then he shows the long-famous "Geminiani grip" (which few violinists today have heard of or can identify), calling it "a method of acquiring the true position of the hand":

The first finger is placed on F on the first string, the second on C on the second string, the third on G on the third string, and the fourth finger on D on the fourth string. This must be done without raising any of the fingers, says Geminiani, until all four have been properly placed; they should then be raised slightly above the strings they touched, "and by so doing the Position is perfect."

The violin rests just below the collarbone, and the right-hand side of the instrument is turned slightly downwards, so there is no need to raise the bow very high when playing on the G string.

Geminiani insists that the head (or scroll) of the violin must be nearly on a level with (that is, slightly below) the part resting against the breast, "that the Hand may be shifted with Facility and without any Danger of dropping the Instrument."

Though these paragraphs are followed by very pertinent remarks on the art of holding and using the bow, it soon becomes apparent that a Geminiani pupil was not encouraged to set bow to string until he had first acquired a firm knowledge of left-hand technique. The positions are to be studied in order, from one through seven.

> It is a constant Rule to keep the Fingers as firm as possible, and not to raise them, till there is a Necessity of doing it, to place them somewhere else; and the Observance of this Rule will very much facilitate the playing double stops. . . .
>
> The fingering, indeed, requires an earnest Application, and therefore it would be most prudent to undertake it without the Use of the Bow, which you should not meddle with till you come to the 7th Example, in which will be found the necessary and proper Method of using it.

Few twentieth-century teachers or pupils have the patience to put up with such a regimen, and Geminiani himself must have received a few complaints, because he concedes that "it cannot be supposed but that this Practice without the Bow is disagreeable, since it gives no Satisfaction to the Ear; but the Benefit which, in Time, will arise from it, will be a Recompence more than adequate to the Disgust it may give."

After the student has worked on the positions, shifting up and down, Geminiani then has him finger-stopping thirty-six scales in all, in order to consolidate his knowledge of the fingerboard before the bow is used at all!

Example 7 is the promised land, with its fourteen bowed scales; but before tackling these the student is required to practice, for several days, the exercise contained in the twenty-fourth example, "in order not to confound the Execution of the Fingers with that of the Bow."

Anybody who wants to delve deeply into the Geminiani technique must acquire a copy of the facsimile edition published by Oxford and work carefully through the scales and bowing exercises; but performers will especially profit from his notes on specific ornamentation and expressiveness. Since dynamic shadings are such an important element of his teaching, however, it is also important to acquaint ourselves with his manner of bow holding and handling. Here it is, broken down into individual sentences for easier reading:

> 1. The bow should be held a small distance from the nut, between thumb and finger; turn the hair inward against the back or outside of the thumb and hold the bow free and easy, not stiffly.

2. Always draw the bow parallel with the bridge and press it upon the strings with the forefinger only.

3. The best performers are least sparing of their bow, and use its entire length "from the point to that Part of it under, and even beyond their Fingers."

4. (Play the scales in different keys) "by drawing the Bow down and up, or up and down alternately; taking Care not to follow that wretched rule of drawing the bow down at the first note of every bar."

Geminiani's objection to the so-called Rule of the Down-Bow is both technical and musical. First, from the earliest bowing exercises he tries to establish the principle that an accent can be produced as well by an up-bow as by a down-bow; this gives an artist far greater flexibility than an automatic physical and mental association of "accent equals down-bow." Second, he objects to the musical absurdity of assuming that the first note in every measure automatically carries an accent and should therefore be played with a down-bow or, conversely, that the first note in every measure should automatically be played with a down-bow and, by implication, should carry an accent:

> In playing Divisions, if by your Manner of Bowing you lay a particular Stress on the Note at the beginning of every Bar, so as to render it predominant over the rest, you alter and spoil the true Air of the Piece, and except where the Composer so intended it, and where it is always marked, there are very few Instances in which it is not very disagreeable.

Here are Geminiani's instructions on ornamentation:

Messa di Voce. "One of the Principal Beauties of the Violin" says Geminiani, "is the swelling or encreasing and softening the Sound; which is done by pressing the Bow upon the Strings with the Fore-finger more or less. In playing all long Notes the Sound should be begun soft, and gradually swelled till the Middle, and from thence gradually softened till the End."

He seems to admit no exceptions to the use of *messa di voce*; not only does he call it "one of the principal beauties of the violin," but he suggests it be applied in playing *all* long notes.

Yet Geminiani goes farther than one would expect by demanding that shorter notes be shaded too. In this he is seconded by Quantz, who (as we have seen in an earlier chapter) insists on expressive shading of individual notes. Although Geminiani wants more expressive playing, like C. P. E. Bach and Quantz he too appeals for more restrained ornamentation:

> playing in good taste doth not consist of frequent Passages, but in expressing with Strength and Delicacy the Intention of the Composer. This Expression is what every one should endeavor to acquire, and it may be easily obtained by any Person, who is not too fond of his own Opinion, and doth not obstinately resist the Force of true Evidence.

135

To express with strength and delicacy the intention of the composer—that sounds very much like a twentieth-Century concept.

Geminiani then recommends the study of fourteen specific "Ornaments of Expression," so that "Lovers of Musick may with more Ease and Certainty arrive at Perfection." Since perfection is something we would all like to achieve, we reproduce the ornaments here with a slight change in the order of presentation to improve the continuity. Further, we are placing the explanatory text directly beneath each musical example for greater ease of understanding; in the Geminiani original, examples and text occur in separate sections of the treatise.

Trillo semplice   T. composto

1. *The plain shake* (simple trill) is proper for quick movements; it may be made on any note, and after trilling you move immediately on to the following note.

2. *The turned shake* (compound trill) when played fast and long expresses gaiety in Geminiani's view; "but if you make it short, and continue the length of the note plain and soft, it may then express some of the more tender passions."

At this point we break Geminiani's sequence to show you three types of compound trill from his example 19:

In slow tempo: a single note with different ornaments and how they should be played.

The eighth note in the first example and the dotted eighth in the third both have a crescendo mark above them. Strict followers of the terraced-dynamics theory of Baroque performance would be horrified at such expressive (and allegedly nineteenth-century Romantic) playing.

Ap.^ra superiore

3. *The superior appoggiatura* "is supposed to express Love, Affection, Pleasure, etc." Geminiani says it should be made quite long and given more than half the value of the note it belongs to. Measure on the left shows how it is written; measure on the right shows how Geminiani says it should be played: the appoggiatura F becomes a dotted eighth note and is played with a crescendo; the E is reduced to a sixteenth. In his words, be sure "to swell the Sound by Degrees, and towards the End to force the Bow a little; if it be made short, it will lose much of the aforesaid Qualities; but will always have a pleasing Effect, and it may be added to any Note you will."

Ap.*ra* *Inferiore*

4. *The inferior appoggiatura* has "the same Qualities with the preceding except that it is much more confin'd." While the superior appoggiatura can be added to any note, the inferior appoggiatura "can only be made when the Melody rises the Interval of a second or third, observing to make a Beat [or mordent] on the following Note." The symbol // in measure 2 signifies a beat or mordent. See no. 13 on page 138 for instructions on how to play it.

Tratten.to sopra la Nota   *Il simile*

5. *On holding a note:* "It is necessary to use this often; for were we to make Beats and Shakes continually without sometimes suffering the pure Note to be heard, the Melody would be too much diversified." The placement of the dash relative to the trill symbol determines how the finished ornament appears. A dash to the left indicates that the plain note is to be played first and the ornament played later; a dash to the right indicates the reverse.

Staccato

6. *The staccato* "expresses Rest, taking Breath, or changing a Word; and for this Reason Singers should be careful to take Breath in a Place where it may not interrupt the sense."

In performance a normal quarter note with appoggiatura can be played ♩ ♪ ; when marked staccato the notes together would have the time-value of a sixteenth.

In a later section, Geminiani describes and illustrates the various ways of bowing a note; and we shall then learn which ways of performing a staccato he considers taboo in a slow tempo, even though they may be acceptable in an allegro or presto.

Agum.^{ne} e dim.^{ne}
di Suono

7 and 8. *On swelling and softening the sound:* "These two Elements may be used after each other; they produce great Beauty and Variety in the Melody, and employ'd alternately, they are proper for any Expression or Measure."

Used together on a long note, they form part of a messa di voce; but Geminiani recommends that they be used together in other contexts too. Since the Geminiani method might well go back to the early years of the eighteenth century, you could use small, expressive crescendos and diminuendos in music written as early as 1700.

piano   forte   for.   pia.

9 and 10. *On piano and forte:* "They are both extremely necessary to express the Intention of the Melody; and as all good Music should be composed in Imitation of a Discourse, these two Ornaments are designed to produce the same Effects that an Orator does by raising and falling his Voice."

Forte followed by piano is by far the more popular order of the two possibilities; but the same or a similar passage first played piano and then repeated forte can give its own flavor to the context.

Mord.^{te}

13. *On the Beat or mordent.* Once again we change the sequence slightly to consider Geminiani's treatment of the beat (ornament no. 13), which he uses in conjunction with ornaments no. 4 (inferior appoggiatura), 11 (anticipation) and 12 (separation). The original paragraph is broken up into its component sentences to make the distinctions clearer:

> (The beat) is proper to express several passions; as for Example,
> If it be perform'd with Strength, and continued long, it expresses Fury, Anger, Resolution, etc.
> If it be play'd less strong and shorter, it expresses Mirth, Satisfaction, etc.

But if you play it quite soft, and swell the Note, it may then denote Horror, Fear, Grief, Lamentation, etc.

By making it short and swelling the Note gently, it may express Affection and Pleasure.

Those sceptics who doubt that this type of affect in music was exercised on Baroque audiences by Baroque performers should read Geminiani's paragraphs on the close shake (ornament 14).

Anticipa.^{ne}

11. *The anticipation* takes its time value from half the duration of the preceding note (to which it is slurred) and its pitch from the succeeding note. Geminiani says this ornament has a greater effect "when it is made with a Beat or a Shake, and swelling the Sound," especially if it is used when the melody rises or falls by the interval of a second. To perform the example shown above, divide the F into two slurred eighth notes, F and G. Following Geminiani's symbols, you now have these options for the quarter note G; in measure 1, you make a beat or long mordent; in measure 2, make a simple trill; in measure 3, a compound trill; in measure 4, a crescendo.

Separassione

12. *The sole purpose of the separation* is to give variety to the melody. Geminiani says it is used best when the note rises a second or third, and also when it descends a second, "and then it will not be amiss to add a Beat, and to swell the Note, and then make the appoggiatura to the following Note. By this, Tenderness is expressed."

Tremolo

14. *On the close shake.* Once again, Geminiani's original paragraph is broken up into separate sentences for an easier visual grasp of his distinctions:

This [ornament] cannot possibly be described by Notes as in former examples. To perform it, you must press the Finger strongly upon the String of the Instrument, and move the Wrist in and out slowly and equally, when it is long continued swelling the

> Sound by Degrees, drawing the Bow nearer to the Bridge, and end-
> ing it very strong it may express Majesty, Dignity, etc.
>
> But making it shorter, lower and softer, it may denote Afflic-
> tion, Fear, etc.
>
> and when it is made on short Notes, it only contributes to make
> their Sound more aggreeable and for this Reason it should be made
> use of as often as possible.

In the musical example for the close shake Geminiani uses the Italian term *Tremolo*, while in the English text he describes it as *the close shake*. While to some English writers the close shake meant a two-finger microtone pulsation, to Gemi-niani it meant a vibrato *with one finger only*—which is actually the *vibrato* of modern violin terminology.

Twentieth-century Western audiences may find it difficult to believe that afflic-tion and fear, or majesty and dignity, could be indicated by the duration of a note, the duration of the vibrato, and the intensity of its pulsation, or by the amount of expressive crescendo or diminuendo used in playing the note. Any East Indian musician, however, trained in the system of ragas, understands how such com-munication of moods is possible; so does anyone who understands the symbolism of ballet gesture in both Western and Indian dance or who has attended an Indian concert given for a musically sophisticated audience. It's as easy (or as difficult) as reading a code; the only requirement is that the recipients (that is, the audience) and the transmitter (the performing musician) both be familiar with the code being used.

We must also remember that Baroque musicians used "body language" to rein-force their message. All contemporary descriptions of performances by Corelli, Vivaldi, and other outstanding violinists of this period speak of flashing eyes, flar-ing nostrils, and various contortions of the body that in those days served to rein-force the message the music was intended to convey; if they were used today they might provoke a modern audience to laughter.

Geminiani had to cope with doubters in his own time, as is evident in this passage:

> Men of purblind Understandings, and half Ideas may perhaps ask,
> is it possible to give Meaning and Expression to Wood and Wire;
> or to bestow upon them the Power of raising and soothing the Pas-
> sions of rational Beings? But whenever I hear such a Question put,
> whether for the Sake of Information, or to convey Ridicule, I shall
> make no difficulty to answer in the Affirmative, and without
> searching over-deeply into the Cause, shall think it sufficient to ap-
> peal to the Effect.

Pointing out that even in speech a change in inflection can give the same word a different meaning, Geminiani continues: "And with Regard to musical Perfor-mances, Experience has shown that the Imagination of the Hearer is in general so much at the Disposal of the Master, that by the help of Variations, Movements, In-tervals and Modulation he may almost stamp what Impression on the Mind he pleases."

This kind of playing on the emotions, or *affect*, is done regularly of course, by various twentieth-century musicians playing Romantic music on modern instruments. It is significant that one of the few recent performers who could produce this same effect with Baroque music was the late Pablo Casals.

The reason he could do so is obvious. Most present day performers were trained to play Romantic music romantically and to play Baroque music like so many automatons. Casals, on the other hand, played Baroque music very freely indeed even though he avoided free figuration. Not only did he shun terraced dynamics, but he used crescendos, diminuendos, fortissimos, pianissimos, and rubatos almost at will, responding to what he felt were the inner impulses of the music with warm heart and soul. He was often criticized for this; I must confess that, when I was not in his presence and under his personal influence, I was among those who felt that his interpretations were exaggerated and stylistically incorrect. Yet at almost every one of his performances at his music festival in Marlboro, Vermont, that I attended, I was invariably swept off my feet. It is now many years since I heard him last and some years since he passed away; but more and more am I convinced, as the result of my own reading and the researches of musicologists such as Kolneder, that Casals was on the right track, at least as far as dynamics were concerned. If only his performances had included the extra dimension of spontaneous and exciting ornamentation, in our own generation we would have seen in that small town in Vermont the type of incandescent music making that Vivaldi often achieved and Bach sought to achieve—though Bach never had the rehearsal time or the extraordinarily skillful musical forces that Vivaldi and Casals had at their disposal.

After this brief digression to the twentieth century we return to Geminiani and his thesis that "the Master . . . may almost stamp what Impression on the Mind he pleases." In his concluding paragraph he points up the one ingredient that all great performances must have in common if they are to move the audience. "[These] extraordinary Emotions," he says "are indeed most easily excited when accompany'd with Words; and I would besides advise, as well the Composer as the Performer, who is ambitious to inspire his Audience, to be first inspired himself; which he cannot fail to be if he chuses a Work of Genius, if he makes himself thoroughly acquainted with all its Beauties; and if while his Imagination is warm and glowing he pours the same exalted Spirit into his own Performance."

The Geminiani book reflects an age of musical sophistication, in which not just the notes but the manner of playing was highly significant. It was not merely ornamentation itself that concerned Geminiani; the problems of bowing, including the type of bow stroke to be used and the amount of weight and dynamic intensity to be built into each stroke were also crucial. Geminiani's treatise includes a table illustrating seven different ways of bowing that we have rearranged in ascending order of acceptability—very bad or the worst, bad, bad but allowable (in particular circumstances), mediocre, good, better, and the very best. We have also juxtaposed the bowings for the same note values in slow and fast tempos, to point up the difference that tempo can make to appropriateness of a given stroke; staccato eighth notes or dotted sixteenths, for example, fall into the bad or special-case area in a slow tempo but are considered good in an allegro or presto. In general, Geminiani prefers a nuanced bow stroke whenever possible; this can be seen in the crescendos he demands on individual eighth notes in slow tempos:

Bowings from *The Art of Playing on the Violin*

Symbols

⌣ crescendo ("swelling of the sound")
⌣ "The Notes are to be play'd plain and the Bow is not to be
taken off the Strings."
| "a Staccato, where the Bow is taken off the Strings at every Note."

The final example from Geminiani's manual illustrates twenty different types of arpeggio.

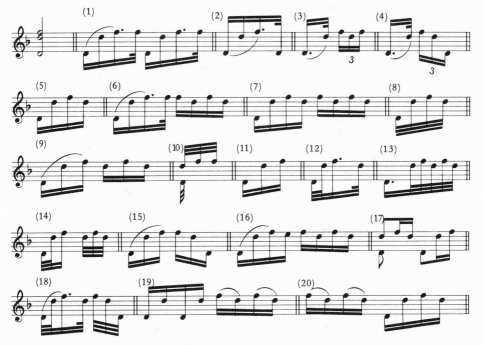

In those variations where only a partial value is shown, the rhythmic units are to be repeated for the value of the half note.

The implications of all this variety in arpeggios are clear. Beginning with the music of Vivaldi, the violinist need not restrict himself to arpeggiating chords in straight sixteenths but can choose from a tremendous variety of rhythmic possibilities that depend on his ability, his mood, and the context.

How many artists will be bold enough to cross this new frontier?

8

Georg Phillip Telemann:
A Blending of Styles

Today many people consider Telemann the stodgiest of the German Baroque composers. But his contemporaries' opinion of him was far different; to them he was a pioneer in an international language that combined Germanic elements with the Italian style of free figuration and the graces, or fixed ornaments, of the French school. He was, moreover, sufficiently master of these styles that his fellow composers held him in very high regard, and Bach counted himself amongst Telemann's admirers.

The Methodical Sonatas

Telemann's tremendous output rivals Bach's and Handel's; however, much of it is chamber music. We will confine ourselves mostly to the set of twelve *Methodical Sonatas* for flute (or violin) and basso continuo, because in these works Telemann himself provides us, in great detail, with carefully worked out embellishments for the slow opening movements of each sonata. They were meant to instruct the amateur in his own day; little did Telemann dream how helpful they would be to the professional in our time. We are doubly fortunate in that the entire set of twelve sonatas can be found in a fine edition by Max Seiffert published by Bärenreiter (BA 2951 in their series) and that the first four in the set have been recorded by the flutist Samuel Baron with Alexander Kougell, cello, and Robert Conant, harpsichord. Baron plays Telemann's variants wherever they occur; then he goes a step further and adds his own elaboration as well.

Although the Bärenreiter score gives us Telemann's plain and embellished lines one below the other with the figured bass underneath, let's begin our study by considering the unadorned line by itself. Work out some Italian-style embellishments for a few minutes, and then see what Telemann actually did with this work. The *Sonata no. 1 in G Minor* begins as follows:

145

Telemann, *Zwölf Methodische Sonaten*, ed. Max Seiffert. Copyright ©
1955 by Bärenreiter. All excerpts are reproduced by permission.

Beginning at measure 2, the possibilities of Italian free figuration are immediately
apparent. In measure 2 alone you could do a lot of filling in just by using running
sixteenths, and the same holds true for the subsequent measures. And what of
measure 1? Would you hold the dotted quarter for as long as possible (using
Corelli's procedure for long notes) and then elaborate?

Here's what Telemann does:

With such an elaborate working out, care must be taken in choosing the right tempo for performance. If one counts a straight four beats to the measure, the adagio melody may sound like a presto; on the other hand if one subdivides the beat and takes an eighth note as the unit, the bass may sound like a funeral procession of elephants in the African veld. The answer lies in a reasonable compromise: count in eight but think in four. Keep the playing light and don't throw in too many accents (they'll interfere with the smooth flow of the music.)

Notice the trill at the end of almost every phrase, the appoggiaturas in measure 2, and the sad, sighing effect of the paired sixteenths in measures 5 and 7. These pairs of sixteenths became one of the trademarks of the very late Baroque *galant* style. Another point to note is the amount of rhythmic flexibility that Telemann encourages the performer to use right from the start.

Here is the balance of the first movement, measures 8 through 15, which leads directly into the Vivace; the example contains a realized keyboard part as well as the plain and ornamented melody line and basso continuo.

The elaboration in Measures 8 and 9 is somewhat different from the one in measures 1 and 2; yet the more these passages are changed, the more they are the same. The same is true of the almost perfectly chromatic scale passages in measures 9–11, and 12–13.

Slow down enough in measure 15 to signify the close of a section but not so much that the music comes to a halt; in other words, give the audience time to un-cross their legs but not enough time to rustle their programs as well. Then take a

149

quick deep breath as you signal the start of the Vivace; if you are a flutist, you have some hard playing to do on that one gulp alone:

While Telemann does not suggest any ornamentation whatever in the fast movements, we know from our study of Vivaldi's works that such ornamentation was not only possible but routinely done.

The second sonata, the *Methodical Sonata in A Major*, offers interesting insights into the Baroque treatment of rests:

An eighth rest is introduced in the first beat of measure 1 with great dramatic impact; you get an off-beat entry and syncopation as well. The last beat of measures 1, 2, and 4 contains the same kind of rhythmic unit—an eighth rest followed by an eighth note. Yet in each instance Telemann treats it differently. In measure 7 a quarter rest is all but obliterated, and in measures 8 and 9 a rest is shortened to make room for the note that follows:

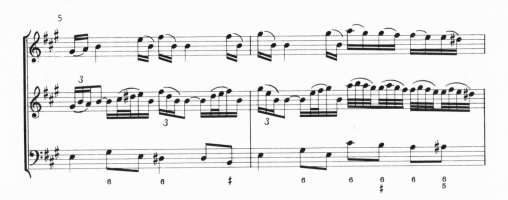

In chapter 2 there were examples of ornamentation in which a rest following a note is pushed aside to make room for an appoggiatura. In every example Telemann has given us in this movement, it is the preceding rest that has been partly preempted by a following note. Notice once again the great rhythmic fluidity in the writing; treated in this manner, and played at the right tempo, Telemann's music sparkles and bubbles like a fresh mountain brook. The pity of it is that Telemann's music is normally played quite incorrectly, with very little ornamentation, and then it is judged for what it is not. After all, Johann Sebastian Bach esteemed Telemann highly enough to make him Carl Philip Emanuel's godfather, and other composers and musicians of his time rated him the greatest composer of the age, greater than either Bach or Handel. When, therefore, in the year of enlightenment 1974, a New York concert reviewer labeled Telemann the "leading bore" of the Baroque period, this opinion is less a reflection on Telemann than a commentary on the dry-as-dust manner in which his music has commonly been performed in our own concert halls.

In the first movement of his third *Methodical Sonata, in E Minor,* Telemann provides a change of pace and a change in ornamentation.

Although in previous movements Telemann plunged abruptly into the use of thirty-seconds sometimes in the very first measure, here he regards the quarter note as his basic unit and uses sixteenths in the ornamented version. Measures 4–6 provide a double surprise; they present the first real opportunity we have come across for a messa di voce in the flute (or violin) part, combined with a melodic treatment of the bass line. A violinist playing the melodic line should make a marked crescendo-decrescendo in these measures, intensifying and diminishing the vibrato as well; a flutist, on the other hand, should try the method prescribed by Quantz and described in detail on page 81. Measures 22–24 should be similarly treated.

Telemann's careful craftsmanship can be seen in the way he goes about building rhythmic variety in this movement; triplet eighth notes are introduced in measure 11 and thirty-seconds in measure 18.

The third movement of this same sonata has a very carefully worked-out melodic part marked "Cunando" (cradling; that is, played like a berceuse):

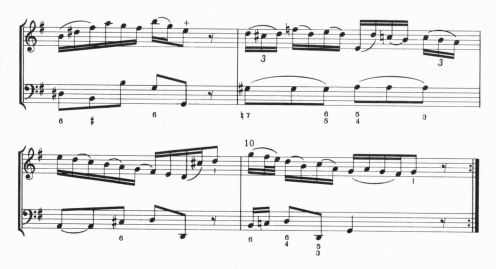

You have the option of playing it as written and varying it on the repeat, or varying it both times. A good way to do that freely is to simplify the part and then ornament your simplified version; you will then be able to compare your efforts with Telemann's own ideas.

The last *Methodical Sonata* we will consider here is the fourth, the *Sonata in D Major*; his treatment of his own melodic line in the first two measures is revealing:

Note that in his elaboration he retains the dotted sixteenths and thirty-seconds wherever they occur; in performance they will be played as double-dotted sixteenths followed by sixty-fourths. But the eighth notes in measure 1 are treated in a variety of ways: and in measure 2 we find eighths are dealt with as follows and in measure 6 the very first eighth becomes : and dotted sixteenths followed by thirty-seconds become

I would urge you once again when faced with such a passage to fly in the face of "tradition" and not twist the dotted rhythm to conform to a triplet; rather, treat the dotted sixteenths as if they were double dotted and the thirty-seconds as if they were sixty-fourths so that the rhythm is sharpened rather than softened. A look at measures 6–8 proves that Telemann kept his options open and while he reworked the figure as a triplet in the right hand, he retained or accentuated the dotted rhythm in the bass:

Note also that, faced with three intervals of a third in measure 6, he leaves the first third untouched but fills in the other two with triplet sixteenths; in measure 7 he similarly fills in two intervals of a third in the same way but widens major and minor seconds in the last part of measure 7 into three pairs of sixths.

What else can one do with triplet sixteenths? If we backtrack a little to measure 3, we find that Telemann can break up an eighth note into a triplet to suggest a broken chord, and in measure 4 use a series of triplets to smoothe out an ascending scale passage.

The *Methodical Sonatas* can yield a wealth of knowledge to those who are willing to spend the time analyzing the music measure by measure. Telemann devised the sonatas as an educational exercise; the fact that they are so ingratiating as music is a testament to his skill.

The Kleine Kammermusik

Telemann's *Kleine Kammermusik* ("Little Chamber Music"), was originally published in Frankfurt in 1716; the instrumentation is "for violin, transverse flute as well as harpsichord, but chiefly for oboe, arranged and composed in an easy and melodious manner so as to make them suitable for beginners as well as virtuosi, by Georg Philipp Telemann." * The *Kammermusik* consists of six *Partias*, or *Suites*. In the Forberg edition that is currently available, the melodic line is given in two versions—Telemann's own above and an embellished line worked out by the editor Richard Lauschmann beneath it. Lauschmann ornamented presto sections as well as slower movements, in a skillful but cautious manner.

Lauschmann made suggestions for handling the repeats in the arias. The first time the sections are played the original texts should be followed, he said; the repetition should be played according to the arrangement or to the individual taste of the performer. But the original text is so bare that one cannot imagine Telemann wanting anyone (except, perhaps, a beginner) to play it that way. The examples provided by the *Methodical Sonatas* show that most often Telemann liked to plunge into ornamentation right away. Lauschmann prepared his edition in 1955; the world was somewhat less prepared then for Baroque ornamentation than it is today; consequently he had to adopt the gradual, or toe-in-cold-water, approach. He preferred to start with light ornamentation or to leave Telemann's own line largely unchanged until the movement was well under way; he then progressively increased the amount of embellishment until it approached Baroque proportions.

* From the preface of the Forberg edition.

Here, for example, are the opening measures of *Partia No. 4 in G Minor:*

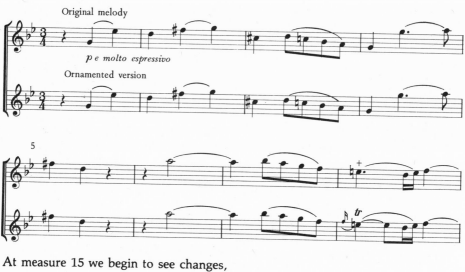

At measure 15 we begin to see changes,

and the movement ends in a flurry of activity.

Exponents of this method argue that twentieth-century audiences tire of overly profuse ornamentation very quickly and that they might even become confused by not hearing the melody stated plainly the first time around. The method is not objectionable so long as one realizes that it is meant only as an intermediate, temporary step until such time as our performers and audiences have not only become used to the idea of ornamentation but are clamoring for more. One cannot avoid feeling, however, that many performers prefer this method because they fear that if they ornament heavily right from the beginning, they will have nothing to add at the end. They really feel silly standing up there in front of audience or friends playing endless trills and runs that sound (to their own ears) just plain repetitive—after all when you've heard one trill you've heard them all.

But is that really so? The secret lies, not in cutting back on ornamental devices, and not in saving some for later, but in using them meaningfully from the beginning. Every trill, turn, mordent—every running passage of sixteenths, thirty-seconds or smaller notes—should pick up the sweep of the ongoing melody and propel it physically to the next scenic peak or valley. It is really a matter of mental conditioning; if we believe in our manner of playing and use it boldly (rather than apologize for it every minute), our audience will accept it that much more readily.

9

Concertos for Keyboard Instruments and Orchestra

Though some of the greatest keyboard concertos ever written belong to the Baroque era, the period as a whole is not particularly known for keyboard concertos. Indeed one looks in vain for works in this genre of any significance whatsoever before the time of Bach and Handel. When one considers that the first true concerto for harpsichord was Bach's *Brandenburg Concerto No. 5*, with its incandescent cadenza, one wonders at the genius that enabled these two contemporaries to bring this strange new form to maturity so quickly.

Here Bach is represented, not by that Brandenburg concerto (which will be dealt with in detail in chapter 12), but by the *Concerto in D Minor for Harpsichord and Strings*, BWV 1052. Certain problems in Bach's concertos for two and three harpsichords will be considered; particularly in the critical area of instrument placement. Handel's concertos "for harpsichord or organ" will be examined briefly; they are works of no great difficulty, but they are charming and historically significant. The survey will end with a double concerto for harpsichord and fortepiano by C. P. E. Bach.

Bach's Keyboard Concertos

For a number of years, Bach's keyboard concertos have been published as "piano concertos" or "concertos for piano and orchestra," and they are so described in some of the most prestigious music catalogues in the world. One wonders why, when they should properly be called harpsichord concertos?

This does not mean that they should not be performed on a piano at all; rather, it means that their small-scale, chamber-music origins should be kept in mind, so that the performer presents them with verve and musicianship and the proper historical perspective.

Let us suppose you are equally comfortable playing either a harpsichord or a piano. You have been asked to play the *Concerto for Harpsichord in D Minor*, BWV 1052. If the hall is large, you opt for the piano. A harpsichord would make a pretty sight on stage, but it simply would not be heard. If the hall is medium-sized, but the string ensemble is large, try to persuade the conductor to cut back on the number of strings. If for some reason he cannot or will not reduce the ensemble, opt for the piano. In a smaller setting, partnered by a small string ensemble, use the harpsichord, provided it has been maintained in top condition.

A few simple rules will greatly help an intelligent pianist give a better-than-normal performance of a Bach concerto on the piano. I would like to emphasize that these rules—or rather guidelines—represent an adjustment in terms of modern technique; a strictly Bach-like technique, that would take into account his own principles of fingering, would take a long time to acquire, and might well interfere with an artist's ability to perform music written in later periods.

Rule 1 for the pianist is: keep your foot off the pedal. A modern concert grand piano has by its very nature too much color—of the water color variety. If the "loud pedal" is depressed, it's like working the color too wet; everything smears. Overtones mesh into one another; blues and yellows blur into messy greens, so to speak. The pedal is the prime destroyer of pre-Romantic keyboard music. It must be used with great discretion in both Mozart and Beethoven (Beethoven supplied explicit pedal markings), and it must never be used in Bach; to use it is to obscure Bach's contrapuntal wizardry.

Rule 2: In a small performing hall keep the lid of the piano down; in medium-sized halls, prop up the lid on the short stick; and in halls seating more than two thousand people open the lid to the fullest extent, but still keep that foot off the pedal.

Rule 3: If you have only a few weeks to prepare yourself, use crisp Czerny-style finger technique to help you skitter around on the keyboard. Forget the twentieth-century ideal of a smoothly flowing legato, induced by rotary wrist-arm movements and backed up by the pedal. But if you have months and years, not scant weeks, in which to prepare, forget about Czerny's finger technique and go back to C. P. E. Bach. His fingering patterns may seem confusing at first, but their logic in Baroque works will soon become apparent to you.

Rule 4: Play with strong, clear metric accents. Add a touch of flamboyance and rhythmic flexibility. This will help you avoid playing Bach in what the musicologist Sol Babitz calls the sewing-machine style.

Rule 5: All dynamic gradations should be controlled by finger action only. The crashing fortissimos that result when hands are brought down on the keyboard from a height, backed up by arm, shoulder, and body weight, are quite out of place. The loudest tone should occur when you strike with your fingers from maximum height above the keyboard without taking your hands off the keys; to make the sound seem louder than it is, work hard at making your pianissimos softer. The audience will learn to listen.

Rule 6: Do everything in your power to clarify phrasing. A combination of rests, finger action, and an intelligent use of staccato can help. Stay alert, listen, and refine your inflection!

Rule 7: In keeping with the preceding rules, which reduce the modern piano's massive sound, the string ensemble should be as small as possible. In small halls use one string player to a part. In medium-sized halls you can use as many as three players on each violin or viola part; the continuo can then be played by two cellos and string bass.

Bach's Concerto in D Minor, BWV 1052

Armed with our seven little rules and the Urtext full score published by Breitkopf & Härtel, we will now take a close look at Bach's *Concerto in D Minor, BWV 1052.*

The tempo of ♩ = 69 seems right for the Allegro, but feel free to try another one if it suits you. (If you are playing a harpsichord, you will want a faster tempo.) The opening theme should be attacked crisply and with absolute unity of phrasing; the opening sixteenths should be strong, the F staccatissimo, the eighth notes E and D played portato on strings and quasi legato at the keyboard with a lift on D, the first A staccato, the quarter-note D held for almost full value, and the succeeding eighth notes A and B flat played on separate bow strokes with a stress on the B flat (first note of measure 2). This B flat as well as the A and G on beats 2 and 3 are to be played deliberately and not too staccato; the A on beat 4 is staccatissimo, however, and the leap to high B flat tied across the bar line creates a marvelous accent and syncopation. The two As in measure 3 are also to be played staccatissimo.

In measure 5 the soloist should play the first C natural in the left hand staccatissimo. Measures 6 and 7 pose a different problem. If they are played through in strict tempo, the performance is stilted; but a ritard is also out of place. What does one do? The answer lies in making a slight *luftpause* ("breath pause") at each of the two eighth rests, with an *a tempo* marking the beginning of measure 7 (page 164). Here the string tone must be thinned out immediately, with a very small bow-length being used to give the keyboard dominance.

All string entries in measure 13 should be forte. Bach left the forte marking out for the viola, but the editor wisely supplied it in parentheses. The keyboard soloist should correct the left-hand part, playing the eighth-note F staccatissimo.

Although measure 13 can be considered a repetition of the beginning, Bach has thinned out and lightened the texture, chiefly by introducing rests in the continuo (measures 14 and 15). Treat the one-measure continuo pedal point in measure 16 as a somewhat ominous introduction to the messa di voce on high A in the viola part (measure 17).

From measure 22 to the first beat of measure 27, the pedal point in the viola must stay subdued. At measure 28 the cello, taking over from the viola, can lead the ensemble downward or upward by firm degrees, with a metric accent on every alternate eighth. The keyboard soloist can reinforce this movement by contrasting the high and low left-hand notes; the high notes can be played staccato and the lower eighths held longer (as indicated in square brackets in the example). The passage would then sound like this:

As a logical extension of this manner of articulation the first violins in measures 34 through 36 can break away from their square eighths and lightly accent and prolong the first note in each pair. The cello can begin a messa di voce on the fourth beat of measure 36, which is tied across the bar line, and alternate with the first violin in the next measure:

Measures 39–41 can be played as written (with the violins playing messa di voce in measures 40 and 41) but in measures 42 through 45 the strings can use the strong-light pattern again. While it may seem fussy to insist on a double-dotted eighth followed by a thirty-second in the second violins in measure 45, such an attack would add snap to that particular close.

The whole point about strong-light accentuation is that it can liven up otherwise square-sounding passages. The gravest danger lies in such measures as 62 through 90; if the soloist has a less than rock-steady sense of rhythm, the entire ensemble can begin picking up speed. The same holds true in passages such as the one beginning with a pick-up eighth note in the first violin part in measure 45; the strings that have the syncopation should play in a relaxed manner, holding back against the pull of the others; the alternating measures of tension and relaxation will heighten the affect of the music.

The cadenza that begins in measure 109 is a masterpiece of brevity, but a trap for less-than-competent conductors, who can have trouble bringing in the orchestra off-beat in the second half of measure 112; since the cadenza is rhythmically so free, cries of "Watch me!" and "Can't you count?" are meaningless, particularly if the conductor insists on giving a preparatory beat before bringing in the orchestra. Instead the conductor should wait with the baton raised so the strings stay at the ready; when he feels the upward rush of the keyboard part in measure 112, he should bring the stick down *sharply* on the third beat *without any preparation*, and the ensemble will jump in without hesitation.

The Adagio of this concerto is the source of more frustration and irritation at rehearsals than any other Bach movement. Conductors as well as soloists complain constantly about the tempo, which always seems to be either too slow or too fast;

they complain equally about the weight of the string sound, which seems too ponderous. In an effort to breathe more life into the movement some conductors treat the music as though it were in a subdivided 3/4, a remedy that makes a bad situation worse. Yet Bach wrote in the clue to the puzzle, and it's right there in the first measure. The problem is that we are separated from him by the mistaken tradition of more than two hundred years; we look at the score, and even though the indications are there, we see absolutely nothing:

However, by reaching out to the authorities of Bach's own time and by getting rid of the prejudices instilled in us by twentieth-century performances, we may discover the Baroque approach to this movement. It is especially important that we refrain from attacking the possible solution by saying: "I've never heard anyone play it that way before." We must resolve several small enigmas.

Enigma 1: Bach wrote six eighth notes to the measure. In very slow tempo, with a lot of ornamentation, this could imply six beats or pulses, or a subdivided three beats. The time signature is 3/4 and each pair of eighths is tied, therefore there must be three pulses, and there's no doubt about it.

Enigma 2: Why did Bach tie the eighth notes together? Did the tie mean that the two eighths are to be played as a quarter? Obviously not, since Bach could have written a quarter note just as easily. It seems to be a bowing indication; both eighth notes are to be on one bow. How they should be played depends on the nature of measures 1 through 12, or enigma 3.

Enigma 3: How important is an accompanying figure involved in measures 1 through 12? It is a basso ostinato; yet it is introduced by the entire ensemble at the beginning of the movement and returns triumphant at the end. I believe that Bach was saying that this is more than an ostinato—that the melodic element in it is very important. The basic difference in concept between accompaniment and melody is itself significant; psychologically, we identify "accompanying" with "bass" and tend to make a bass line more or less important by the manner in which we underline it and give it weight and substance; on the other hand we are all well aware that a melodic line can be made to stand out by lightening it and making it airier.

Enigma 4: How can we lighten measures 1 through 12? This takes us back to enigma 2 and what Bach meant by the tied pairs of eighths.

Here's what we have discovered so far: Measures 1 through 12 are more than just a basso ostinato—they have a melodic function; they are to be counted three beats to the measure, and each pair of tied eighths is to be played two eighths to the bow.

But in separating eighths, the method and manner of separation are both important. We want to break away from weight, squareness, and stodginess in favor of lightness and movement. They can be brought about by dwelling on the first note of each pair of eighths and lightening the second note. The unison passage is played as follows in an easy tempo of $\quarternote = 48$ (L, long; s, short):

The third movement is fairly straightforward, but these details should be observed by pianists: In measure 1, the opening eighth note should be held for its full value, but the remaining eighths should be played staccato. In measure 2 the first two eighths are to be paired while the others should be played staccato. In measures 5, 6, and 13 the first eighth is to be held and the others are to be played staccato; follow this articulation for similar passages throughout the movement. Measure 272 has a trill followed by a measure and a half of adagio—an obvious place for a small cadenza. The eighth note leading into the tempo primo should be played staccato with a very slight luftpause after it, but the tempo primo itself should go without a break until the second half of measure 285, where a slight ritard will signal the end.

Performances with Two or More Harpsichords

Beware of concertos involving more than one harpsichord! One recent Bach marathon performance in New Jersey featured three harpsichord concertos, beginning with the fifth Brandenburg at 1 P.M., going on to the Concerto in C for Two Harpsichords (BWV 1061) at 4 P.M., and ending with the Concerto in C for Three Harpsichords, (BWV 1064) at 7 P.M. Various other works were played in between, all involving the use of one of the instruments. All three harpsichords had been most competently tuned just before the beginning of the concert at 1 P.M. That was the only time when they were in tune with one another—and that, of course, is when the Concerto in C for Three Harpsichords should have been played.

This could have been followed by the *Concerto in C for Two Harpsichords*, picking the two instruments most in tune with one another; and at 7 P.M. the *Brandenburg Concerto No. 5* could have been scheduled, picking the instrument most in tune with itself. Incidentally, if a really fine quartet of string players is available, both these Bach concertos in C can be performed with no more than an hour's rehearsal for both works. There are a few stylistic pitfalls; traditionally trained string players do not like to double dot. Nor do they like the idea of a messa di voce on every note that lasts for half a measure or more.

Avoid orchestral parts other than an Urtext; in BWV 1061 the first slur then occurs in measure 44 of the first violin part. The second violin part has slurs in measures 65 and 66, the viola has its first slur with a pick-up note in measure 101, and the cello has no slurred notes at all. With so much detaché playing in the string quartet, a special responsibility falls on each player and on the conductor to see that the music is not performed squarely; the endings of phrases in particular should be tapered off in musicianly fashion. This concerto has very few technical problems. The main problems concern the balance of one harpsichord against the other and of the harpsichords singly or together against the string ensemble. The latter problem can be eased considerably if a group no larger than a string quartet is employed—just two violins, viola, and cello. All the players should be good, solid musicians, or else the ensemble will not sound right. The opening should be crisp, allegro, and forte; the rhythmic figure ♩. ♪ ♩. ♪ ♪ should be played double dotted, thus:

The adagio section at the end of the first movement may present another problem—who leads? Theoretically harpsichord 1 should lead, but it may be better for the conductor to take the initiative and carry the ensemble through to the end. A ritard on the final trill is possible.

The amount of control the conductor exercises will depend on the amount of rehearsal time available; with adequate time a certain amount of flexibility can be successfully introduced, allowing the music to breathe. If the time available is short, the conductor should keep a tight hold of the reins even when the soloists are playing on their own. Three treacherous patches occur in the Adagio (the second movement) of BWV 1064, where in measures 36, 37, and 41 the entire ensemble has fermatas on the first beat followed by three short cadenzas for the first, third, and first harpsichord respectively. The conductor should hold the fermata and then treat the cut-off as a resumption of the beat, which should proceed rather strictly to keep the ensemble together.

The fact that the orchestral parts present no particular difficulty does not mean that they can be dispensed with and the concertos played by two or three harpsichords on their own. On the contrary the sound of the four accompanying instrumental parts is integral to these concertos, but it does not matter unduly whether they are played by a string quartet or a compatible wind instrument is substituted for one of the strings. A number of substitutions are suitable for this concerto; a flute can replace either violin, and a bassoon or a bass gamba can be used instead of a cello.

The placement of the instruments for performing these concertos must be very carefully considered. It is self-defeating to place two harpsichords side by side, keyboards next to each other. If both instruments keep their lids open, the harpsichord nearest the audience shuts out the sound of the farther instrument, and if the lid of the first one is removed, its sound is dissipated and the second instrument prevails. It is equally futile to have the two instruments facing one another. We found by experiment that the best way to place the two harpsichords is at right angles to one another:

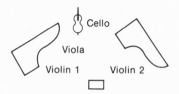

The first violin sits to the conductor's left. The second violin sits at the conductor's right.

With three harpsichords the solution is similar. The harpsichords are placed in a semicircle with their keyboards on the left. Violin 1 is seated in front of the left harpsichord, the viola in front of the center harpsichord, and violin 2 in front of the right harpsichord. The cello is close to the end of the center harpsichord and slightly behind it.

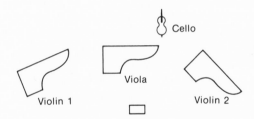

If these seating arrangements are followed, you will find that the harpsichords will complement one another and yet be heard as distinct entities; the cellist, who may feel that he will not be heard at all, will still come through very clearly if he is at all a sensitive, confident player; and the other strings will add their distinctive voices to the ensemble without erecting a wall of sound between the harpsichords and the audience.

Handel's Organ Concertos

Handel's *Concerto for Organ or Harpsichord in F Major, opus No. 5* (with strings, two oboes, ad libitum bassoon and basso continuo), turns out to be an old friend in a new guise—the recorder sonata we so valiantly tried to ornament as our first experiment. We have already explored some of the possibilities of the first movement, but with your new skills and confidence you might want to rework the ornamentation in greater detail and also ornament the "Alla Siciliana." Here the Bärenreiter editor Karl Matthaei suggests a tempo of ♪ = circa 92, which in a 12/8 seems far too deliberate. In both movements you will have to insert short cadenzas; aside from this challenge to ingenuity, the concerto itself holds no terrors. The choice of solo instrument will determine the number of string players. With a harpsichord keep it one to a part; with organ, you can use up to three players on first and second violin parts and the viola part plus one cello and a double bass. Though violins and oboes share the same line they can alternate in parts of the Siciliana to provide interesting tonal contrasts.

During most of the rousing finale the soloist is on his own. If you play too fast, you may have to restrict ornamentation to a snappy mordent now and again; on the other hand, by holding back the tempo slightly you may be able to add some really dazzling figuration.

Some of Handel's other organ concertos call for the interpolation, not only of figuration, but of entire movements. In his third set, which was published posthumously as opus 7, the fourth concerto is a work in D (minor and major!); it contains only three movements—Adagio, Allegro, and Allegro. But between the two Allegros Handel specifies "organo ad libitum". The soloist is expected to play here a movement of his own composition or choosing: he is also expected to supply entire movements in the second and third concertos of opus 7. (In this last concerto

Handel is more specific; he asks for "Organo adagio e fuga ad libitum.") You have these options in supplying the missing movement:

You can improvise an entire movement in Handel's own style, or you can find a suitable work by another composer and use it without shame. In Handel's own time you could even have used it without attributing it to its composer, a practice that would not be acceptable today.

A Double Concerto by C.P.E. Bach

Although many publishing houses issue confusing and misleading editions of Baroque music, Bärenreiter usually makes the extent of its editing of original manuscripts very clear. For example, here are the first two paragraphs of the Bärenreiter editor Erwin R. Jacobi's "Notes on Execution" for C.P.E. Bach's *Double Concerto in E Flat* for Harpsichord and Fortepiano, with flutes, horns and strings, BA 2043. The edition is based on the only manuscript parts now extant, at the Conservatoire Royal de Musique in Brussels:

> Every individual indication of tempo, phrasing, articulation, ornamentation, etc., is that given in the original; in a few instances, obvious errors committed by the copyist have been tacitly emended whenever it appeared necessary.
>
> With regard to apparent inconsistencies in indication of phrasing, as for example in different arrangement of slurs for the notes of rhythmically-identical motifs, it should be noted that the slur marks in the Brussels manuscript are frequently unclear; moreover, the copyist, and hence also the composer, would appear (in the editor's view) to have purposely desired that the phrasing of rhythmically-similar passages be varied. Such deliberate variation is not only quite permissible in this type of concert music but is, indeed, most desirable, for it imparts vitality and interest to the musical setting.

The editor ends his notes with almost a full page of examples listing C.P.E. Bach's ornaments and the way they should be performed. He also provides a page and a half of historical commentary, setting the work in proper perspective. Now that's a practical performing edition! The date of publication of this edition is 1958, but it is years ahead of many works being published today in terms of clarity and helpfulness.

The C.P.E. Bach double concerto can be performed with a conductor, or either soloist can conduct the ensemble from his keyboard. From the first measure we are aware that one of the archpriests and codifiers of the Baroque tradition is deviating from that tradition. The tempo indication is Allegro di molto. In Baroque practice that would indicate a forte; yet C.P.E. Bach specifically asks for a quiet start and entrusts the opening to the first and second violins only:

All excerpts from C. P. E. Bach concertos copyright © 1958 by Bärenreiter. Reproduced by permission.

In the keyboard concertos we looked at earlier, the soloists entered within a very few measures of the start of the movement. In this C.P.E. Bach concerto the solo entries are preceded by thirty-five measures of orchestral introduction during which both harpsichord and fortepiano serve in unobtrusive roles as continuo instruments. In measure 34 the strings transmute the opening violin figure into a motif, consisting of a sharply staccato double-dotted eighth note followed by a thirty-second, ending with a chord on the third beat of measure 35. Treat the ensuing one-beat rest as a gran pausa.

The harpsichord now plays the theme as a solo for the first time, with the piano repeating it half a measure later. Sixteenths are aped by sixteenths, and triplet figures imitate triplets. In measure 42 the pianist tires of playing follow the leader

173

and for five measures plays everything that the harpsichordist plays simultaneously and upside down. Having made the point that both instruments are quite compatible as continuo instruments, C.P.E. now adroitly contrasts their tone colors and compares their strong points. The orchestral techniques too are worthy of mention. No longer do we have just the stark Baroque contrast between tutti and solo passages; quite often instruments are used individually or in small groups, with a fine ear to their tonal characteristics. In measure 69 C.P.E. uses a device that later became a Beethoven trademark—a sudden, short, sharply off-beat entry by strings to provide a dramatic comment on the dialogue of the soloists.

C.P.E. uses every Baroque device known to the keyboard, including tasto solo for both instruments in measure 100. Since the orchestra is playing forte at the same time and in the next measure will go into a tenuto fortissimo, we can safely assume that the harpsichord here is supposed to use two eight-foot registers, or at least an eight-foot and a four-foot register, depending on the instrument. Incidentally, the tenuto fortissimo half note is followed immediately by a drop to subito piano—foreshadowing another Beethoven-like device.

Starting at measure 100, against a background provided by soft flutes and violas, the harpsichord has some dazzling passages to play:

At measures 109 and 110 there are fast runs against strongly rhythmic orchestral punctuation:

Though passages of this nature are electrifying to listen to when played at great speed, they lie easily within the hand, and both the harpsichord and forte piano of C. P. E. Bach's time had a sufficiently light and responsive action to make very fast tempos possible.

By measure 134 Bach abandons the fireworks in favor of imitation of a more elegant kind, replete with turns (a sixteenth rest is missing in the harpsichord part in measure 136):

The first and second movements of this concerto contain a few interesting clues about the type of harpsichord C. P. E. Bach had in mind when he wrote (and presumably played) it. Here is a passage from the first movement;

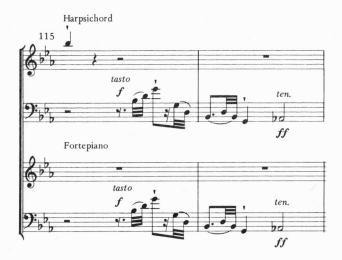

Note that the left hand playing alone goes from a forte to a subito fortissimo. In the second and third movements the dynamic indications include fortissimo, forte, mezzo forte, piano, and pianissimo; sometimes several changes take place within the space of a few measures.

These quick dynamic changes are not possible with the normal harpsichord. As we mentioned previously, C. P. E. Bach had come across a harpsichord with a pedal mechanism some years earlier; using this, he could add or subtract registers while playing without taking his hands off the keys. It seems logical to assume that the concerto was written for performance on just such an instrument. By restricting most of these changes to passages marked tasto, however, Bach also made it possible for some of them to be made on a harpsichord with hand stops, since these can be operated by the right hand. In this example from the first movement, the change to a sudden fortissimo might involve coupling two manuals; if any of these dynamic changes involved sliding a manual forward or back, the harpsichordist is advised to avoid this adjustment and pretend he played and heard a fortissimo, because the end result otherwise will hardly justify the clatter and the effort.

It is noteworthy that in certain aspects of orchestration C. P. E. Bach seems to anticipate Beethoven. He wrote this concerto in 1788, the last year of his life; Padre Martini had already been dead four years, and Mozart had four more years to live; Beethoven, then just eighteen, stood defiantly at the gates. The world would soon be Beethoven's.

10
Vocal Music of The
High Baroque

The supreme misfortune is when theory outstrips performance.

Leonardo da Vinci

Are twentieth-century musicians more technically proficient at their craft than their Baroque ancestors? Perhaps it can be argued that instrumentalists are far ahead of their Baroque counterparts except for their inability to improvise. It seems obvious, however, that present-day singers lag so far behind their predecessors that despite the millions of singers in the world today, only a handful—Joan Sutherland among them—come anywhere near approaching the legendary feats of singers of Baroque times. The falling-off in technique has not been sudden but has gone on for generations. Yet, despite the fact that voice teachers have been searching for the lost secrets of bel canto for many decades, no one seems to have quite found them. Why do they remain so elusive?

Vocal art flourished in the Baroque period. It was the age of *bel canto*, of Porpora the teacher, and of Caffarelli, Farinelli, Crescentini, and countless other singers of the highest caliber. We know that they sang in a brilliant and highly ornamented fashion. We also know that Baroque singers worked on their voices as pure instruments for years and years. As a result they were able to sing phrases of disproportionate length, apparently without taking a second breath, and they could indulge in messa di voce, trills, arpeggios, turns, and rapid runs up and down the scale without becoming vocally tired. This much is fact, not legend.

Somehow between then and now the secret of voice production and of voice training—of bel canto—got lost. Today we cannot perform Baroque vocal music the way it should be performed because our singers lack the following skills: (1) the breath control they need to spin out the long, Baroque phrases; (2) vocal flexibility; (3) the right vocal quality; and (4) training in the art of embellishment and improvisation.

Although the picture is bleak, we do not mean to imply that, since they do not have the awesome technique of Farinelli, our singers should refrain from performing Baroque music altogether. For the present, we should perform Baroque music as best we can, compromising as necessary. The ideals of bel canto should be before us at all times, but we should only use as much ornamentation as the voice can take smoothly. And we should take advantage of the license accorded Baroque performers to ornament as much as possible (and as little as necessary) to ensure a good performance.

The future of Baroque vocal performance is a different story. It is important for singers to set a series of short-term and long-term goals for themselves. The easiest of the problems to deal with is training oneself to embellish and ornament. Yet although a singer can intellectually master the concept of the messa di voce, the trill, the mordent, the appoggiatura, and the turn within five minutes, months and years of practice are needed to ensure perfection in performance. Furthermore countless hours must be spent in acquiring breath control, the right vocal quality, and flexibility.

Voice Training in the Baroque and Today

In order to find the right vocal techniques it is necessary to examine the attempts made over the past one hundred years and more to revive the ancient art of bel canto. Why do several basic technical questions still remain unresolved? Explanations for the decline in the art of singing abound. Much of the blame has been placed on the disruption of society caused by two world wars. Some people blame voice teachers, who do not always agree among themselves. Take the question of breathing; the old Italians said that he who knows how to breathe knows how to sing. Almost every teacher today claims to have the true secret of breath control; but the proof lies with their pupils—how many of them can sing even an eight-measure phrase without gasping for air? The argument about breathing from the diaphragm rages on; does anyone know exactly what is meant by diaphragmatic breathing?

The young singer today ostensibly has the same ideals as his counterpart in the Baroque era; he values purity of tone and of intonation, clear diction, and subtlety of phrasing and of musicianship. Gone are the days when a singer could slide and scoop all over the place; the vocal style of Bjoerling is preferred to that of Gigli. Largely because of the pedagogical influence of men such as Hindemith, many young singers can sight sing far better than singers of a previous generation. But high ideals do not guarantee high artistry, and sight singing skills are only a part of total performance. Perhaps where the twentieth century has failed most is in neglecting to channel the natural impatience of the young and gifted singer. A young violinist of our times may start at the age of four and even if making a Carnegie debut at the age of ten will continue intensive technical and musical studies until twenty years old and more. A young singer, on the other hand, may have sung casually in a choir in childhood. He is told he has a bright future at nineteen, and he decides to be a superstar at twenty—all *without* the benefit of any sort of musical apprenticeship. As students have become impatient, teachers have acquiesced. Today most singers seem to be studying vocal repertoire rather than the culture of the voice.

Even where a modern singer goes through a rigorous system of vocal training, the purpose of such training needs to be reexamined in terms of true bel canto and Baroque ideals. Just about every vocal exercise practiced in the twentieth century has one goal in mind—the development of a more powerful voice. Just as the Stradivarius and Amati violins made during the Baroque period were altered over the centuries to give them a bigger and better (?) tone, so the goal of voice teachers has changed since Baroque times. Today we have to fill bigger halls and cope with larger orchestras; therefore a large voice with some quality is valued over a voice of good quality alone.

The Baroque ideal was rather different. It was not the large voice that was prized but the flexible voice. In the Baroque period the voice was treated like an instrument, and even in the early 1800s vocal exercises continued to be instrumental in nature; some of these bear a striking resemblance to the Czerny velocity and dexterity exercises for piano, but they were written several decades earlier! It is true that some recent composers have once again begun to treat the human voice as a pure instrument, but except in the case of Alan Hovhaness this has placed them even further in opposition to Baroque ideals; the modern singer is now expected to produce disparate and disjunct and even harsh tones outside the old scale structure, while Baroque singers were praised highly for their ability to blend the various vocal registers and to meld one set of notes smoothly into another.

Although the controversy over voice training continues, this much is certain: the present-day singer who wants to acquire Baroque skills must be prepared to put in long hours of hard work. The practice schedule at the papal singing school in Rome during the early 1600s, when it became famous for the calibre of its young singers, shows the amount of work aspiring Baroque singers were expected to do. They spent four hours a day on vocal skills:

> messa di voce and intervals of special difficulty, one hour
> the trill, one hour
> flexibility exercises, one hour
> ornamentation and figuration, one hour

That's four hours a day, day after day, week after week, year after year—is there any other way to become a serious musician?

Bel Canto Vocal Exercises

Here are a few of the vocal exercises that were practiced daily during the heyday of bel canto; no vocal method in wide use today approaches these studies in complexity and brilliance.

The pupil began by floating a soft tone and letting it hang in the air, in the same way some violinists test the "ring" of a violin or guitarists test the resonance of a guitar; once he learned to produce this soft tone on a comfortable note, the pupil then moved a few steps up and down the scale.

His introduction to messa di voce came early. (Only towards the middle of the nineteenth century did voice teachers insist that messa di voce was too difficult to be learned in the early stages of vocal training.) It is significant that this technique was learned in reverse: the pupil floated a mezzoforte tone on a comfortable note and then shaded it down to piano:

Once this diminuendo technique was mastered, the pupil then sang the exercise up and down the scale on all vowels. The pattern was then reversed, and the pupil began to sing a crescendo from piano to mezzo forte:

Finally, when the pupil had enough control, he would be expected to make a crescendo-diminuendo on each note.

The above exercises are taken from the famous text by Gaetano Nava, who was born in 1802 but whose training was within the mainstream of the old bel-canto tradition.

Earlier, in the most celebrated period of bel canto, Isaac Nathan, a pupil of Domenico Corri (who was himself a pupil of the great Porpora), wrote a treatise on singing called *An Essay on the History and Theory of Music, and on the Qualities, Capabilities, and Management of the Human Voice;* in it he included a whole page of crescendo-diminuendo exercises designed to achieve the most subtle gradations in messa di voce. Franklyn Kelsey reproduced these exercises in Grove's *Dictionary of Music and Musicians,* speculating that they might in fact be the fabled exercises on which Porpora kept Caffarelli for five years before sending him out into the world.*

Will someone who assiduously practices these sixty-odd exercises for five years, day in and day out, end up being a great singer? Not necessarily, but he or she may well have acquired one of the major technical skills associated with bel canto.

We will now look at material Gaetano Nava designed to help singers learn to trill, to use the voice as subtly as any stringed instrument, and even to snatch a quick breath on a single staccato eighth note at a brisk tempo. Some examples are reproduced here; they are all from the section of Nava's treatise, *Elements of Vocalization,* dealing with embellishments.

Nava's Vocal Exercises

Trills. Nava says that the trill was indispensable to singing in "former" (that is, Baroque) times. Although the trill was used less often in "modern" music (that is,

---

* *Groves Dictionary of Music and Musicians,* "Voice Training," vol. 9, pp. 57–58.

nineteenth-century music) it should be practiced because it is "of great use in freeing the voice, and rendering it *softer and lighter*" (italics ours).

This introductory exercise is to be practiced on all degrees of the scale with the crescendo and diminuendo:

The exercise that follows—trilling from the upper note—does not include the long crescendo-diminuendo of the messa di voce; instead, the pupil is exhorted to sing it softly and lightly, with the first eighth note in each measure detached or staccato; the exercise is to be performed on each degree of the scale:

Triplets. For the kind of bravura singing that Nava called "interesting and brilliant enough to deserve a special exercise," he recommends a succession of triplets. Each measure begins mezzo forte and is sung crescendo; the figure is repeated on each degree of the scale:

Articulation. The instrumental approach to the voice may be seen in the following exercises, where the aspiring young singer, like any string, keyboard, or wind player of his day, learned to distinguish very carefully between slurred and staccato notes. In this exercise Nava wants the first of each pair of slurred notes to be lightly accented; the staccato notes are to be sung pianissimo; again the emphasis is on lightness in the voice:

Breathing. The art of breathing consists of concealing breathing; the young singer must learn how to take a quick breath even on isolated staccato notes in a quick tempo:

Yet another exercise focuses special attention on notes slurred in pairs, where each pair is separated by a very short rest. Nava asks that "the first of the two notes must be slightly accented, and the second extinguished and stopped. This kind of ornament may serve in graceful singing, and it is also excellent to express vivid emotion or pain."

Repeated notes. After doing exercises on arpeggios to firm up the intonation, the singer performs a series of agility exercises on repeated notes, and *gorgheggii* ("warblings") that are like Czerny finger exercises in character:

Though Nava does not explicitly say so, the singer can take a breath following each staccato eighth note as he did in one of the earlier exercises. This exercise, like the others, is to be done in all keys.

Throughout these exercises Nava exhorts and admonishes the singer to use less, not more, power, in producing the voice.

Breath control for long phrases. The singer eventually progresses to eight-measure phrases to be sung in one breath:

Cadenzas. The final lesson in Gaetano Nava's treatise deals with cadenzas, which, he says, must be founded mainly on the messa di voce; after that the singer is allowed to show off his vocal agility. Nava's requirements are few and sensible; the singer should be sure and free in modulating; he should sing the gorgheggio in one breath; and he should sing only cadenzas that are best suited to his own vocal ability. Nava's examples range from relatively simple cadenzas

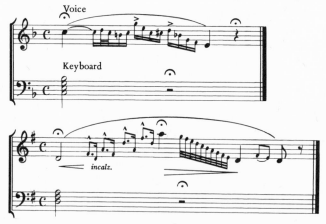

through more elaborate ones

to these two final cadenzas:

If you are able to negotiate these cadenzas with ease, you will have successfully completed part of a course in bel canto. So far the title of Nava's treatise has not been mentioned. The full title is *Elements of Vocalization*—and this part may surprise you—*for Young Beginners*. What sufficed for young beginners then could be considered a master course today.

A Baroque Song: Stölzel's "Bist Du Bei Mir"

The exquisite miniature, "Bist du bei mir," was long known only as an air in the *Little Notebook for Anna Magdalena Bach,* where it had been transcribed in her own handwriting. It was generally attributed to J. S. Bach and revered as his work, until recent research unearthed another copy of it together with several other songs in the Berlin Library—all ascribed to Gottfried Heinrich Stölzel. Stölzel was much better known in his own time than he is today, but if enough people can be persuaded to sing "Bist du bei mir" with flair and imagination, perhaps his name will become a household word.

There is a great quantity of brilliant vocal writing in the Baroque period. Even though there is so much, we have chosen "Bist du bei mir" to work on for special reasons. First of all, its great simplicity places it well within the powers of even the most modest singers; at the same time, this same simplicity can pose a challenge to the greatest interpreters. Also, I am an incurable romantic; I can't help feeling that since Anna Magdalena copied this work in her notebook herself, it was in fact "their song"—that either Anna Magdalena sang it to Johann Sebastian or he sang it to her. In any case their love, which lasted many years until death, can stand celebrating as much as Romeo and Juliet's. Since the young couple from Verona had Shakespeare on their side, we might as well sing about Anna Magdalena and Johann Sebastian, to balance the scales, so to speak.

The melody itself is starkly simple and of great expressive beauty. Indeed it is so beautiful that one is strongly tempted to leave it alone. Since in the Baroque period, however, one seldom left beauty unadorned, we will embellish the music and see how it turns out. Here is the original song with the voice part and bass line.

Structurally, the entire air consists of a four-measure phrase that is varied and a five-measure answering phrase, forming a nine-measure sentence. The words are simple:

> *With you beside me*
> *I can go forth with joy*
> *To meet my end, and seek my peace—*
> *To meet my end, and seek my peace.*
>
> *How beautiful*
> *Will my passing be*
> *If yours will be the lovely hands*
> *That will close my faithful eyes!*

Though the words might seem somewhat morbid to twentieth-century eyes and ears, this *is* a tender love song. The relationship between love and death forms a recurrent theme in German poetry, as it does in English poetry of the same style. There are in fact love poems in both languages where "death" and "sweet death" are used to signify the more earthly pleasures of ecstasy in love.

The kind of love portrayed in "Bist du bei mir" is the love that endures "till Death do us part." Any ornamentation undertaken here therefore has to reflect the rather special, almost transcendental nature of the words; there must be smoothness rather than hard brilliance and tenderness rather than bravura.

If the musical structure and the structure of the words is compared side by side, a clearer picture of the major difficulty appears; the iteration and reiteration of words as well as music:

	Music	Words
Section 1:	A (4 measures) and B (5 measures)	Stanza 1
	Repeat A and B	Repeat stanza 1
Section 2:	A1 and B1	Repeat stanza 1
Section 3:	A2 and B2	Stanza 2
Section 4:	A3 and B3	Repeat stanza 2
	Repeat A1 and B1	Repeat stanza 1

Sections 2 through 4 of the music are all variations of section 1.

When a piece has so much repetition, a special responsibility falls on both the embellisher and the singer; at all times the words must be given their full weight. For example, the opening phrase, "Bist du bei mir," can be sung expressively in a variety of ways. The stress can be laid on "Bist," on "du," or "bei," or "mir," or on any combination of these words; in any of these ways it can be made to sound convincing. The subtle interplay of ornamentation and vocal stress will help prevent monotony and provide a true test of artistry. Here is how we have worked out the entire piece.

Original voice by G. H. Stölzel
Ornamentation by V. Rangel-Ribeiro

En - de, es drück - ten__ dei - ne schö - nen__ Hän - de mir__

die ge - treu - en Au - gen zu. Bist du __ bei __ mir,

geh ich mit Freu - den zum Ster - ben__

und zu mei - ner__ Ruh, zum __ Ster-ben und zu mei - ner Ruh.

Measure 1: The word "Bist" is to be sung staccato. The stress is thereby thrown psychologically (and not physically) onto "du;" the upward-pointing turn absorbs some of this stress and transfers it to the highest note of the original phrase, which we have reduced in value to a sixteenth. Measure 2: Sing a beautifully shaded messa di voce on "mir," pushing aside the quarter-note rest if you feel like it. Measure 3: By splitting the E flat into four sixteenths we make a smooth transition to "ich" and we also match the movement suggested by "geh." Since "mit" is the least important word in this measure, we have dotted the "ich" and reduced "mit" to an eighth note. Measure 4: Trill on the syllable "Freu" and combine the trill with a messa di voce if you can.

Here are a few brief comments on the rest of the elaboration. Measure 10: Sing legato from "Bist" to "du," but make a short break before and a slight stress on "bei." Measures 19–20: These measures should be completely legato. Measures 46–47: It should be legato here as well. Measure 52: Begin a ritard on "zum" and continue pulling back to measure 54, where there should be a strongly affective messa di voce on the half-note D that fades to a pianissimo on the final E flat.

A Vivaldi Motet: O Qui Coeli Terraeque

Vivaldi's motet, *O Qui Coeli Terraeque*, is currently available in two editions; one is published by Heugel and the other by Brockmans en Van Poppel. The Heugel version, edited by Roger Blanchard, provides a full score for this motet and five others as well; not only can one work well with the motet itself in this edition, but by studying the other motets one can arrive at a better understanding of Vivaldi's style in motet composition. Neither edition gave figures for the bass; the Heugel edition is more imaginatively realized, but Jan de Hoog, the Broekmans en Van Poppel editor, has been absolutely scrupulous in keeping the harpsichord silent in those measures in which Vivaldi indicated rests. (See Chapter 3, p. 41, for C. P. E. Bach's comments on this practice by Italian composers.) On the other hand Blanchard for Heugel filled in the continuo part but showed that it was the editor's choice by using smaller notes, which are to be played when the singer is accompanied by a keyboard instrument alone. The motet is best performed with small string forces; either have one instrument to a part or use three first violins, three seconds, three violas, a cello, a bass, and harpsichord.

The voice part is demanding: there are no extremely high notes to be sung—Vivaldi does not go beyond A flat above the staff—but the tessitura lies high and the phrases are quite lengthy.

Blanchard's allegretto tempo indication for the first movement accurately describes the feel of this section. All strings should use small bow strokes; the playing should be altogether light and airy. Instead of using alternate down-bow and up-bow strokes, try the following as an experiment to get the required lift on the strings: the first six measures, written thus

should come out sounding as follows:

Will it work? Even if it doesn't, if it at least makes your string players conscious of the need for airiness and lightness in these passages, the experiment will have served its purpose.

Blanchard points out that the text of the motet is a rather crude Latin; here is a free rendering of the text alongside the original:

1

O qui coeli terraeque serenitas
et fons lucis et arbiter es;

Unde regis aeterna tua sydera,
mitis considera nostra vota,
clamores et spes.

1

You who are peace on heaven
and earth and the fountain and ar-
biter of life;
From where you rule your stars
eternally, graciously hear our
prayers, hopes and cries.

2

Fac ut virescat tellus
dum respicimus coelum;
Fac ut bona superna constanter
diligamus et sperantes aeterna
quidquid cadudum est,
odio habeamus.

2

Make the earth green
while we marvel at the sky;
Order it so that good things
we shall constantly praise,
and so that we shall despise
all that is worldly:

3

Rosa quae moritur
unda quae labitur,
mundi delicias docent fugaces.
Vix fronte amabili
mulcent cum labili
pede praetervolant larvae
fallaces

3

The rose that dies,
the wave lapping by,
sweet fleeting worldly delights!
The lovely brow
cannot be touched by false spirits
gliding by on faltering feet.

4

Alleluia

4

Alleluia

At the voice entry in measure 20 the harpsichord should fall silent. The bass line is then carried by the viola (or violas). The natural tendency at this point for a twentieth-century soprano is to sing the next four measures in an absolute legato:

O___ qui coe - li ter - rae- que se - re - ni - tas,

195

Yet the musicologist Sol Babitz has pointed out that the modern legato is basically a Wagnerian invention that is indiscriminately applied to older music; Baroque vocal music, he insists, depended a great deal on a *parlando* or "spoken" style. Looking again at the four measures in question, one can see how cleverly Vivaldi shaped the melody to the words so that the accent and phrasing of the words are reflected in the string parts:

Here one has a four-measure phrase that is held together by sense and rhythm rather than just by a vocal legato. Once this basic principle is understood and accepted, the remainder of the movement presents no problem whatsoever.

In the Recitativo of the second movement a great deal of freedom should be accorded the singer. The vocal line follows the natural rhythm of the words, and the singer should play on it at will. The conductor then becomes a simple accompanist, whose sole task is holding the keyboard and the continuo parts in line. From this point of view Blanchard's keyboard realization in the Heugel full score is far too elaborate, rhythmically as well as melodically. Both Blanchard and de Hoog have edited the keyboard part so that it overlaps the voice in the final measure. Since the original manuscript of this motet does not exist and both editors were working from other sources, it is impossible to say with any certainty whether this was in fact Vivaldi's own intention; nevertheless de Hoog's realization of the separate part for harpsichord has the conventional, safe, and right-sounding approach; the keyboard comes into play as the voice ceases its statement:

There is no real reason to be stuck with a five-beat final measure. In fact the strong dramatic feeling of this close calls for a "luft-pause" after the soprano has spoken; both the keyboard chords then are played with a strong cadential feeling, and the passage works out rhythmically thus:

The contrasts Vivaldi achieves in the Largo are more than a matter of alternating strings and voice. The strings play a syncopated theme that is based on the vocal material; the texture of the vocal passages, however, is light and airy, while the string playing should convey a mood of clinging, of indolence, and almost of lethargy. The keyboard reduction is by de Hoog.

This mood can most easily be achieved by breaking away from the conventional alternation of down and up bow strokes. In a spirit of experimentation, try the following: Use the lower half of the bow only and alternate up-bow and down-bow for entire measures. Use very small strokes—small enough that a circular movement of the wrist suffices to bring the bow back to its starting point at the end of each stroke. Play the eighths in a detached and dry manner and play the quarter notes espressivo and with a light vibrato:

The bowing pattern is broken at the end of measure 6.

Here is the vocal line from measures 8 through 23, which shows how Antonio Vivaldi, the composer and master violinist, treats the human voice:

Vivaldi's vocal writing is clean, singable, and even idiomatic until measure 18. We are now in the middle of an extended passage on a pure "ah" sound; the rising scale passage after the breath mark in measure 18, with its three-note pattern of two sixteenths and an eighth repeated three times, gives rise to a suspicion that is confirmed by the eighth rest in measure 20. Vivaldi is now treating the voice as another instrument, pure and simple.

Let's reexamine the vocal writing preceding this measure. In measures 8 through 15 every even-numbered bar has a pattern of three quarter notes followed by a strongly rhythmic figure in the next measure. We are going to break that pattern, letting measures 8 and 10 stand as they are but changing measures 12 on as follows:

This brings us to three rhythmically identical syncopated measures. Leaving the first one undisturbed, we can try:

By introducing staccato and sometimes legato eighths, according to the purely rhythmic demands of the music, we too are treating the voice as an instrument as Vivaldi does. Measure 20 duplicates measure 18; in measure 21 the skillful vocalist can sing a mordent on F and D, trill on the A natural in measure 22, and conclude strongly on G without messa di voce. We can let the rest of the movement pass without further comment.

The final movement of the motet is one long Alleluia. The tessitura here lies uncomfortably high; there are high A flats thrown in every few measures, an A natural in measure 15, a B flat in measure 37, and another B flat in measure 40. Only once does the accented syllable "lu" coincide with the first beat in the bar; in the first two measures, in fact, it occurs on the last eighth, creating a most interesting effect:

In choosing a tempo bear in mind that lightness and clarity are all-important; try a tempo of ♩ = 80. The strings should match the vocal quality by playing with light, short strokes; the harpsichordist may want to change his part from a series of plodding eighths to something more linear and rhythmically imaginative. In vocal passages such as measures 9–12, if the length of the phrase becomes a problem, a quick breath can be snatched at either of the points indicated in parentheses, so that the melodic features can be brought out without interrupting the long phrase:

In measures 13–16, a joyous lightness can be imparted to the singing by keeping the eighth notes staccatissimo until the A natural in measure 15 (an A flat is suggested by de Hoog; see example below); the last two eighths should be mezzo staccato and the quarter notes in the following measure should be legato and held for their full value. This will help make an effective crescendo:

In the same passage the strings should play their eighths staccatissimo, or they will destroy the soprano's best efforts. The remainder of the movement follows much the same pattern. Make a strong ritard on the final alleluia (in the second half of measure 42) and follow through to the end of the piece.

A Handel Aria: "Flammende Rose"

It is interesting to compare the edition of Handel's German aria for soprano, "Flammende Rose," as published in miniature score by Breitkopf & Härtel, with the version published in the Organum series by Kistner & Siegel. The different approaches of the two editors work out to our benefit; Roth, the Breitkopf and Härtel editor, went back to the original, while Seiffert, the Kistner & Siegel editor, provided some detailed ornamentation. The Seiffert score should be used as a handy guide to what can actually be done in performance; the Roth score reveals Handel's original intentions.

For example, the Seiffert score is peppered with dynamic markings right from the start of the instrumental introduction. This of course is the type of alteration that we have become used to and can readily ignore. But there are also differences in bowing and phrasing that the performer would be unable to spot without actually comparing the scores. Here are measures 5–8 according to the Roth miniature score

and according to Seiffert:

Measures 9–12 according to Roth look like this:

but Seiffert's version is this:

In evening out the bowing in measures 11 and 12 Seiffert's version has lost one of Handel's subtleties.

The text of "Flammende Rose" itself is slight. What seems to be an endless paean of praise when it is sung in German, resolves itself into just five lines of English:

> *Flaming rose, ornament of the earth,*
> *Enchanting splendor of the brilliant garden!*
> *Eyes that have seen your excellence*
> *Must, astonished by your grace, admit*
> *That a divine hand has created you!*

An Alban Berg or Webern or other gifted composer of our time would have set this text in a dozen or so pithy measures of music; Handel chose to lavish 126 measures on it, plus a huge repeat!

The two editions vary in their treatment of the vocal line; when the voice first enters, at measure 22, the main difference between the two versions is that Seiffert's has additional slurs, which are shown here in brackets:

Flam - men - de   Ro - se,   Zier - de   der   Er - den,

The first major difficulty occurs in measures 36–47, a passage originally meant to be sung in one breath. If you find yourself running out of air, as most singers will, snatch a quick breath in measure 44;

glän - zen - der   Gär - ten   be - zau - - - -

- - -   bern - de   Pracht!

Although the greater part of this lengthy passage is sung on the dipthong "au," the dipthong itself should be broken up into a long "ah" sound that lasts eight measures plus the first sixteenth in measure 46 and only becomes "au" on the second sixteenth of that measure. Seiffert suggested that two breaths be taken, the first immediately after the word "Gärten" in measure 37, and the second in measure 44; we feel strongly that a breath in measure 37 comes much too soon and destroys the sense of the passage. A similar lengthy section, measures 68–78, includes a messa di voce in measures 74–77.

The Breitkopf & Härtel miniature score has an ornamented alternative to measure 79, to be used on the repeat:

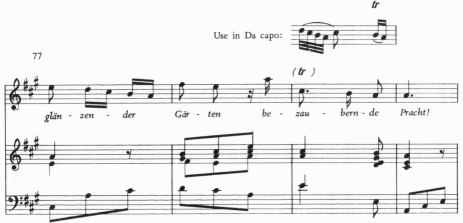

Use in Da capo:

77

glän - zen - der   Gär - ten   be - zau - bern - de   Pracht!

But the Seiffert has interpolated a one-measure cadenza between that very same bar and the preceding measure:

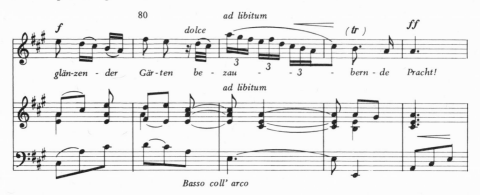

Seiffert follows up with an eight-measure instrumental passage; Roth's passage runs to sixteen measures, and it should be followed. Later, however, Seiffert's vocal line is considerably more varied; the four measures preceding the da capo repeat give an inkling of what's to come.

In Roth's edition the vocal line is rather spare:

Seiffert's version is much more elaborate (measure numbers no longer match):

Seiffert further greatly shortens the da capo section, but makes the vocal line much more florid. Study both scores well to see what imagination and knowledge can achieve. In Seiffert's recapitulation he skips the entire instrumental interlude and begins directly with the vocal entry in measure 21, transforming it as follows:

From measure 27 he jumps to the instrumental interlude at measure 47 and follows the text through measure 61, cutting there in the middle of a florid passage and skillfully tacking on measure 70. At measure 72 he jumps to measure 77 and then alters measure 78 by introducing a sweeping octave run on the last beat to prepare the singer as well as the audience for the cadenza. He offers a choice of five cadenzas, all very brief:

Try them all and then prepare your own cadenza; if you sing that final high A, remember that the fortissimo is more suited to an operatic cry of triumph than to the present context. A messa di voce, mezzo forte to forte to triple piano, is much more appropriate.

Seiffert has cut the instrumental close from the original fifteen measures to eight. The reasoning behind all this cutting and splicing is probably that Seiffert felt that today audiences will not sit through all of Handel's repetitions. This is true if the music is performed strictly as written; but when the singer provides sufficient variety in ornamentation and nuance and the performance moves at a fairly quick tempo, there is no feeling of monotony.

With almost any Baroque air you choose, the chances are that, like "Bist du bei mir," it has long been sung "straight." Now, as you begin to ornament it, people will begin to re-hear it as if it were for the first time. One of your more difficult tasks is to maintain this feeling of freshness by radically or subtly varying the ornamentation each time you perform the air. The ornamented versions that we have given here and in other chapters of this book are only suggestions. We want to encourage artists to be free; but by the very act of writing the ornaments down we can sometimes inhibit freedom of choice. You may feel, "It's already been done; it's all here, frozen for all time. Why change anything?" And yet the soul of Baroque music making is change; this is why, we repeat over and over again, the models you find in this book are meant to serve only as starting points for performance. What you actually do should depend entirely on you, your mood, and the moment. That way you will maintain freshness; you will create, and not merely follow.

11

Music for the Viola da Gamba

The repertoire for viola da gamba and cembalo or basso continuo is quite extensive, but only a small portion of it is available in modern editions. That portion, such as it is, is dominated by Bach's three sonatas for viola da gamba and cembalo.

Bach's Sonatas for Viola da Gamba

The best edition of these sonatas now available (1980) is still Rolf van Leyden's for Peters, which was prepared in 1935. There have been a number of pertinent musicological advances since then, and this edition should be revised in light of them. It should be stated, however, that Van Leyden cannot easily be faulted for the job he did. For the text of the first sonata in D he went back to a Bach manuscript; for the second and third sonatas he relied on copies made by C. F. Penzel in 1753. His phrasing marks were based on suggestions by Albert Schweitzer and Ernst Kurth. He has included a table of ornaments that follows "to a great extent" the table given in Bach's own *Klavierbüchlein für Wilhelm Friedemann Bach* ("Little Piano Book for Wilhelm Friedemann Bach").

These three sonatas were written at Cöthen between 1717 and 1723, when Bach was between thirty-two and thirty-eight years old. The soprano, alto, and tenor gambas were fast disappearing from the musical scene, displaced by the violin and the viola. Only the bass viola da gamba still maintained its position, even though it too was threatened by the cello. Several famous gamba players were Bach's contemporaries, among them Marin Marais (1656–1728), Antoine Forqueray (1671–1745), Jean Rousseau (dates unknown), and Louis de Caix d'Hervelois (circa 1680–1760), all of whom lived in France; Ernst Christian Hesse (1676–1762) and Jean Schenk (1660–circa 1715) were well-known German players. Specifically at the court of Cöthen with Bach was Christian Ferdinand Abel, a member of the famous Abel family of musicians; he played both violin and bass viola da gamba. Prince Leopold of Cöthen was also a gamba player, and it is surmised that the first of the sonatas was transcribed for him from its original form as a sonata for two transverse flutes and harpsichord. The other two sonatas may have been written for the prince.

Sonata No. 1 in G begins with a curiously halting rhythm in the gamba part;

since the harpsichord repeats these rhythms moments later, the whole effect can be rather wobbly, particularly if it is taken at the very slow tempo suggested by van Leyden:

If, however, instead of measuring this movement out in eighth notes, one adopts a tempo of ♪ = 96–104 and takes each measure in four beats, then the picture changes dramatically. The music already flows far more smoothly and seems altogether more Bach-like in character.

The question of what the gamba does in measure 4, where it plays A above middle C for more than a measure and a half, now arises. The harpsichordist who strikes the D once in measure 1 and holds the note for the prescribed length of time is trapped by his instrument—either he goes into a long trill or he lets the note die. But the gamba player who in measure 4 plays the long-held A above middle C can and should take advantage of the flexibility provided by bow and bow arm to make an extended messa di voce. The gamba should make a similar crescendo-diminuendo in measures 13–14, 26 (twice, on each dotted half note), 27, and 28. The gamba and harpsichord should also find ways to overcome the end-stopped, halting effect of the two eighth notes by ornamenting them, bearing in mind particularly C. P. E. Bach's dictum that "the primary aim of all embellishments is to connect notes" (*Essay*, p. 48).

The recommended metronome marking of ♩ = 80 for the second movement seems eminently reasonable. The gamba player must make a crescendo-diminuendo in measures 38–39 and also on the half notes in measures 42 and 45; more messa di voce should be used in measures 71–72, 78–79, 94–95, 96, 98, 100, 102, 113, 115, 117–18, and finally in measure 141.

In the Andante third movement, van Leyden fell into the trap he fell into in the first movement—he based his tempo on a fraction of the beat. In this instance he came up with an Andante at ♪ = 72; a far better tempo is ♩ = 52–60.

The tempo set for the fourth and final movement is far more justified (♩ = 76–80). There are no great technical difficulties here; Prince Leopold must have been a player with a rather modest technique. Since a virtuoso display is out of the question, gambist and harpsichordist must combine forces and decide to play as musically, expressively, and idiomatically as possible. For example, when one instrument imitates the other, the performers should not be satisfied with slavish imitation but should ornament by connecting notes, recalling another dictum of C. P. E. Bach that is very much apropos: "I believe that that style of performance is the best, regardless of the instrument, which artfully combines the correctness and brilliance of French ornaments with the suavity of Italian singing" (*Essay*, p. 85).

Bach's *Sonata No. 2 in D*, like the earlier sonata, has the first movement running into the second, and the third into the fourth. The opening Adagio has the suggested metronome marking of ♩ =40. Again that seems to me to be very much on the slow side; ♩ = 60 would be much more flowing. A mordent on the first note and a messa di voce on this same high D in measures 2 and 3 would be appropriate here.

If it seems fatuous to list every instance that calls for a messa di voce, may I point out that the idea of playing terraced dynamics in Bach, with each dynamic held for entire sections, is so deeply ingrained in most musicians that they must constantly be reminded to use the messa di voce. Of all the cries of surprise and astonishment at rehearsals, the one most frequently heard is, "You want a crescendo and a diminuendo, *here?*" The patient answer must be: "Yes, and here and here! It was a simple but basic rule of Baroque playing! Let's apply it!"

Nathalie Dolmetsch and her father, Arnold, devoted their lives to research on the music, instruments, and musical practices of the Baroque period; Nathalie Dolmetsch confirms the fact that the messa di voce was an important part of a gamba player's technique: "A mode of expression which was much favoured on the viol was the swelling of the note, either with or without vibrato. Musical phrases were also swelled and diminished," she writes. A quote from Hubert le Blanc, an eighteenth-century writer on music, corroborates her point: "The grace of Musical Discourse consists in making the appropriate decrease follow the Increase, as in the well-formed leg of a Lady, which the Queen of Navarre held to have such power over the heart of Man." Only some of the gamba players around today seem to agree with Nathalie Dolmetsch, Hubert le Blanc, and the well-formed Queen of Navarre; in fact the best-known recording of Bach's gamba sonatas available in the United States until now uses no messa di voce on long notes or crescendos and diminuendos in phrases and is played mostly in a curiously inexpressive manner.

Going back to the adagio of the second sonata, the gamba part calls for a messa di voce in measures 2 and 3, 10 and 11, 16, 18, 21–22, and 23. It can be argued that the harpsichord has similar long held notes and no way of simulating the messa di voce of the gamba. How does one get a crescendo and diminuendo on a long held harpsichord note when the harpsichordist has enough trouble getting the note to sound beyond a fleeting second or two? The answer lies in the nature of the messa di voce, particularly as defined by Quantz. Quantz recommended that while a flutist was making a crescendo and diminuendo on a long note, he should simultaneously make a pulsation with the finger on the nearest open hole (*On Playing the Flute*, 165–166). A harpsichordist in a similar situation has the option of letting the note die away or of making a long trill on it. If he decides on the trill, he can begin the trill slowly and then let it increase in intensity and slacken off towards the end, making an effective crescendo and diminuendo. Tartini described such a trill for the violin: "Finally, there are other ways of trilling with regard to *piano* or *forte*. As a voice or instrument pleases by passing from *piano* to *forte*, a trill will sound well when it begins slowly and softly and increases both in strength and speed." Here is Tartini's example of a trill that begins slowly and gathers speed, volume, and intensity:

piano   moins piano   demi fort   et plus fort

This device has long been used by some harpsichordists, as well as organists. Fernando Germani's organ method has a section dealing specifically with trills in the slow movements of J. S. Bach. It states that "it is well to remember once more with regard to trills (especially in expressive passages) that they are begun at a moderate speed and quickened almost imperceptibly until their conclusion" (p. 58). Since the conclusion of a trill almost invariably involves notes that are progressively longer in character, a diminuendo at the end is assured.

Quantz had an odd suggestion for the keyboard player who has to accompany a messa di voce in a melodic part: "If in the Adagio a singer or solo player allows the tone of a long note to swell and diminish, and the movement of the bass beneath it is in different values, it is good for the accompanist likewise to stroke each note more strongly and again more softly, in accordance with the example of the principal part" (On Playing the Flute, p. 262).

C. P. E. Bach also has some advice on accompanying a long-held note in the principal part; in his chapter on accompaniment, he says: "When the principal part has a long held note which, according to the rules of good performance, should commence pianissimo, grow by degrees to a fortissimo, and return similarly to a pianissimo, the accompanist must follow with the greatest exactness. Every means available to him must be employed to attain a forte and piano. His increase and decrease must coincide with that of the principal part; nothing more, nothing less" (Essay, pp. 371–372).

According to principles C. P. E. set forth in earlier articles in the same chapter, "every means" includes an increase or decrease in the number of parts and, we would assume, the use of a pedal, on those harpsichords that have such a device, to bring into play one or more additional set of strings.

It is curious how J. S. Bach refrains from exploring the full range of the solo instrument in these three sonatas. He particularly shuns the lowest notes; only once, in the fourth movement of the second sonata, does he go down by leap to B below the bass clef. For the most part, the music lies between third-line D and the D two octaves above that. The second sonata thus calls for a seven-stringed viola da gamba, but the other two works can be played on an instrument with six strings. Contrast Bach's use of the gamba here with his treatment of it in the Saint Matthew Passion, where in the bass aria, "Komm, süsses Kreuz," it was the Bach historian Charles Sanford Terry's opinion that Bach wrote "his only typical viola da gamba part." Says Terry "It yields a colour the violoncello cannot impart, is eloquent over a compass that instrument could not equal, and reaches to depths it could not plumb." And he speculates that Christian Ferdinand Abel from Cöthen was a guest performer when the passion was first given.

Buxtehude's Viola Da Gamba Sonatas

Dietrich Buxtehude published his first set of sonatas for viola da gamba and other instruments at Lübeck the year before Bach was born. Two further sets were published (as opus 1 and opus 2) in that same city in 1696, when Bach was eleven years old. A few years after that young Bach made a special pilgrimage to Lübeck to hear Buxtehude play the organ. Since his stay in that city extended far beyond the short term he had anticipated, we can safely assume that not Buxtehude's organ playing alone, but his chamber music as well, held Bach's attention.

Four of Buxtehude's sonatas from opus 1, for violin, viola da gamba, and harpsichord, have been published by Bärenreiter. They all share the typical Buxtehude characteristics—very short slow movements, brisk, almost motor-driven fast movements, and an assurance in compositional skill and inventiveness that explains why Bach undertook that long trek in the first place and what magic then held him spellbound.

Sonata No. 2 in G has a short three-measure Lento introduction followed by a subito Vivace:

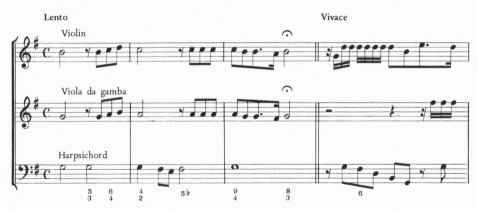

The introduction is best left unornamented, since it represents—in slow motion, as it were—some of the rhythms of the Vivace. The nine-measure Adagio that forms the third movement does invite ornamentation, however:

It is up to us to turn the violin line into an ornamented melodic line; we do this by breaking up some of the long held notes, by filling in between skips, and by extending the range upwards. The bass part stays as written, and a minimum of alteration suffices in the gamba part:

An eight-measure Largo introduces an Arioso with Variations:

In the Bärenreiter realization the gamba and the harpsichordist's right hand play for the most part in unison. The keyboard player should not use this realization if it inhibits the gamba player and the violinist from ornamenting the way they should.

In the *Sonata in B Flat*, opus 1 no. 4, Buxtehude wrote a Vivace in ₵ that runs into an Allegro; the upper two parts of the Allegro are in triplets, and the ground bass is the same one used in the Vivace. The bass itself runs to a cycle of fourteen pulses that blithely ignores bar lines; you can spend many a lively session figuring out subdivisions; it certainly works out to two groups of 7+7 but is it (4+3) + (4+3) or (3+4) + (3+4)? Or is it (4+3) + (3+4)? Could it be some other subdivision?

The transition from Vivace to Allegro and the change in rhythm are particularly interesting:

Since the rhythm of the ground bass has to remain absolutely solid, the passage beginning at measure 92 plays havoc with the theory that three against two is not a genuine Baroque rhythm (see the discussion of this complex problem in the epilogue).

A Telemann Sonata for Treble Gamba

Among the 25 issues of Telemann's music periodical, *Der getreue Musikmeister*, that have survived until today, we are fortunate to have a sonata for treble gamba and basso continuo. The first movement is a graceful "Siziliana" in two sections of fourteen measures each, with repeats. You have had so much practice by now that the ornamentation of the following passage should give you no trouble at all:

Like so much of Telemann's music the sonata can be played effectively by the amateur musician as well as by the virtuoso; where the virtuoso might wish to dazzle with brilliant technique, the amateur might aim at a noble simplicity.

Another Telemann work that uses the gamba as a melodic instrument is the *Trio in F* for alto recorder, gamba, and basso continuo (Nagel's Musik-Archiv 131). It is not an extensive work—only a hundred and thirty-five measures long—and it contains two fast movements flanking a ten-measure movement marked *Mesto* ("wistful or melancholy"). A solid technique is an absolute necessity; the writing for both melody instruments is too brilliant and too transparent to allow easy faking.

A Marais Chaconne

Marin Marais was one of the greatest gamba players of all time, and he was also a composer of renown. One of his compositions, which is still played today, was probably one of the earliest musical "sick jokes": it is a portrayal of a gall-stone operation. A work that is more serious in content, which you might want to study, is the *Chaconne in D* for viola da gamba and basso continuo (number 4993 in the Peters edition).

This work is certainly not to be treated lightly; the musicianly soloist will be able to embellish the melody and find and reveal new depths and new beauties each time he presents this music. Ornamentation should consist of a judicious combination of the French and Italian styles, and broken chords should be freely employed in those variations marked grave.

12

Two Brandenburg Concertos
for Small Ensembles

The six Brandenburg concertos by J. S. Bach can—and should—be performed by a small group of musicians. Even with the first concerto, which is the most extensively scored, what we really have is a group of six winds balanced by six bowed instruments and harpsichord. In the second concerto we have three winds, six strings and harpsichord; only in the third do we find a specific call for at least 10 stringed instruments—violins 1, 2 and 3, violas 1–3, cellos 1–3, string bass and harpsichord. On paper this combination seems to suggest that the violins will need reinforcing, or else they will not be heard; since at this period, however, the cellos and basses were still using relatively weak strings that lacked power and brilliance, the concerto can still be performed with just one instrument to a part and come out sounding right.

The idea that every wind instrument needs to be pitted against a disproportionately large complement of strings is essentially a modern one. Today, the smallest symphony orchestras anywhere have two flutes, two oboes, two clarinets, two bassoons, two or three French horns, two trumpets, a couple of trombones and percussion, and these same fifteen musicians will be opposed by fifty or more string players. True, a group such as this does make a brave show on stage and quite a photograph for the local papers; but for the music of Beethoven and all those before him, the same visual black-and-white contrasts and a far better balance of sound can be achieved if half the strings are replaced by a flock of muted penguins.

Bach's Instrumental Resources

Bach himself has left us documentary evidence on what he considered a well-balanced group. We know from public records exactly who most of his performers at Cöthen were. He had a select inner group of eight chamber players, plus four local musicians who were retained as substitutes at low wages. There were also two trumpeters who could play other brass instruments, and a drummer. Fifteen men in all. A few years later, in Leipzig, he wrote a famous letter asking for additions to the seven-man municipal orchestra he had there. Here are the total forces he felt he needed:

> First violins 2 (better still, 3)
> Second violins 2 (better still, 3)
> Violas 4
> Cellos 2
> Bass 1
> Oboists 2 (or 3)
> Bassoon 1 (or 2)
> Trumpeters 3 (they could also double on other brass instruments)
> Timpanist 1

Bach thus felt he could balance a total of eleven or thirteen strings against six or eight winds, plus timpanist.

The Brandenburg concertos were commissioned by the Margrave Christian Ludwig of Brandenburg while Bach was still at Cöthen, and the Margrave's orchestra was if anything even smaller than Bach's own group. The scoring seems to suggest that Bach planned the works so that they could be performed by either one of the two ensembles, and there is a strong likelihood that he in fact performed them at Cöthen. We can even pinpoint with reasonable accuracy the players he used for three of the concertos:

"I'll make this a showpiece for transverse flute, violin, and that new harpsichord I've just picked up in Berlin. Good Josephus Spiess can play solo violin once again. Perhaps Ludwig Rose can put aside his oboe and play the solo flute. This once—just this once!—I'll not play viola, but instead I'll give the harpsichord a real workout. Who'll play viola? Abel is able. Hmm, good, that means I need not write a second violin part after all. Linigke can play cello and what's-his-name the violone." Hence no second violin part in Brandenburg No. 5. (The reasoning—but not the language —is Heinrich Besseler's.)

Once we are prepared to accept the fact that Bach wrote the Brandenburg concertos for a small chamber group, and performed them that way, we can see immediately where most twentieth-century performances go wrong: we have more musicians on stage than the music can bear. Even before they begin to play we have destroyed all possibility of achieving a true balance or the right tonal quality. A second area where we go wrong is that we fuss with intonation and twentieth-century techniques when we should be fussing with intonation and eighteenth-century styles.

This chapter will be devoted to a study of two of the Brandenburgs—the fourth concerto in G, and the fifth concerto in D. Both works will be discussed in detail, some of which may seem trifling if you have already resolved the issues to your own satisfaction; some of the suggestions may seem quite new. Once in a while, we will throw up our hands and admit we don't have the final answer, but most times, we will stick our necks out and make recommendations even when these may seem highly controversial. Indeed, they may prove to be the most valuable sections of this book, for through discussion and controversy one often finds the truth.

Brandenburg Concerto No. 4

Peters some years ago published a very clean set of parts to Bach's *Brandenburg Concerto no. 4*, BWV 1049; it has since been joined by two excellent modern editions—Breitkopf & Härtel and Bärenreiter. As a full score, I recommend the one-volume Urtext collection in the Neue Bach Ausgabe (Bärenreiter's BA 5005). The individual scores and sets of parts published separately by Bärenreiter as "practical editions" have editorial markings; they should be treated with caution. If you are using a Breitkopf & Härtel score and set of parts, make sure all the parts are labeled Urtext; a mixed set was available until recently. The best results can be achieved if you use the Neue Bach Ausgabe Urtext, BA 5005, for a score and match it with a Breitkopf & Härtel set of parts; you can then use one to balance the other, and your players will recognize any penciled markings you make as your own unique contribution.

Recommended instrumental forces: besides a very fine violinist, you will need two more-than-competent recorder players for the other solo voices. If recorder players are not available you should consider using two one-keyed Baroque flutes. As a third choice, two modern metal flutes may be used. With recorders or wooden flutes, the orchestral ripieno should be held down to one instrumentalist to a part. Where metal flutes are used, the number of string players may be increased to Bach's Leipzig list of three first violins, three second violins, four violas, two cellos and one bass. And what if the performance is to take place in a very large auditorium, such as New York's Avery Fisher Hall? The Brandenburg Concertos are particularly unsuited for performance in large modern halls; but if they must be played under such conditions, take advantage of the excellent facilities for electronic amplification that such halls normally have. Discreet amplification of tightly-knit playing is immensely preferable to an unbalanced performance by a bloated string orchestra.

We come now to the music itself, and the positioning of our forces. The soloists stand in an arc a little to the right of the conductor; to the left sits the "ripieno"—first violin, second violin, viola, and cello; between the two groups, in the center and to the rear, are harpsichord and string bass. Bach's tempo indication is "allegro" in 3/8. We will beat time (in one!) in a leisurely $\quarternote = 46$ to 52, which will seem too slow to your instrumentalists at this point, but may seem horrendously fast to your principal violinist by the time he gets to measure 187. Now it should become quickly apparent from an examination of the music, that though the time signature is 3/8 and we are beating time in one, the measures are really grouped in pairs—strong, weak, strong, weak. We will feel more comfortable, and the music will sound better, if we therefore modify our beat to a kind of two: strong pulse to the right, weak pulse to the left:

In the first measure there are two problems, and two decisions to be made, involving matters of style and dynamics. We have been told repeatedly that in Baroque times an allegro tempo almost automatically implied a forte beginning; yet here we have two alto recorders that are allowed to float serenely up in the stratosphere. It is obvious that mezzo forte is a better choice here. The next problem is that recorder 1 has a high held D for the first two measures. In almost every performance today, this note is played in a perfectly level manner; instead, we should use the messa di voce; begin softly, make a crescendo in measure 1, and then make a diminuendo in measure 2. Intonation should be carefully watched; if the recorder player begins too softly, he will sound flat, and if he makes too big a crescendo, he will go sharp. The three eighth notes in measures 3 and 5 are to be played legato—not staccato as they are so often rendered today. Both recorders are expected to ease up on the third eighth in these measures; however, they can play a mordent on the second eighth in measure 3 and on the first eighth in measure 5. The first few measures will then sound like this:

We have now set the pattern for the tempo, dynamics, and articulation for the entire first movement. There is one important proviso: while the use of the messa di voce will be binding on the soloists and other instrumentalists at all times, the inverted mordent and similar ornaments may be used by the three soloists at will, so that they always come unexpectedly upon the audience.

The off-beat principal violin entry in measure 13 and the ripieno string entries beginning at measure 14, are most effectively pulled off with the bow already on the string, waiting to go. Be very insistent on this point, because if bows are going to be dropped on strings from various heights there is a danger of imprecise and scrambled attacks, and the brisk pace of the music generates enough excitement without adding the risk of error. Ask your players to use very short strokes in the upper half of the bow, with hardly any weight on the strings at all. Notice that the principal violin has his own extended *messa di voce* in measures 25–28 and 31–35.

Bach has the two recorders playing without interruption from measure 35 through measure 59. To preserve this feeling of an unending line they can arrange to take breath at different times, each covering for the other; the most logical places occur at the tied notes across bar-lines, where the tied notes can be released a fraction of a second ahead of time without disrupting the flow of melody.

At measure 50 we come across proof of how closely Bach tailored this concerto to the instrumental forces at his command at Cöthen. Recorders 1 and 2 are treated exactly alike in this Concerto except that three times in the first movement—in measures 50, 278, and 394—recorder 2 ducks the challenge of the high F sharp above the treble staff and recorder 1 accepts it in the following measure. Obviously F sharp was a problematical note for recorders in the eighteenth century and it still is a doubtful note today; only the best instruments were capable of producing it, and special fingerings were needed to make it sound true. Here's the way the passage is scored:

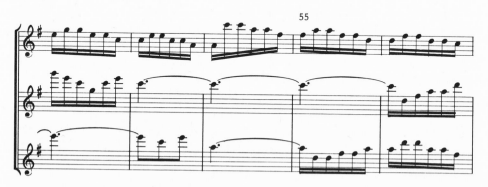

Had recorder 2 been capable of producing the high F sharp at all (to say nothing of its being in tune) Bach would have written the note marked with an x a full octave higher. What note do present-day performers play? If we too have on hand just one recorder capable of playing that high F sharp, the question is academic—we are forced to accept Bach's solution. However, if the second recorder can play the note, then there is a dilemma; should we be true to the printed score or to Bach's presumed intentions? My choice is to play the note an octave higher than written in each of the three passages where it occurs; your choice is your own.

We suggested earlier that the three eighth notes that form part of the principal theme and descend in seconds should be played legato. There are a few instances where Bach used eighth notes followed by a leap—in recorder 1's measures 19 and 49; in recorder 2's measures 39, 43, 47, 51, and 53; and the ripieno instruments' beginning at measure 43. These eighths should all be played staccato.

Problems are sure to arise in measures 79 through 82 when these are played by a less-than-professional group of musicians. The difficulties however are psychological rather than rhythmic in nature, and they tend to disappear when the conductor keeps a smoothly-flowing beat and the musicians themselves do not hesitate. Errors are apparent in the Urtext at this point. In measure 80 the solo violin has a printed staccato quarter note instead of an eighth note. In measure 81 the rhythmic pattern for recorder 1 shows a staccato eighth note, a sixteenth rest, an eighth note and a staccato sixteenth; the values of the last two notes should be reversed.

The recorder parts in measures 157–159 need special attention:

If the music is played exactly as written, it comes out sounding as though the same recorder player were playing the identical passage three times in exactly the same manner—a mindless procedure. There are more interesting alternatives. Recorder 2 can play measure 158 more softly, as an echo; this would demand a similar scaling down of tone by the entire ensemble. Also short mordents can be used effectively; in measure 157 recorder 1 plays the phrase as written, in measure 158 recorder 2 plays a short inverted mordent on the first A, and in measure 159 recorder 1 plays a short mordent on F sharp:

Beginning at measure 165 Bach allowed the principal violinist plenty of rest until a messa di voce entry at measure 185; this period can be gainfully spent in yoga exercises or transcendental meditation, whichever calms the nerves best. At measure 187 the violinist begins playing twenty-two measures of onrushing slurred thirty-seconds that allow absolutely no room for miscalculation. Once this passage is safely past, even the triple and double stops beginning in measure 215 are a relief—half the movement is already over. The G below middle C held by the ripieno violins and viola from measures 211 to 221 should be treated as a pedal point.

At measure 235 we come across one of those rare instances where Bach demanded a pianissimo; the conductor should make sure that the players observe it and that all violinists observe Bach's bow slurs, however unorthodox or illogical these might seem to be:

Bach specified a return to forte at measure 241 and to the pianissimo again at measure 251. He neglected to cancel out the second pianissimo, however, and this omission raises some interesting possibilities. If the ripieno violins come in pianissimo at measure 263, the cello, bass, and harpsichord enter pianissimo at measure 264, and the two recorder soloists enter pianissimo at measure 267, the individual playing level is still very soft, but Bach has achieved a cumulative crescendo; with a messa di voce in the ripieno violins, one can easily (and logically) slip into a forte at measure 271:

270

275

In the Andante a tempo slower than ♩ = 46 tends to drag. Ornamentation becomes difficult here when all three soloists move together. Yet, what a difference small touches can make! Observe the slurs in paired notes: lean lightly on the first note, ease off on the second. There are other essential refinements you can make on the very first page: a messa di voce in measures 3 and 4 of the principal violin part, and in measures 13–16 in principal violin, recorder 1, and ripieno violin 1.

A curious shift of emphasis occurs with the viola, which in the first movement, had allied itself closely with the violins rather than with cello and bass. In the second movement, cello, string bass, and harpsichord work closely together, with the viola playing related rhythmic patterns in conjunct as well as disjunct motion.

Where the first movement has an almost orchestral brilliance, the second is much more contemplative in character. Moreover, here Bach has both ripieno violins securely tied to first and second recorder during forte passages; when the recorders are playing softly, the violins fall silent. Bach, however, in playing the viola obviously felt he could now indulge himself a little, and he demands a chamber-music-like intensity and felicity in passages such as the one beginning in measure 13. No noisy contrasts can be employed here, no big crescendos and diminuendos can intrude on the listening ear; rather the violist must seek to draw attention to the importance of his own part by very subtle dynamic coloration and by the quiet intensity of his playing.

In measure 39–42, the three violins play two quarter notes in each measure. These notes should be played semi-detached; in measures 39, 41, and 42, the first beat is strong while the second beat is relatively weak. In measure 40, however, both the principal violin and the first ripieno violin should make an accent on the second beat. In measures 59–60, Bach left out the slurs for some instruments and wrote them in for others; it is easy to assume that Bach erred and to correct him by slurring everything. But first try it this way:

Since one of the goals of normal editorial practice is to secure uniformity at all costs, many modern editors slur recorder 1's two eighths on the third beat of measure 59 and the eighths making up the first and last beats of measure 60; try leaving off the slurs in the principal violin and second violin parts in measure 60. Listen closely; you might find this an interesting manner of playing.

However, a look ahead at measure 66 will raise fresh doubts. There the principal violin and the ripieno violin 1 play identical notes, but the violin 1 part lacks a slur; for that matter, so does the first recorder part. Did Bach really get caught in two minds—or was he just plain tired? And what of the last two measures: why do we have a trill in recorder 2 and violins 1 and 2, but no trill in the principal violin and recorder 1? Was it perhaps three A.M. of a winter morning, and the fire was burning low? Whatever the reason, here is an instance where an "urtext" does not provide a clear answer, and you will have to make up your own mind.

Four measures before the end of this movement, Bach provides his own cadenza. It's one of the simplest cadenzas ever; one need only play it with taste—and let it go at that.

Because of the bold theme of the final Presto, the temptation is to begin forte, but we should begin no louder than a mezzo forte. The viola starts off with the main theme, and the cellos and continuo come in off-beat to provide strong support. (Bach, playing viola at the first performance, was able to maintain strong control over tempo and dynamics.) In measure 5, violin 2 enters, but within three measures cello and harpsichord drop out. In measure 11, principal violin as well as violin 1 make a strong entry; four measures later, so do cello, bass and harpsichord. The entire string ensemble keeps playing when the recorders enter in measure 23. Had we started the movement forte, the recorders would have been quite inaudible at this point.

Going back to the beginning of this movement, how does one play measure 1? Not with smoothly connected bow strokes, as one so often hears it played. Rather, the first half-note should be played staccato, and the second should take the mesa di voce. This device should also apply to the cello part in measures 3 and 4 and to all similar passages. Only those quarter notes that move by leap should be played staccato.

The paired seconds shown by the sign ⌐——⌐ , when played legato, will give the entire passage far more clarity and definition than normally possible.

The messa di voce must be observed wherever it is called for: by the two recorders and second violin in measures 23–24, by solo violin and violin 1 in measure 24, by the second violin in 24–25, by the principal violin and violin 1 in 27–30, by the viola in the passage beginning at measure 28, and by the two recorders in the passage beginning at measure 31. The thought of so many small crescendos and diminuendos following one another so quickly might seem mannered and fussy at first thinking, and yet we have to accept the fact that they were indeed a baroque mannerism. An especially intense and dramatic effect is created when the device is used in different voices in close sequence, as in the passage beginning at measure 38.

In the extended section that follows in which the three soloists play on their own, a special responsibility devolves on the principal violin to play as lightly as possible, so as not to obscure the interplay between the two recorders. When, beginning at measure 63, Bach begins to pull in the ripieno instruments one at a time, he not only uses these carefully spaced entries to build up intensity, but the two recorders are soon joined by principal violin and violin 1 in what must surely be one of the most extended messa di voce passages ever written, since it is only phased out in measure 87. When Bach has the messa di voce occurring within bar lines for the violins, he writes across bar lines for the recorders, and vice versa; the crescendos and diminuendos overlap and interlock with a subtlety that can be brought out with great clarity by a small and sensitive ensemble.

Beginning at measure 87 the solo violin is king; the accompanying instruments do no more than break in with their comments as the violinist storms on in an extended cadenza. Only in measure 105, when the first ripieno violin breaks in with a delightful variant of the principal theme, does the ensemble itself attempt to bring the soloist under control; do not allow him to drown out this challenge with a barrage of bariolage. Throughout these measures the accompaniment, though played softly, must be firm and dynamically incisive, to give the principal violinist a rhythmically rock-solid foundation; else he may be carried away by his own enthusiasm. By the time the cadenza ends in measure 127, the movement is just past its halfway mark. The conductor should be especially alert to forewarn violins 1 and 2 about their entries here; and as soon as he has brought in violin 2 he should prepare the viola for its off-beat entrance in measure 129. In measure 175 the situation is slightly different; there, after he has alerted the entire ensemble in advance with his eyes, the careful conductor will bring in the long-silent violins and bass with his left hand, but the right-hand beat of "one" will be directed specifically at the viola with enough bounce in it to get a controlled off-beat response. In such a spot either sloppy preparation on the conductor's part or an overly anxious viola player can bring chaos to the ensemble.

The rest of the movement covers familiar ground. Here are a few additional suggestions: in measures 220 and 223 Bach indicates staccato half notes for the two violins and viola; keep these accented, incisive, and short. Staccato half notes are indicated in the second half of measures 229, 231, and 233. In measure 229 the accent should fall lightly on the second beat, and in measure 231 it should fall lightly on the first beat; in measure 233 it should fall very sharply, almost sforzando, on the second beat.

A slight, hardly noticeable pullback in tempo is permissible to heighten the tension in these measures. From measure 234 on, however, the tempo should be held firm until the concluding trill in measure 243; a ritard should be made here on the repeated octave D (remember C. P. E.'s rules!) and a strong crescendo and diminuendo on the final chord.

How does this performance of the *Brandenburg Concerto No. 4* differ from the performances we are accustomed to hearing? Leaving minor detail aside, these are the major points that we have insisted upon:

1. One instrument to a part, a small ensemble, and extreme clarity!
2. Use of recorders as solo instruments. Most conductors and groups use two modern metal flutes.
3. More flexibility in the use of fortes, pianos, and in-between gradations than allowed by terraced dynamics
4. Observance of Bach's device of creating natural extended crescendos by adding instruments at carefully calculated intervals
5. Greater use of ornamentation, particularly in the second movement
6. Extensive use of messa di voce. Bach provides so much opportunity for the use of this device that it seems as though he wanted it to be a distinctive feature of this particular concerto—yet this aspect has been ignored by almost every group of performers up to now.

In spite of the small musical forces involved, *the Brandenburg Concerto No. 4* has heroic proportions. In terms of mood, it is a happy work. Yet most performers have insisted on giving it a somewhat somber character, mainly by playing the second movement too slowly and giving it a particularly lugubrious feeling. We can and must enliven the slow movement while still being true to the Baroque spirit; we can play it somewhat faster, we can observe the slurrings in the solo parts as well as in the ripieno, and we can ornament. The end result might well be a performance to remember.

Brandenburg Concerto No. 5

We have already seen how, in the *Brandenburg Concerto No. 5*, Bach placed himself at the manuals of a new harpsichord from Berlin. We see him now, ready to begin, with the two other soloists playing a one-keyed flute and a violin. But although our combination time machine–crystal ball shows us the ripieno string players, this writer sees no sign of a second harpsichord player to cope with the accompaniment, even though Spitta suggests he must have been around, and quite a few twentieth-century performers agree with Spitta. My personal feeling is that a second harpsichord would diffuse the texture and muddy the sound. Besides, we know now that it was established practice in Bach's time—and right through Mozart's—for a keyboard soloist to function as a continuo player in tutti passages when the solo part fell silent. Unlike Mozart, however, who contented himself with writing a skeletal bass line for the pianist's left hand in orchestral tuttis, Bach here takes care to identify the non-solo keyboard sections as "accompagnement" and figures the bass:

This figured bass line raises the important question of how elaborate the accompaniment should be. A comparison of the accompaniment with the harpsichord concertato writing may yield some information. The harpsichord concertato first enters in measure 9:

Certain differences immediately become apparent; however, further ahead in the movement are two half measures of accompaniment sandwiched between two onrushing solo sections. This type of passage is important because of the problems raised by the use of a second harpsichord:

Even from such a brief look at early portions of the movement, some conclusions can be drawn:

The solo cembalo part

1. is linear in both hands, except for right-hand passages such as those in measures 20–21
2. its right-hand part moves freely in sixteenths, triplet sixteenths, occasional thirty-seconds, and equally occasional eighth notes
3. its left-hand part (up to this point) moves in sixteenth notes, with a fair sprinkling of eighths thrown in

In contrast, the "accompagnement"

1. is chordal in concept
2. should have fewer running sixteenths in the right hand
3. has a bass that moves steadily in eighth notes

The skill of the harpsichordist will be seen not only in the brilliance the artist brings to the interpretation of the solo part, but also in the musicianly restraint, finely balanced by imaginativeness, with which the figured bass accompaniment is realized. The "accompagnement" must be restrained without being dull; far from causing the performance to drag, it must at all times bring liveliness to the ensemble.

Since the use of a second harpsichord is being seriously recommended by many performers, the following points are offered for your consideration: First, at no time should a second harpsichord play while the solo harpsichord is playing the solo part—or the chords of the continuo harpsichord will obscure the soloist's clean lines.

Second, the soloist should avoid playing the continuo along with the accompanying harpsichord; for if the realizations of the two match each other absolutely, the reinforced harpsichord sound may well unbalance the ensemble; and if the realizations do not match, we will have a blur of keyboard sound instead of a strong foundation.

Third, as a corollary, at measure 9 the accompanying harpsichordist will play a chord on D, and the soloist will enter with the right hand only, observing the sixteenth rest.

Fourth, in measure 19 and similar passages, the accompanist will take over in the second half of the second beat and play to the first sixteenth E in measure 20; the soloist will then reenter with the left hand on high E, as though starting after a sixteenth rest:

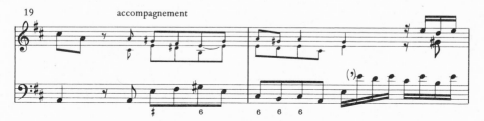

The phrase mark in measure 20 between the first two sixteenths in the left hand, shows where an accompanying harpsichordist would leave off and the soloist would take over. The chord immediately preceding the phrase mark should be kept extremely short, whether one or two harpsichords are used; only then will the soloist's attack on the E above middle C in the left hand be seen as a distinct off-beat entry. Similarly the accompanist will have to play a staccatissimo chord on the first beat of measure 42, to avoid obscuring an off-beat right-hand entry by the soloist.

If these measures already seem complicated to you, there is worse to follow. In measure 61 a significant fragment of solo in both hands surfaces like a rock in a sea of accompaniment. In the following measure the tide of accompaniment recedes and the solo part takes over.

Within seconds we come to six brief accompanying chords in the midst of an extended passage:

The accompanying harpsichordist drops out on the first beat of measure 66, where the soloist enters. And yet the bass line at this point is one smooth continuous line, as it is in measure 62. These complications give us pause and we must ask ourselves whether all these comings and goings of two harpsichordists are really necessary or are they just so much windy drama and visual and aural gimmickry superimposed on a magnificent score. It seems to me that with this concerto at least, the old adage no longer holds true—one head (and one pair of hands) is definitely better than two.

The other musical aspects of this movement also pose problems for consideration. The dynamic level for the opening tutti is forte. We know that this is so because (1) the tempo indication is allegro; (2) the music is of a robust nature and seems to demand a loud dynamic; and (3) Bach specifically marked measure 10 piano, implying that the preceding measures were louder. The tempo should be $\quarternote$ = 66–72; anything faster would turn this into a race with the devil.

The principal violinist and the ripieno group wait with their bows on the strings and their eyes on the harpsichordist if there is no separate conductor. In such cases the harpsichord player usually conducts; but nothing prevents the principal violinist, or any other member of the group, from conducting the ensemble by mutual consent. The general dynamic level of this opening section stays at forte, but note in the second half of measure 5 Bach creates a strong natural crescendo by having all the strings plus the harpsichord play a scale passage in running sixteenths. This gathering up of forces, this forward thrust, implies an intensification of attack in measure 6, and the string players must provide such an intensification either by lengthening the bow stroke slightly or by applying more pressure to the bow, but not by doing both.

In measure 9 the harpsichordist ceases to be an accompanist and instantly becomes the soloist. Now this transformation from compliant citizen into defiant hero has to be achieved without benefit of telephone booth and superman cape; the answer lies in registration. We have seen that a harpsichordist who is a purist generally sets the registration ahead of time and deviates from it as little as possible for the duration of the movement. If the keyboard player has the use of a harpsichord with pedal stops rather than hand stops, we should (like C. P. E. Bach) consider ourselves fortunate, because considerations of musicianship can now prevail over mere convention. If we assume that a two-manual harpsichord is being used, with an eight-foot set of strings on the upper manual and an eight-foot and a four-foot set on the lower manual, we would have these options:

In passages marked "piano", the accompaniment would use the upper 8' register only; the solo part would use upper 8' and lower 4'.

In passages marked "forte", the accompaniment would use upper 8' plus 4'; the solo part would use upper and lower 8' registers, adding the 4' for a fortissimo.

In single-manual instruments look for a knee lever, and if your harpsichord does not have one, then you pray Bach will not desert you in your hour of need.

And indeed he won't. In measure 9, for example, he has the strings fall silent even as the solo harpsichord makes an entry. The preeminence of the harpsichord is thereby proclaimed, though it is not yet established. The harpsichord enters off-beat; hard on its heels, also off-beat, comes the flute. But while the harpsichordist is playing sixteenths, the flutist is dealing in eighth notes; care should be taken to prevent a subconscious broadening of the tempo.

The flutist plays the first messa di voce in measures 9 and 10 and the violinist plays it in measure 12. All three soloists continue to play forte even though the ripieno plays softly starting from measure 10. In measure 19 the ripieno forte must be sustained to the second beat of measure 20, when a diminuendo may be made. Bach indicates a pianissimo for the ripieno strings immediately thereafter; it must be strictly enforced, particularly since the flute is now playing in a weak part of its register and can easily be drowned out.

Balance is particularly crucial in these measures because in reality we now have four soloists to contend with: the principal violin, the flute, and the harpsichordist's two hands—the left hand must know exactly what the right hand is doing. (See our earlier comment on phrasing in measure 20, on page 241). Meanwhile the ripieno violin, viola, and cello carry on a rhythmic commentary interrupted by silences. The routine conductor beats these passages in a four-square manner and the audience is none the wiser; the flamboyant conductor unnecessarily conducts the soloists, who are better left alone. The musicianly conductor turns to the ripieno, and with small Reiner-like beats illuminates the silences as well as the soft rhythmic attacks, leading the audience in spite of itself to listen closely, not only to the loudest parts of the music, but to the soft, too-often-neglected inner voices. How beautiful is music—particularly Bach—when it is performed and listened to in this way! The same approach should be used in measures 50–56.

The entire ripieno makes a forte return beginning with the pick-up note to measure 29, and by measure 31 we are faced with another enigma. The harpsichord does a quick change from accompaniment to solo; the double bass drops out; the cello is marked pianissimo, and an eighth note later so is the viola; the principal violin is marked piano. In measure 32 the flute reenters without a dynamic marking, followed by the ripieno violin, marked pianissimo. Since the flute, like the principal violin, is playing what is essentially an accompanying figure, it should play softly; both instruments should make a slight messa di voce. But what does the harpsichordist do? Should he shift to a softer registration, or continue to play forte? There is no final answer, except to repeat that the harpsichordist in this concerto is, if not *the* star, at least "first amongst equals"—either forte or piano can sound right. Try them both, then decide.

The situation here is far different from the one we encountered earlier. Here we have only one solo line, provided by the harpsichordist's right hand; the left hand teams up with the cellist to provide a broken-chord accompaniment. The viola and ripieno violin together provide a different strand; the principal violin and the flute provide yet a third. Here again the conductor's role should be that of illuminator rather than time beater. The more acutely the conductor listens, and the more subtly he directs the audience's attention through his control of inner voices and his physical attitude, the more listening pleasure his audience will derive from the performance.

In measure 35, the conductor should beat sharply on one to help the ripieno violin break the across-the-bar tie; he should then immediately turn his attention to the double bass's pianissimo entry on the third beat (to prepare the double bass for his entry the conductor should have caught that instrumentalist's eye a couple of measures earlier). The entry should be light but distinct—it is especially important in performing Bach that no notes get thrown away. In this entire section starting at measure 31 on, the conductor should make sure that the ripieno strings draw their bows lightly above the finger-board, so that a true pianissimo is obtained.

Beginning at measure 47 Bach silences the lower strings while indicating a staccato, piano attack for the ripieno violin and viola. The playing should be airy. Pianissimos are marked in measure 50; does this imply that a diminuendo can occur in between? The single bass note in the same measure is there for a purpose; while soft, it should be clearly audible. Between measures 61 and 71 the ripieno group plays just two pockets of sound; the conductor here should "pulse" four beats to a bar to hold the ensemble together and ensure a smooth break in tied notes.

At measure 71 Bach introduces ten measures of extensive imitation between flute and principal violin. How many generations of musicians have played this section "straight" while the ripieno and the harpsichord just doodle along! Here's how the parts for transverse flute and violin appear in the score:

Custom so dulls the ear, that until recently I was able to sit through performance after performance of this music "as written," and to find it perfectly satisfying. One day, however, the nagging question presented itself: did Bach really want the music to be performed this way? The more I thought about it, the less likely it seemed, and the more strongly I felt that Bach was merely providing the framework in which artists were expected to elaborate. So I set about ornamenting it, beginning straight off with measure 71, and very quickly reached a dead end. But the pattern had already presented itself—whoever began the ornamentation would do so in the second half of the measure. The other instrumentalist would then pick up the ornamented version and repeat it immediately in the first half of the following measure, and tease the partner and titillate the audience—by introducing a new variant in the second half. And so it would go, until somebody called time. In our example it is the principal violinist who calls time in measure 80, so I finally decided to begin with this measure and work backward.

Before you begin to play and appraise the following variants, please play over and over again the measures as they were originally written. Then try variants of your own; finally, try my suggestions. Do the variants flow naturally? Are they smooth enough? Are they logical in their development? The goal is to find variants that are so natural, smooth, and logical that you will not ever be satisfied with playing just the framework again—well, hardly ever. If you agree, you may even be tempted to go back to the beginning of the movement and look over some of the other imitative passages to see what you can do. But that's an "if"—the first hurdle lies right here, in your reaction to this reworking of the flute and principal violin parts, measures 71–81:

Another long sequential passage begins at measure 81. The flute and principal violin play staccato broken chords in eighths, the harpsichordist's right hand plays broken chords in sixteenths, the string bass with single quarter notes on the first beat of each measure underlines the steady descent of the bass line. If at measure 81 the conductor, while holding the ensemble together, quietly turns to face the string bass, he can without fuss or ostentation, merely through the focus of his attention, make his audience aware of this descending bass line, and the harmonic changes that logically go along with it. At measure 93 we get the feeling that we are there: the bass has arrived; but while it tries to hold on to this low E for another eight measures, the inexorable pull of the music continues. At measure 95 Bach indicates

a 2-measure trill, pianissimo, for flute and principal violin, followed by four more measures of whole notes for these two instruments. In spite of the very soft playing, the harmonic tension builds dramatically, until at measure 101 we are brought back to the original theme, forte.

The marking of this entire passage is very ambiguous and subject to varying interpretations. First, does the long trill extend for the first two measures only, or should it extend over all six? Does the pianissimo marking preclude a messa di voce in measures 95 and 96? Does the pianissimo really extend all the way through measure 100? If you maintain the pianissimo in all parts, the forte in 101 comes through as a sudden burst of glory. There are other possibilities as well. You can maintain the pianissimo in the two solo instruments, while the ripieno makes a gradual four-to-six measure crescendo. The solo instruments can join in the crescendo starting at measure 97, or they can trill, with messa di voce, from measure

95. The ripieno violin, viola, and bass can remain subdued; only the cello doubling the harpsichordist's left hand, will become more and more insistent with every passing measure. In this interpretation the harpsichord and cello between them pull the entire ensemble, against its will, into a new tonality and a new dynamic at measure 101.

This last alternative seems to me to be the best way in which to bring out the inner tensions and conflicts and resolutions of the music at this point; but of course this is a momentary and personal point of view, which only the inflexibility of cold print freezes in time. I would like to be free to feel differently tomorrow. Discuss and try out all the possibilities with your group, and bear in mind that no matter how you rehearse it, it may well come out sounding quite different in the heat of performance.

Since from measure 101 the entire ensemble is playing forte, at measure 105 the conductor should prepare for a piano in the ripieno violin and viola only, and he should bring in the bass softly in measure 109. Dynamic ambiguities occur in measures 128 and 132. Does the ripieno play forte or piano? Look ahead at measure 136; you will find the ripieno parts marked forte there. This implies that they

should be played piano at measure 132, and quite possibly at measure 128 as well. Bach introduces thirty-seconds in the solo harpsichord part in measure 139 and begins to thin out the rest of the structure. The scattered low As played alternately by the ripieno violin and viola from measure 147 are a foretaste of the viola pedal-point that begins in measure 151. With a messa di voce successively in ripieno violin, principal violin, and flute (measures 152 and 153) we come to the solo harp-sichord cadenza in measure 154—a historic "first."

A bar-by-bar analysis of this cadenza lies outside the scope of our book. If necessary, detailed help should be sought from a first-rate harpsichordist, but a few general remarks are in order. If you must choose between cool control and white heat, choose white heat. It is not enough merely to get through this cadenza—it *must* excite. In the two hundred and fifty years that have elapsed since the concerto was written, no other cadenza, whether original or not, has had quite the same power to stir the intellect and bring a lump to one's throat—not even the great

Beethoven cadenzas to his Concertos in C minor and E flat major. Whether you are using a harpsichord, a fortepiano, or a pianoforte, be sure to establish the right balances between your two hands; for instance, the left hand dominates at the outset (measure 154), and the right hand dominates at measure 155. When Bach's contemporaries played the half-notes in the left hand in measures 189–194, these notes must have been short indeed, because many Baroque keyboard players avoided the use of the thumb. Since Bach strongly advocated its use, however, you should be able to hold that important and persistent A for full value throughout almost the whole of this passage, particularly if your instrument has narrow German-style keys. Beginning at measure 195, you face thirty-seconds only; so be careful! In measure 198, play the left hand staccato and marcatissimo; in measure 202 maintain rhythmic sharpness and think how much easier things are going to be. In measures 203–212, the left-hand eighth notes should be played somewhat pesante, almost sostenuto, and yet detached; the low A should be quite insistent. In

251

the second half of measure 213 the ominous A sharps are to be held for almost their full value. Cautionary triplets are suddenly heard in the left hand in measure 214. If the conductor is still in a trance, this is his cue to come awake; he signals the ensemble quietly with his left hand at the beginning of measure 215—four measures to go. In measures 216 and 217 he gives the first beat only. With his left hand index finger cautioning "1 still to go," he gives the first beat of measure 218 and continues to beat quietly; the entire ensemble should now quietly have all instruments in place. At the count of two the conductor's left hand comes up to the ready, and bows should be poised on the string. The soloist, aware of the preparations, will be sufficiently reassured if eye contact is established by the third beat; the conductor gives the fourth beat with the soloist and holds fractionally, maintaining the ready position and eye contact, establishing with the soloist the precise moment when the final tutti begins. This should be played incisively, joyously, even triumphantly, with a ritard in the second half of measure 226 signaling the end.

The "affetuoso" second movement of the concerto should be taken at a pace somewhere between ♪ = 66 and 72. We are faced with four, not three, soloists—the transverse flute, the principal violin, and the harpsichordist's two hands. The violin is the control and the flute is the rebel; the harpsichord, whether as soloist or accompanist, is the wise compromiser who resolves the disputes and establishes the overall unity of the movement. What a challenge have we here, not in terms of technique, but of musicianship! Anyone who believes in the theory of terraced dynamics should be given half an hour to work out the terraces in this Affetuoso—and he should then be condemned to play it that way for thirty days. The music's ebb and flow cannot be suppressed.

At first glance the ornamentation in this movement might seem to be a problem; yet it can be worked out with patience. Obviously it is most difficult where four voices are involved and easiest when there are only one or two. Another point to consider is the style; since Bach wrote his dedication to the Margrave of Brandenburg, not in elegant German, but in courtly French one may surmise that the French influence at the margrave's court was quite strong. Therefore it seems fitting that in the second movement of this concerto Bach should resort to the French style of embellishment, using the ornaments indicated by signs (mordents, trills and so on) rather than the filling in by smoothly flowing notes that was typical of the Italian style.

The manner in which we begin the third movement is crucial; Bach has built a trap into the very first measure. The principal violin starts off-beat, the flute enters in measure 3, the harpsichordist's left hand enters in measure 9, and the right hand measure 11. Around measure 25 the ripieno strings begin to get restless and start shaking their heads, and at measure 29 the viola misses his entry. There is now a chorus of "where are we?" The confusion results because the ripieno parts show twenty-eight measures of rest before the viola entry, but they do not indicate that the first notes the principal violin plays (in fact, the first notes anyone plays in this movement) are off the beat. The problem should not arise with professional musicians or with amateurs who are completely familiar with the score; it is, however, a very real danger at other times. The solution is twofold; the conductor should cau-

tion the players that the entry is on the second beat with a pick-up sixteenth, and he should give this definite preparation:

In recent years most orchestras and chamber groups have played the rhythmic figure ♪ ♪♪. ♪ as though it were composed of two sets of triplets: ♪ ♪ ♪♪♪.

The Bärenreiter parts recommend such a treatment, and Robert Donington makes a similar recommendation, quoting both C. P. E. Bach and Quantz. I believe, however, that such a recommendation is based on a misreading of these sources; despite the statement that "three against two" is a rhythm that does not belong in the Baroque period, not even in Bach, "three against two" is exactly what we should be playing in this movement of the fifth Brandenburg. Since the reasoning for and against such a procedure is long and involved and would only get in the way of this discussion it is included in the epilogue. My recommendation is that in this movement, ♪ ♪♪. ♪ should not be played triplet fashion; further, I strongly urge that it be played instead with a greatly sharpened double-dotted rhythm:

♪ ♪♪.. ♪

(See the epilogue for my reasoning here also.)

The nature of this extended opening section is such that it is not enough for a conductor merely to mark time passively while the soloists play. The beats should be unostentatious, to be sure, so as not to downgrade the soloists; but the conductor should maintain an alert attitude and eye-contact with the ripieno. This keeps the soloists from pulling in different directions and is also reassuring to the ripieno. In rehearsal the conductor may have to remind the soloists to use messa di voce—the solo flute in measures 13–15, the violin in measures 15–17, and the two of them starting from measure 22. In actual performance at these points the conductor does nothing. At measure 26 he catches the eyes of the viola and low strings and indicates that there are three measures to go; in measure 29 he brings them in, even as he alerts the ripieno violin that there are two measures to go.

As the movement progresses, notice the brilliance and feeling of exaltation that Bach achieves through his use of "three against two." Although the conductor's beat will be firm and almost marcato, the second beat in each measure is best indicated sideways, to convey some of the lilt of the triplets without diminishing the intensity of the contrasting rhythm; in places such as measure 62, however, where all the strings have the dotted figure at once, the first beat should be given with even more incisiveness than normal. At measure 79 Bach begins an extraordinary passage in which the flute plays forte against a soft triplet accompaniment by the principal violin and harpsichord (the keyboard part is not marked piano here but it should be). The ripieno violin and viola enter with an angry outburst in measure 87; the viola drops out in measure 89, while the ripieno violin drops to a subito pianissimo. The ripieno violin part is also marked solo. This does not imply that Bach necessarily demanded more than one ripieno violin to the part in the earlier sections, but it does emphasize the point that a tone of the utmost delicacy is called for in these measures. Similarly, in the same part, a forte in measure 97 is followed by a solo pianissimo indication in the same part two measures later. Here the harpsichordist becomes the soloist; on his behalf, the conductor demands the softest possible playing by the two other principals and the entire ripieno.

Starting at measure 115 the flute and the principal violin have messa di voce across bar lines. At measure 148 the ripieno violin and viola get their turn; they should play this section *cantabile*. At measures 157–159 and 161, the conductor beats crisply as at the beginning, but his gestures are very small to ensure piano. At measure 177, after several measures of rest, the principal violin and flute reenter, supported by the ripieno violin and viola. In measure 189, the dynamic marking for the two soloists is piano; therefore we can assume that the entry by these four instruments in measure 177 should be forte. Measure 198 and similar passages yet to come have pedal point; no messa di voce should be used with them.

At measure 231 make a very slight ritard, but in measure 232, where a quarter note is followed by a quarter rest, stretch the quarter note into almost a half-note, preempting the quarter note rest. Then make a small *luftpause*, and attack measure 233 with vigor, a tempo. Starting from measure 261 the conductor brings in the ripieno once again after adequate preparation; be careful beginning at measure 273—these are real eighth notes! Give them full value, and the triplet and dotted-note passages will become sprightlier by contrast.

At measure 303 the conductor maintains the tempo but increases the tension in his beat. At measure 307, he increases the size of the beat, in preparation for a ritard in measure 308; make a marked ritard in measure 309, and in measure 310 there should be a strong final chord; the forte may either be sustained or allowed to die away as you wish. This should have been a joyous movement, with an ecstatic, exhilarating ending. Tumultuous and spontaneous applause will tell you whether you have succeeded.

13

Tartini, Leopold Mozart, and the Slide into Decadence

If a violinist wishes to do justice to music of the late, late Baroque, he should acquire a solid technical foundation based on Corelli's principles. One would have to do this in a slightly roundabout way, since Corelli himself left no written method behind him. But his star pupil, Geminiani, did—as we have seen in a preceding chapter. A thorough study of Geminiani's *The Art of Playing on the Violin* is therefore called for. Having mastered that, one should do what young violinists of that time were continually exhorted to do: study Corelli's *Sonatas*, Opus 5. Tartini demanded of his pupils that they study this opus; according to Burney, Tartini regarded Opus 5 as a prerequisite to further studies. As late as 1791 we find another famous violin teacher, Francesco Galeazzi, recommending that his pupils study Opus 5 every day, particularly the sixteenth-note allegros of the first, the third, and the sixth sonatas.

So much for the foundation. To acquire dazzling virtuosity, the violinist would then have to go on to Tartini. Tartini perhaps expected more from his pupils than any teacher who had preceded him; he showed just how much he expected of them in a set of fifty well-thought-out variations on a Corelli gavotte. Tartini was writing not just for the average or good violinist, but for the ones who are truly gifted, and his high standards have persisted. Even today, a young violinist must be able to perform Tartini's *Art of Bowing* with the requisite clarity, verve, and brilliance before he can regard himself as a potential virtuoso.

One must remember that no organized, advanced teaching material for the violin was available before the appearance of Corelli's *La Follia* in 1700. Fifty-one years later, Geminiani's extensive method became publicly available; this work presented organized teaching material up to the eighth position. Leopold Mozart's *Treatise on the Fundamental Principles of Violin Playing*, published in 1756, presented material (some of it borrowed from Tartini) suitable for levels from beginning to quite advanced.* Two years later thirty-eight variations from Tartini's *Art of Bowing* were published; although the complete set of fifty variations was not published until it was included in Cartier's *L'Art du Violon* in 1798, all the variations must have been

---

* An English translation by Editha Knocker is published by Oxford University Press (New York, 1951).

256

accessible and in use well before Tartini's death in 1770. Tartini's work demanded not only the development of a phenomenal bowing technique, but great left-hand finger dexterity as well. When L'Abbé le Fils' treatise appeared in 1761, with its own special contribution in the field of harmonics, the post-Tartini violinist had at his disposal a tremendous battery of technical devices plus all the agility and dexterity he needed.

Tartini's renown as a teacher was already established when he founded an international school of violin playing in Padua in 1728; there he taught brilliant young violinists from various parts of Europe. His influence grew with the years: the composers Johann Gottlieb Graun and de Tremais were his pupils; Graun had already studied the violin with Pisendel before coming to Tartini. Locatelli had many Tartini scores in his library; and the French violin teacher Baillot, a power in the late eighteenth century, was Tartini's admirer, as was the publisher Cartier. The impact of his teaching was felt all over Europe. As the direct result of Tartini's teaching methods and personal influence, the difficult not only became easy, it became almost commonplace.

For example, in a section of his treatise illustrating various ornaments, Leopold Mozart describes the *tirata* as an ascending or descending scale thrown in on the spur of the moment to connect two notes. In a brisk tempo he says it resembles a shot, and he gives the following example for a quick ascending tirata. Here is the passage, in a molto allegro tempo, without ornamentation:

The same passage (in the same tempo) now has two quick tiratas:

Ey! ist das nicht ein Schuß?

"Ey!" cries Leopold Mozart exuberantly, "Isn't that some shot?" Now here is the fiftieth variation from Tartini's *Art of Bowing:*

If Leopold Mozart fired a shot, Tartini has set off a fusillade! Where other composers dealt in sixteenths and thirty-seconds, Tartini made sixty-fourths the common musical coin of the realm. As we shall see, his pupils soon outdid their master.

Tartini was a driven man, driven in youth and age to excel above all others. Quite early in his career he felt he had been publicly outplayed and humiliated by the violinist-composer, Francesco Maria Veracini; Tartini then retired from public life for two years of intensive study and self-criticism and returned only when he felt his bow arm was at least as good as Veracini's. At one time he dreamed that the devil appeared at the foot of his bed holding a violin, and played a sonata that surpassed in tonal beauty and technical virtuosity anything Tartini had ever heard. Did the dream-devil perhaps look a little like Veracini with wig and cloven hoof? (The dates of the two incidents are uncertain.) Was his violin baked in the ovens of Hades, as Vuillaume's were baked in the kilns of Paris some decades later? No matter—Tartini awoke, the devil was gone, but the dream remained.

The "Devil's Trill" Sonata

The *"Devil's Trill" Sonata* is Tartini's attempt to recreate that dream. The sonata was known and admired as a virtuoso challenge in Tartini's own lifetime; it was not published, however, until 1798, when Cartier included it in his *L'Art du Violon.* * The manuscript that Baillot lent to him to copy disappeared without a trace. The devil again, perhaps, was reclaiming his own?

* A facsimile of Cartier's *L'Art du Violon*, Paris (1803?) Edition, has been published by Broude Brothers Limited, New York. Monuments of Music and Music Literature in Facsimile, First Series—Music, vol. XIV, 1973.

Be that as it may, ever since this sonata first appeared, editors have worked feverishly at making it simpler. These editors include some of the most respected names in violin literature; the latest one is Gunter Kehr, who prepared an edition for Schott; he makes a great to-do about the Cartier version in his foreword, and then departs from it without ceremony. It behooves us (excuse *me*, Satan!) to reproduce the original Larghetto here and see how we can make it *more* complicated, not less so.

In the preface to his *Rules for Learning to Play the Violin* Tartini gave his rules for bowing. A knowledge of these rules will help us play his music the way he wanted it played. A synopsis of Tartini's bowing rules follows:

> We must distinguish, he says, between two types of passages—the cantabile and suonabile. (Do not look for this word in your Italian dictionary—it is the eighteenth-century spelling of *sonabile.*)
>
> In cantabile passages the melody moves by step; these passages should be played absolutely legato.
>
> In suonabile passages the melody moves by leap; the notes should be played detached. Use short bow strokes to achieve a true suonabile in allegro movements!
>
> If the accompaniment matches the principal part rhythmically, the music should be played suonabile and allegro. If the two parts have a different rhythm, the piece should be played cantabile. Be consistent in repeating passages. If a cantabile passage is repeated it should be repeated cantabile, and a suonabile passage should be repeated suonabile.
>
> If a passage has been ornamented and needs to be repeated, it should be repeated with the same ornaments in order to achieve perfect consistency. (This is peculiar to Tartini.)
>
> Notes that move in sequence by half step should be played in one bow.
>
> If the first of several slurred notes has a different time value, it should be played with a separate bow.
>
> To draw a beautiful tone from the instrument, place bow on strings gently and then increase the pressure. If you press too hard from the start, a harsh scratchy sound will be produced. Always use the middle of the bow, but try to play spiccato notes at the point.

Now for the *"Devil's Trill" Sonata* itself. This is the way twentieth-century audiences have heard the first measure performed by almost every violinist:

Larghetto Affectuoso [sic]

It sounds like sugar and spice and everything nice. What it lacks is *bite*—this devil has no teeth! But the Cartier first edition, which is based on the original manuscript, is far different. It contains melodic as well as harmonic surprises, and it is more difficult to play.

The double stops should be held as long as possible; where this presents unusual difficulties, the violinist touches the lower note lightly to suggest the harmony and then moves on. This sort of escape, however, must be considered a temporary expedient; it is only to be used until one's technique has caught up with one's ambition.

The bass in the Cartier edition is not figured. The keyboard part should be realized in as light a manner as possible; the violinist carries the major portion of the weight and all of the fireworks; the keyboard player should subordinate his part to that of the violinist, remembering to enjoy—rather than wince at—whatever dissonances might arise.

The first movement of the Tartini *Sonata in G Minor*, (the "Devil's Trill") is reproduced here in full as it appears in Cartier's *L'Art du Violon*. Study it closely, run it through your mind over and over again, and before long, ornamentation will begin to suggest itself to you:

On the basis of Tartini's own rules, this movement should obviously be played very cantabile, or legato. The presence of double stops limits the amount of ornamentation that is practicable, but the double stops should not be used as an excuse to forego ornamentation entirely. Turns, mordents, appoggiaturas, and an occasional double appoggiatura should suffice. The tempo should be around ♩ = 96. If the piece is ornamented lightly the first time around, should it be ornamented more heavily on the repeat, or should it just be ornamented differently? Neither way is the right one; remember that Tartini wanted the repeat played exactly the way the original measures were played, for the sake of consistency.

Here are the first twelve measures of the *"Devil's Trill" Sonata*, very simply ornamented. In some double stops the lower note will have to be touched hardly at all so as not to interfere with the melody.

Here are some suggestions for dynamics in these first measures. Since the movement is marked Larghetto Affectuoso, begin it piano but be prepared to play with a lot of nuance. For example, there should be a small crescendo-diminuendo on the second, third, and fourth beats. In measure 3 pick up the tempo slightly, build a crescendo, linger a little on that C sharp (like a tenor who's *afraid* of the conductor), and ease into the D in measure 4 to release the tension. Your eyes do not deceive you; the third note on the second beat of measure 4 is a delightful B flat (it is in the Cartier edition), and itself introduces a suspension. Play mezzo forte in measure 5, make a diminuendo in measure 6; play mezzo forte in measure 7, make a pianissimo echo in measure 8 (use very little bow, over the fingerboard), play mezzo forte and make a crescendo in measure 9. In measure 10 play the unison B flat on beat 3 staccato, and then accent the double stops, playing them forte. The remaining two measures can be played slightly diminuendo or slightly crescendo to the double bar, and a pronounced messa di voce should be made on the final note. (Tartini specifically prohibits using any type of vibrato while making a messa di voce).*

The entire first movement should be played quite flexibly in a tempo rubato. Look for points of tension and release in each bar and savor the harmonic clashes where they occur, either as the result of a deliberate progression by the composer or as passing notes in the ornamentation.

The proper justification for the tempo rubato is found, first of all, in the nature of the music itself. It ebbs and flows, and this must be indicated; at the same time care must be taken that the general forward momentum is not lost. Second, the next movement is marked "Tempo guisto [sic] della Scuola Tartinista" ("strict time of the Tartini school"). The implicit indication is that the preceding movement is to be played not in tempo giusto, but in tempo rubato.

* Tartini, *Rules to Learn to Play the Violin*, facsimile of copy by his pupil, G. F. Nicolai. Moeck Verlag, p. 16.

Use a slow vibrato most of the time, except where you want to increase the tension.

In the second movement minor differences abound between the Kehr edition and the Carrier first edition; these differences are mainly in bowing slurs and in the placement of trills. The changes introduced by Kehr would be more acceptable if they were shown clearly as editorial suggestions.

The divergences in the Kehr edition from the Cartier text that have been allowed in the third movement are far less acceptable than those in the first movement. Incidentally Cartier identified this movement as "Dreams of the Author," and marked the introductory seven measures Andante; the Kehr edition carries only the Andante marking. Kehr indicated a forte in measure 1, while the Cartier has the forte in measure 3; piano is therefore implied in measures 1 and 2. This makes good sense musically, and it also conforms to what we know of Baroque practice.

Far more crucial and interesting, however, are the sections that deal with "the devil trilling at the foot of the bed." This is the trill in Kehr's version:

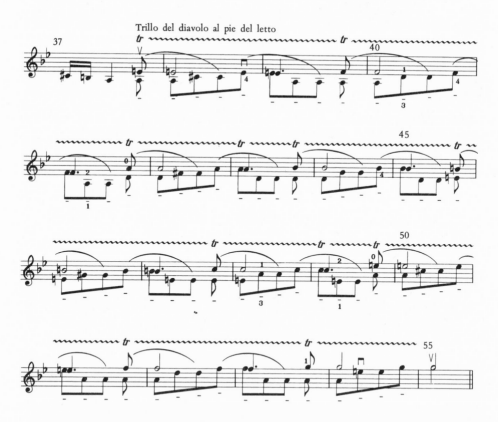

This shows a continuous trill that begins with the eighth note pick-up in measure 37 and goes right up to but stops short of the final G in measures 55. Twentieth-century violinists have practiced mightily to achieve this continuous trill; it seems they have been hoaxed by the devil. The Cartier text shows the following:

trill beginning on the half-note E natural in measure 38, not on the pick-up eighth note in measure 37; there is no trill on the eighth-note F in measures 39 or 41.

Furthermore there is no trill on the half-note A in measure 42; could this be an error? The trill resumes again in measure 44. There is no trill on B natural in measure 45 or on the half-note C in measure 48, but there is a trill on the second A in the lower voice. There are no trills on the E-natural pick-up in measure 49, on F in measure 51, on G in measure 53, or on the final G in measure 55.

Leopold Mozart quotes the same passage in his treatise, and he also shows the trill beginning, not on the pick-up eighth, but in the first complete measure. Also in the fourth measure there is no trill on the A (it is an F in the Cartier edition), but he does trill on the final G:

The trill sequence occurs two more times in the course of the movement:

In the Cartier edition the trill begins on a half note in measure 88; modern editions begin the trill with a pick-up eighth in measure 87. Cartier shows no trill on the E-flat in the upper voice in measures 89 and 90, but there is a trill on the E-flat eighth note in the lower voice—the only example of a trill in the lower voice. In measures 91 and 92 the E natural in the upper voice is trilled; it is also trilled in measure 93, where there is no trill on F; measure 95 has no trill on the A. In measure 97 the Cartier edition shows no trill on the A or the B flat; in measure 99 there is no trill on the C. The final appearance of the trill in the Cartier edition provides the conclusive evidence—here the eighth notes are treated as pick-up notes only, and none of them carries the trill:

Oh, all you unfortunate violinists who have been spending days, weeks, years perfecting this continuous trill—to what purpose have you labored! You have been giving Beelzebub more than his due, and what the devil has once taken, he does not fork over lightly.

A Nardini Violin Sonata

Pietro Nardini (1722–1793), one of Tartini's most brilliant pupils, became a famous violinist and composer in his own right. Unfortunately, very few of his works are available today in a reputable edition; one of them is the Sonata in B flat, for violin and basso continuo, realized and edited by M. Abbado and published by Ricordi. Here are the first eight measures: Should they be ornamented?

Let us put that question in historical perspective. One of the earliest sonatas we have examined here is a work for violin, gamba, and continuo by Buxtehude. Had we been asked, should the Buxtehude work be ornamented? the answer would have been an immediate yes, of course it should. And had we been asked the same question about the sonatas in Corelli's Opus 5, written at the beginning of the eighteenth century, or the sonatas of Vivaldi written a few years later, or those of Quantz and C. P. E. Bach, the answer would also be a spontaneous "yes." All these works have opening movements that can demonstrably be improved through ornamentation.

With Handel, and later with Tartini, we come across opening movements that already have both melody and form, and they still call for skillful ornamentation. But *Nardini?* In the popular mind, and in highly regarded books on music appreciation, and in quite a few music conservatoires, Nardini is regarded as being well outside the confines of the Baroque period. Dare we then ornament his music?

For a simple answer, let us first look at Nardini's own playing, as seen through the eyes of his contemporaries. Christian Schubart (1739–1791), German poet, musician and composer, tells us that Nardini's playing brought courtiers to tears; in fact his (Nardini's) own tears "run down on his violin." Obviously, Nardini fitted into the Baroque prototype of a performer, as one who not only made music but emoted at the same time. Leopold Mozart heard Nardini perform in 1763, three years after the sonata we are considering was published in Venice. He praised Nardini's evenness of tone and its singing quality, adding the puzzling comment, "But he plays rather lightly." You might well wonder why Tartini's star pupil, with all the bow control and dexterity that this reputation implies, should be playing "rather lightly"?

It is most reasonable to suspect that Nardini was playing the music, not as it was written, but in a highly ornamented version. (How full a tone can one produce when playing a whole string of notes in a single bow stroke?) Cartier includes an elaborate version of this sonata in his reprint of the Venetian edition in his *L'Art du Violon.* Before we examine it, however, let us look at a few ornaments that Leopold Mozart commends to violinists in his *Treatise on the Fundamental Principles of Violin Playing.*

Section 27 of chapter 9 deals with a melody and appoggiaturas, to which the performer adds a rapid *doppelschlag*, or turn. Here is the appoggiatura alone:

and the appoggiatura with a turn.

This is the way it is to be performed.

The turn is also effective whether a melody rises by step

or by leap

Longer notes can be broken up by using a half trill. Here is the actual notation, with the half trill indicated:

and here is the passage as it is to be played, with the longer notes broken up:

The *groppo*, a cluster of four notes, is one of the most useful of all ornaments. Its purpose is familiar to us in a social context; it's like driving that extra block or two to make sure we don't arrive at a party ahead of the other guests. In a rising groppo the second note moves back a pace. To move smoothly from B flat to F and from E flat to B flat two groppos per move will do admirably:

Similarly, in a descending groppo the second note moves up a step. To get from F to C in one beat using thirty-seconds alone, two groppos are all you need:

The *half circle* is like a groppo, except that the first three notes either rise or descend and the fourth note moves in the opposite direction; although there is no such thing as half a groppo, there is something called a *full circle*, which consists of two half circles following one another. In a melody that moves up and down by step a rising circle and a falling circle will get us there and back:

A half circle can be extremely useful when you want to give the impression of movement while staying in the same place. Here is the melody as it is written and as it is enlivened by a half circle:

Although the tirata was discussed at the beginning of this chapter, two other examples of this ornamental device are included here because they are very pertinent to our discussion. To get from F to D

we use a quick tirata in semitones:

To climb from D to A

we use a tirata in thirds:

We are now ready to go back to the ornamented version of Nardini's B flat major sonata, as published by Cartier. It appears on three staves; the plain melody is on top, the ornamented melody is below it, and the unfigured and unrealized bass is on the bottom line. Whoever embellished the melody in the late eighteenth century did it in accordance with the principles set forth by Leopold Mozart in the 1750s. The ornamentation is therefore very much in keeping with Nardini's own style. Remember that Mozart relied on Tartini and Tartini was Nardini's teacher.

Here is the opening eight-measure sentence:

The devices used are easily identified; we will ignore the appoggiaturas and the trills because they are quite obvious. There is a tirata in measures 1 and 5, two ascending groppos and a descending tirata in measure 7, and there should of course be a messa di voce in measure 8.

So far the elaboration follows the general sweep of the original melody fairly closely. In measure 10 an ascending tirata in thirds and a descending tirata in triplet sixteenths changes the appearance and sound, but not the intent, of the passage,

which is very simply to descend from an E flat through D and C to B natural:

In measure 11 a tirata is again used to provide smooth and rapid movement within the confines of the melody; in measure 13, a tirata followed by a descending groppo tempts the violinist to an upward leap to E flat, and the downward plunge of an octave is no problem whatever. Space does not permit us to look at the remainder of this movement; but the measures already considered have a wealth of instructive material in them.

Ah, yes. About that slide into decadence, mentioned in the title of this chapter. Turn to Appendix 2—the opening Adagio from Nardini's *Sonata No. 6* as published by Cartier, and you will see exactly what we mean. It includes, incidentally, one of the longest chromatic tiratas you are ever likely to see, and enough tiratas of every sort to decimate an army of violinists. At this point the musicians of the late eighteenth century had to face up squarely to the question: Where could they go from there? Clearly, the move had to be toward simplicity. The question was no longer "how many more notes can we pile on?" but "how many can we leave out?" As more became less, less became more. Leopold Mozart, C. P. E. Bach, Quantz, and Geminiani had all realized this by the middle of the eighteenth century and tried to control the excesses of ornamentation, to no avail. A few years after their passing, the Baroque period itself lay dead, killed by a surfeit of notes.

Epilogue:
A Non-Final Note on Baroque Dynamics and Bach's Rhythms

With so many scholars now looking closely at original manuscripts and microfilms, as well as at the earliest possible printed sources, much new light is being shed on the question of Baroque dynamics. Until recently, the theory of terraced dynamics held sway: music marked piano was to be played softly until it was marked forte, and the forte mark held good until it was contradicted once again. The reasoning was that all Baroque music was strongly influenced by the limitations of two of the principal instruments of the era—the organ and the harpsichord. Both of these played at "levels" of sound; in general, music for these instruments was made louder or softer by adding or taking off a register, or by thickening or lightening the texture. Not all twentieth-century performers of Baroque music subscribed to the terraced dynamics theory; among the most notable exceptions were Pablo Casals and his merry men of Marlboro, Vt., who played Bach strictly by note and by inspiration—with absolutely no ornamentation—and yet introduced what seemed to be the most anachronistically romantic crescendos, diminuendos, and rubatos ever heard. Away from Marlboro, I rejected such a concept of Bach, but when physically present at a Casals performance I must confess I was invariably swept off my feet.

Now it turns out that Casals was at least partly right. Researches by Walter Kolneder on Vivaldi and by other musicologists on Baroque performance, together with my own readings in the literature and music of the period, have convinced me beyond the shadow of a doubt that the old Baroque musicians were men and women of flesh and blood after all. They responded to musical stimuli as musicians more than other people are supposed to do—passionately and expressively. The question is: how expressively?

The indications are seldom absolutely clear. If in a Bach cantata we come across a progression that he marks from forte through piano to pianissimo, are we to infer from this a continuous diminuendo, or are we to play the passage at these various levels of intensity, each with its own nuances? And if one finds only scattered fortes and pianos or pianissimos in Vivaldi's printed scores, does one then infer that Vivaldi meant these passages to be played merely as blocks of contrasting dynamics without expressive shadings? Faced with such "evidence," might one not assume that the performance of a Bach cantata under Bach's own direction would be a much more musicianly, a much more subtle event than a Vivaldi performance under Vivaldi?

If we made this assumption, we would be quite wrong. Kolneder and others have written about Vivaldi's extraordinary situation. Alone amongst the giants of his time, he was not only a virtuoso violinist-composer capable of exploiting the flexibility of a stringed instrument to the fullest, but he also had at his disposal a highly-trained resident orchestra that was regarded by many observers as being the finest in Europe. Further, this orchestra consisted of young orphan girls whom Vivaldi taught himself; he had ample rehearsal time, and they played in church in pin-drop silence—with even applause forbidden. Kolneder has established the fact that Vivaldi could fuss with nuances as well as with large-scale dynamics; he examined scores used by Vivaldi for his concerts and found thirteen gradations of tone between pianissimo and ff! Obviously, the master could demand, and has. Group could deliver great refinements in light and shade. Contrast this with the situation of J. S. Bach, whose often difficult cantatas were sometimes read at sight Sunday mornings by a motley group of singers and instrumentalists. He may have had trouble enough holding them together, without having to cope with the added burden of a sophisticated range of dynamics.

Vivaldi's subtleties are reflected in the writings of Quantz. On his visit to Venice in 1726, Quantz attended concerts by Vivaldi's orchestra and was impressed by the style. So impressed was he that by the time he published his own book on performance practice in 1752, Quantz had refined Vivaldi's practice to the point of demanding that each and every note have its own dynamic crescendo-diminuendo within itself.

The rule for Vivaldi then is simple: in slow movements, shade, by all means. In fast movements use nuances wherever possible, but notice how often the orchestration calls for broad contrasts, including echo effects. For composers such as Pisendel and Quantz, who came under Vivaldi's influence, the guidelines are the same. We are less certain with Bach, and it would be wise to take a new look at the layout of each individual score to see how he coped with a particular situation. Where he has massed strings playing forte followed by one or two instruments playing softly, he is obviously looking for broad contrasts; but when in an extended passage marked forte he begins to use his skills as an orchestrator, thinning out the texture, introducing rests, weeding out notes, eliminating parts, winding up in piano, then he is making sure he gets a diminuendo along the way, whether or not the performers are capable of seeing beyond the tips of their noses. Truly Bachiavellian!

As for other composers, should we recommend prudence? The eyewitness accounts that have come down to us of performances by men like Corelli and Geminiani—the demonic expressions, the flashing eyes, the scowling, the gnashing of teeth—are hard to reconcile with the proper, formal, restrictive view of Baroque performance we have inherited. Perhaps Sol Babitz is right after all, and the rest of us are truly howling in exterior darkness. The Baroque era, he never tires of preaching, is an age of glorious exaggeration; so if we must err in our use of dynamics, we should err on the side of too much rather than too little. For myself, I would rather attend a Bach performance that is exciting, than one that is scrupulously correct and dreadfully dull; and if by some chance you and I should stumble across a performance that is correct as well as exciting, we should consider ourselves fortunate indeed.

Duple and Triple Rhythms in Bach

Our final concern will be with Bach's rhythms, which for several years now have been under attack. Specifically, we will begin with the three-note figure that launches the final movement of the *Brandenburg Concerto No. 5:*

The manner in which this tiny rhythmic fragment is performed vitally affects the character of the entire movement. A footnote in the Bärenreiter edition of the parts says tersely:

"All dotted rhythms (♩ ⌐⌐♪) are played as triplets (♩ ♩ ♩)."

A good question to ask is: Why?

And it must be asked, since the Bärenreiter edition states as an established fact what has been until now a matter of some dispute. It quotes no authority for the statement, nor does it cite any precedent. In fairness to Bärenreiter it must be acknowledged that the "play it as a triplet" point of view is supported by many musicologists, including Robert Donington. We will therefore have to examine the statement more fully in order to arrive at a proper conclusion.

Answers to the question "why?" include the following:

1. This was normal practice for those times.

2. Bach himself meant ⅜ ♪ ♩ ♪ when he wrote ♩. ♩ ⌐⌐♪ .

3. Bach was careless about the manner in which he indicated rhythms.

4. There was no way Bach could indicate this triplet rhythm in 2/4 meter in his day.

Many musicians who give answers 1, 2, or 3 quote the writings of Robert Donington in their own defense. Those who give the fourth alternative for an answer shrug their shoulders when challenged and say, "Well, if he could have, he would have, wouldn't he?" Unfortunately, some sophisticated musicians are among those who share this view.

Each of these answers is fallacious, and we should examine them individually.

Fallacy: There was no way Bach could indicate ♪ ♩ ♩ ♩ *in 2/4.*

Those who advance this argument are obviously unaware of the fact that Bach had been writing triplets for years, and had also been using the rhythmic figure ♪ ^{3} ♪ . What's more, had he wanted he could have changed the time signature to 6/8 and then all the triplet rhythms would have fallen into place right away.

Donington, who on occasion fearlessly attacks Bach for sloppy rhythmic writing, himself admits that Bach "was perfectly capable of writing out the most elaborate simple-plus-compound triple, dotted and double-dotted rhythms with complete precision, using all the necessary triplets and ties (the double-dot itself though known earlier only came into fashion a generation later) when he so chose. . . . But he did not always so choose."* As proof of Bach's skill, Donington refers to the fourteenth prelude from Book 2 of *The Well-Tempered Clavier* (BWV 883). Book 2 was only completed in 1742, however; since the Brandenburg concertos date from 1721, we shall have to look for much earlier examples to clinch our case.

If anyone really doubts that Bach used this rhythmic figure and its variants as a unit in 6/8, 9/8 or 12/8 meter before 1721, those doubts can be dispelled by a look at *Cantata No. 131* (1707), where these rhythmic units are used with a time signature of 12/8.

In *Cantata No. 150* (1708–1710), *Cantata No. 31* and *Cantata No. 132* (both 1715), and *Cantata No. 208* (1716) we find the same rhythmic units of notes and rests in 6/8. There are also other instances that the interested reader can easily find on his own.

If Bach could write these units in 6/8 and 12/8, he could write them out just as easily in 2/4, either by using a three with a slur above it, a slur alone, a three alone, or nothing at all. The musicians of his time would have coped.

Fallacy: It was normal practice to play a dotted rhythm as a triplet when played against ♩♩♩ ; *and Bach himself meant a triplet when he wrote the dotted rhythm* against ♩♩♩ .

Once we admit the fact that Bach could have written out the passage in 6/8 time, it is illogical to state that Bach was implying the triplet rhythm when he wrote something quite different.

Both Quantz and C. P. E. Bach have strong views on the subject, and they are quoted briefly in Donington's *The Interpretation of Early Music*, New Version (New York: St. Martin's Press, 1979), in his chapter on triplet rhythm. Donington chose the right quotations but somehow arrived at the wrong conclusion. He states:

> Quantz, like C. P. E. Bach, treats the standard compression of dot-
> ted rhythm into triplet rhythm (bringing the little note after the dot
> into line with the last note of the triplet) as the strict meaning of
> the notation; he treats what to us is the strict meaning of the nota-
> tion (bringing the little note after the last note of the triplet) as a
> case of "over-dotting"—no doubt because if the dot is thus taken at

* Robert Donington, *Tempo and Rhythm in Bach's Organ Music* (New York: Hinrichsen, 1960): p. 45.

all, it should be "over-dotted" to emphasise the effect. He prefers this to the standard interpretation, which is that given by C. P. E. Bach.

Donington gives as his reference chapter 5, section 22 of Quantz's *Essay*, in the Berlin edition of 1752.

Now if we refer to the Quantz passage in the excellent translation by Edward R. Reilly, we will realize just what it was that Quantz said.

First of all Quantz is absolutely clear in his instructions about the duration of a dotted note. In Chapter 5, subsection 20 he states that a dotted half note followed by a quarter and a dotted quarter note followed by an eighth are to be treated in exactly the same way; if the two notes and the dot make up four rhythmic pulses, three pulses are to be assigned to the note with the dot, and the fourth pulse to the smaller note.

In section 21 Quantz states that with dotted notes of *smaller value* (eighths, sixteenths, and thirty-seconds), no matter what the tempo, the dotted note is held as long as possible, and the other note is played as short as possible, so it will almost invariably sound like a sixty-fourth.

Quantz feels that it should be done this way "because of the animation that these notes must express."

In Chapter 5, section 22 Quantz develops the argument further, applying it to mixed rhythms:

> This rule likewise must be observed when there are triplets in one part and dotted notes against them in the other part . . . .

> Hence you must not strike the short note after the dot with the third note of the triplet, but after it. Otherwise it will sound like six-eight or twelve-eight time, ...

> The two passages must be treated quite differently. . . . If you were to play all the dotted notes found beneath the triplets in accordance with their ordinary value, the expression would be very lame and insipid, rather than brilliant and majestic.

My reading of section 22 is as follows:

Where there are triplets against dotted notes, you *must* double-dot. Otherwise, (1) if you fit the short note against the last note of the triplet, it will sound like 6/8 or 12/8, which would be misleading, or (2) if you merely give the dot its theoretical or true mathematical value, your performance will be tame and lacking in brilliance.

In spite of Quantz's view, Donington, writing on triplets in his chapter on Rhythm (*A Performer's Guide to Baroque Music*, p. 276), states:

> In baroque music (other than certain rather late baroque music in the galant style) triplet rhythms against duplet or quadruplet rhythms were as a whole not favoured.

To buttress this opinion he quotes one Giannantonio Banner:

> Observe in composing, never to put three Notes against two, this being one of the most prohibited musical situations. (Banner, *Compendio musico*, II, Padua, 1745, p. 111.)

Against this Banner with the strange advice, we have C. P. E. Bach's statement that "triplets have come increasingly into use in common or 4/4 time, as well as in 2/4 and 3/4" (*Essay*, Berlin, 1753, III, 27). How could triplets have come increasingly into use in these time signatures, one wonders, if this was indeed "one of the most prohibited musical situations"? Prohibited when, and by whom? Could the learned Giannantonio—a champion exhumed and resurrected from the Limbo of the Forgotten—be a real-life musical Rip Van Winkle, awakening from prolonged sleep to shout: "Long live the prohibition of three against two!"? How much weight should we accord his views, as against those of men of the stature of C. P. E. Bach and Quantz?

Donington concedes that "in 'galant music', two against three, and three against four, became fashionable, the intention being as notated." And he quotes such passages from Telemann's Gamba Sonata in A minor, "both intended to be performed as notated." (*Performer's Guide*, p. 278). He does not, however, extend his "perform as notated" recommendation to include Telemann's contemporary and friend, J. S. Bach.

Donington's views must be considered seriously because of his stature as a scholar and the very large following he has acquired among musicians involved in the Baroque revival. His paragraphs in the *Performer's Guide* should be read in conjunction with the rather more extended treatment he gives the subject of triplet rhythm in *The Interpretation of Early Music*, New Version. The reader is urged to read the Donington chapter in its entirety; only a brief summary of his views can be given here.

Under the subhead "Two Against Three Not a Normal Baroque Rhythm", Donington advances the following opinions:

> Through the baroque period, an appearance of "two against three" or "three against four" is deceptive. . . . Neither . . . had an accepted place in true baroque rhythm. . . .

Triplets as such are common. . . . But the duple notes set against them in baroque music are not meant for cross rhythms; they are meant to accommodate themselves to, or be accommodated by, the rhythm of the triplet. . . .

The notation is a mixture of half-remembered propositions [in the old sixteenth-century sense] and loose conventions. The convenient flexibility of the dot and the familiar practice of inequality were both pressed into service: ♪. ♪ was softened, and ♪♪ was sharpened, to produce the same result (i.e. ♩ ♪)."

    3

Inasmuch as the opinions are those of an eminent scholar, they should be given due consideration; in spite of their air of finality, however, it should be borne in mind that they are opinions, not facts, and hence subject to scrutiny.

Donington quotes C. P. E. Bach's *Essay* (the 1753 Berlin edition, 3: 27) to support his stand on triplet rhythms:

Now that triplets have come increasingly into use in common or 4/4 time, as well as in 2/4 and 3/4, many pieces have made their appearance which could with greater convenience be notated in 12/8, 9/8 or 6/8. The performance of other values against these (triplet) notes is shown at:

Does this passage really prove that an appearance of two against three, or of three against four, is deceptive "through the baroque period"? It can reasonably be argued that it proves exactly the opposite.

The signficant phrase is "now that triplets have come increasingly into use." C. P. E. Bach's book was published in 1753; the "now" therefore would refer to 1740–1750 or thereabouts, and his ruling would apply to music written around that time, and not in the 1720s.

Also significant are the words "many pieces have made their appearance." The use of the present tense again pinpoints the period C. P. E. is writing about as being close to 1750.

Yet another significant qualification is contained in the very next phrase: "which could with greater convenience be notated in 12/8, 9/8 or 6/8."

Logically, C. P. E. Bach's argument so far runs as follows:

Pieces using triplets in 4/4, 2/4 and 3/4 are now being written more and more often.

Many such pieces can be better rewritten in 12/8, 9/8, or 6/8. Others cannot.

C. P. E. Bach's recommendation, as I see it: In those works that are better rewritten, adapt the dotted notes to conform to the triplet rhythm.

The implied corollary: In works that cannot be rewritten, keep the rhythms distinct.

Looked at in this light, the two statements by C. P. E. Bach and Quantz on "three against two" are not at all contradictory but merely refinements of a position. We should also bear in mind that C. P. E. was writing largely about keyboard performance practice, and Quantz had a wider field in mind. Though both men were innovators with broad cultural backgrounds, C. P. E. Bach, who was born in 1714, seventeen years after Quantz, was more likely to represent the permissive new wave; Quantz was more likely to be the stricter traditionalist.

The other argument against "three against two" in Bach accuses him of being casual, if not downright sloppy, in his notation of rhythms. It is true that he did not always write in his slurs and staccato marks (see the earlier discussion of the slow movement in the *Brandenburg Concerto No. 4*); but internal evidence seems to indicate that when he wrote a variety of rhythms, he meant it. As early as 1708, in *Cantata No. 71*, he was using a dotted figure to set off triplets, and vice versa:

In *Cantata No. 70*, dated 1716, we have such measures as:

In *Cantata No. 147* (also 1716) the famous chorale "Jesu, Joy of Man's Desiring" is set in 3/4, and starts off with triplet eighths moving against two other rhythms:

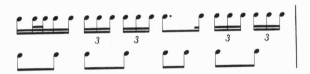

In measure 16 of the same chorale we come across the following:

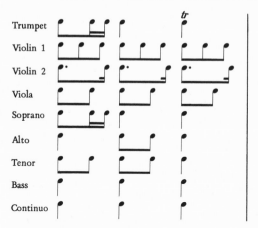

that's nine different voices, eight rhythmic patterns. How dreadful it would be were we to take this great variety of rhythms and reduce it to one smooth melange of homogenized triplets!

We still need a clue, however, some bit of clinching internal evidence, that is beyond dispute, and perhaps in the time signatures we have it.

Consider: In the cantata movements with time signatures of 6/8, 9/8 and 12/8, we have found a dotted rhythm within a triplet—like ♩♪♩ ♩♩♩ —but never ♪ ♩♩ Movements in simple meters, however—2/4, 3/4, 4/4—quite often have no triplets at all, or may have a preponderance of triplets combined with the sharply dotted ♪ ♩♩ rhythm.

Cantata No. 208 (1716) is particularly significant. There we have an aria in strict 6/8, and later on another aria in 4/4 that juxtaposes triplets against the dotted rhythm, much in the manner of the *Brandenburg Concerto No. 5:*

More complicated rhythms are introduced as the movement progresses, and in measure 37 triplets and the dotted rhythm alternate in a manner that suggests deliberate choice, beyond the shadow of a doubt:

This, then, is the clue: When Bach wanted a smoothly flowing set of triplets, he chose to write in a compound meter; but when he wanted to mix his rhythms and still keep them very distinct, one from the other, he chose a simple time signature.

Hence, in the last movement of the *Brandenburg Concerto No. 5*, the 2/4 time signature is Bach's way of saying, in effect: "Friends, I want a duple meter throughout, but some of it is 2/4 and most of it is in 6/8; I just want you to be careful and sée that they are kept distinct, and that the 2/4 does not get swallowed up into the 6/8."

If one follows through on this reasoning and repeatedly sets double-dotted eighth notes and thirty-seconds in sharp contrast with smooth triplets, the last movement acquires a crispness, a buouyancy, a sparkle that is quite exhilarating. Too bad that until now so few performers have read Bach's intentions in this manner, and that so many others probably never will.

Yet who am I to blame them? For I too have sinned.

Appendix 1
A Vivaldi Violin Concerto:
As Written,
and as Ornamented by Bach

The original version of the slow movement from Vivaldi's Concerto in G Major for Violin, Strings, and Organ (or Harpsichord), Fanna 1, no. 203 (Ricordi edition, Vol. 449):

140

155

The same Vivaldi concerto as transcribed by Bach for keyboard. The bass has been changed and the solo part ornamented:

Largo

Here Bach's elaboration is juxtaposed with the Vivaldi original:

Appendix 2

A Sonata for Violin and Continuo by Nardini as Published in the Late Eighteenth Century

The Adagio from Pietro Nardini's Sonata No. 6 in D Major for Violin and Continuo as it appeared in Cartier's L'Art du Violon (Paris, 1798). The original melodic line is on the first staff, the elaboration on the second staff, and the unfigured unrealized bass is on the third. The elaboration uses devices familiar to Baroque musicians in the 1750s (see chapter 9) but the note values are smaller than normal.

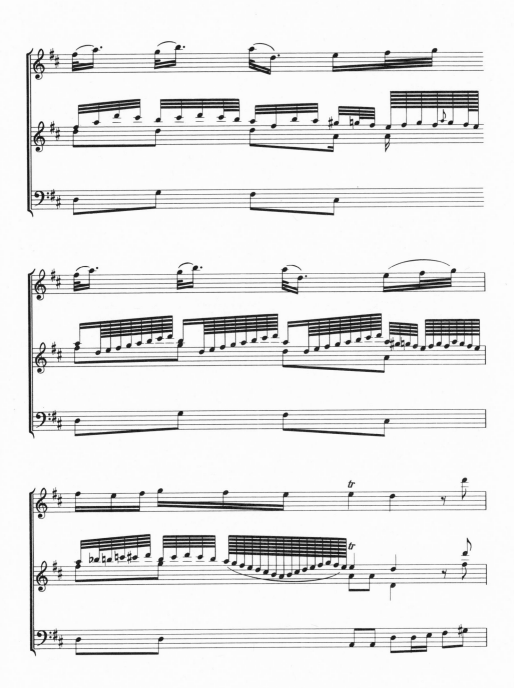

INDEX